GLOBAL DEVELOPMENT AND HUMAN RIGHTS

The Sustainable Development Goals and Beyond

From 2000 to 2015 the Millennium Development Goals (MDGs) mobilized external aid to finance life-changing services in the global South. However, in doing so, the organization failed to meet the challenges often associated with human rights initiatives, which are to make underprivileged communities independently prosperous, equitable, and sustainable.

In *Global Development and Human Rights*, Paul Nelson assesses the current thirty-year effort to make transformative changes in the global South by exploring how this disconnect from human rights weakened the MDGs reputation as a successful aid organization. To overcome the failings of the MDGs, the Sustainable Development Goals (SDGs) were formed in 2016 with the intention of managing the issues fundamentally ignored by the MDGs.

Drawing on twenty-five years of research on development goals, human rights, and the organizations that promote them, Nelson reasons that transformative change arises out of national and local movements, and shows how human rights can offer leverage and political support that help drive transformative national initiatives.

PAUL NELSON is an associate professor of international development at the University of Pittsburgh.

UTP insights

UTP Insights is an innovative collection of brief books offering accessible introductions to the ideas that shape our world. Each volume in
the series focuses on a contemporary issue, offering a fresh perspective anchored in scholarship. Spanning a broad range of disciplines
in the social sciences and humanities, the books in the UTP Insights
series contribute to public discourse and debate and provide a valuable
resource for instructors and students.

For a list of the books published in this series, see page 245.

GLOBAL DEVELOPMENT AND HUMAN RIGHTS

The Sustainable Development Goals and Beyond

Paul Nelson

UNIVERSITY OF TORONTO PRESS
Toronto Buffalo London

ISBN 978-1-4875-0116-7 (cloth)   ISBN 978-1-4875-1262-0 (EPUB)
ISBN 978-1-4875-2125-7 (paper)   ISBN 978-1-4875-1261-3 (PDF)

Library and Archives Canada Cataloguing in Publication

Title: Global development and human rights : the sustainable
   development goals and beyond / Paul Nelson.
Names: Nelson, Paul J., 1956– author.
Series: UTP insights.
Description: Series statement: UTP insights | Includes bibliographical
   references and index.
Identifiers: Canadiana (print) 20210155248 | Canadiana (ebook)
   20210155310 | ISBN 9781487501167 (cloth) | ISBN 9781487521257
   (paper) | ISBN 9781487512620 (EPUB) | ISBN 9781487512613 (PDF)
Subjects: LCSH: Sustainable Development Goals. | LCSH: Sustainable
   development. | LCSH: Human rights.
Classification: LCC HC79.E5 N47 2021 | DDC 338.9/27 – dc23

University of Toronto Press acknowledges the financial assistance to its
publishing program of the Canada Council for the Arts and the Ontario
Arts Council, an agency of the Government of Ontario.

Canada Council   Conseil des Arts
for the Arts   du Canada

ONTARIO ARTS COUNCIL
CONSEIL DES ARTS DE L'ONTARIO
an Ontario government agency
un organisme du gouvernement de l'Ontario

Funded by the   Financé par le
Government   gouvernement   Canada
of Canada   du Canada

Contents

Figures and Tables

Figures

Tables

Preface

I have many debts of gratitude to acknowledge. For fifteen years I have collaborated with Dr. Ellen Dorsey, executive director of the Wallace Global Fund, and my thinking about human rights and development owes a great deal to Ellen. (She disagrees, however, with some of my optimistic views about the SDGs.) My dean and colleague at the University of Pittsburgh, John Keeler, supported and encouraged this project, and I had the pleasure of working with him for four years as associate dean, an experience that slowed the writing but enriched me as a person. My thanks, too, to three exceptionally able research assistants, K.C. Euler, Rachel Vinciguerra, and Kayla Kuziola.

Various chapters have benefited from discussions in panels at the International Studies Association, Association for Nonprofit Organizations and Voluntary Action (ARNOVA), and at the University of Dayton's biennial conferences on the Social Practice of Human Rights. Two reviewers' careful, thorough critiques have sharpened the argument and its presentation, and Jennifer DiDomenico at University of Toronto Press has been enthusiastic and supportive throughout. Portions of chapters 1 and 2 are adapted from articles that appeared in *World Development*, used here with permission, and portions of chapter 4 are adapted from an article that appeared in the *Brown Journal of World Affairs*. Thanks to both publishers for their kind permission.

I have written much of this book in a lovely hilltop house situated among glacial moraines in south-central Wisconsin, and I thank my parents-in-law, Antonio and Lillian Scommegna, for making it available. Red-tailed hawks and sandhill cranes provided the best possible kinds of distractions. My spouse, Paola Scommegna, patiently put up with my preoccupation and provided important editorial suggestions, which I happily add to the long list of gifts for which I thank her.

The last stages of this writing came during a period of intense testing for my society and many others: a global pandemic, punctuated by episodes of deadly police violence against US people of color and the sustained protests for racial justice that have followed. The connections between these events and this book's themes have sometimes been clear to me, sometimes obscured by the fear, anger, and distress of living through these days. The pandemic challenges the entire idea of a fifteen-year global campaign against poverty and for sustainability, and my perspective on this challenge is summarized at the end of the introduction, and discussed in many of the chapters.

In the midst of these traumas, John Lewis, the distinguished civil rights leader and longtime member of the US Congress, died and was memorialized. President Barack Obama began his moving eulogy by quoting from scripture, the letter of James to the early Christian churches: "the testing of your faith develops perseverance. Perseverance must finish its work so that you may be mature and complete, not lacking anything." The message can be generalized, I think, by reading "the testing of your *principles* develops perseverance," and I hope that, in time, the perseverance I admire and argue for in the principled pursuit of economic and social justice can have the effect that the ancient writer wished for us as individuals and as societies, making us more mature and complete, lacking nothing.

Paul Nelson, Pittsburgh

Abbreviations

ARV	anti-retroviral
CESCR	Committee on Economic, Social, and Cultural Rights
CESR	Center for Economic and Social Rights
CHW	community health worker
DFID	Department for International Development (UK official aid agency)
DIHR	Danish Institute for Human Rights
FAO	Food and Agriculture Organization of the United Nations
FIAN	Food Information and Action Network
GI-ESCR	Global Initiative for Economic, Social and Cultural Rights
HRMI	Human Rights Measurement Initiative
ILC	International Land Coalition
ILO	International Labour Organization
ITC	International Tax Center
LMIC	low- and middle-income countries
MDG	Millennium Development Goals
OECD	Organisation for Economic Co-operation and Development
OHCHR	Office of the High Commissioner for Human Rights
OOPS	out-of-pocket spending
OPERA	outcomes, policy efforts, resources, and assessment
PHC	primary health care

SERF Index	Social and Economic Rights Fulfillment Index
SBA	skilled birth attendant
SDG	Sustainable Development Goals
Sida	Swedish International Development Agency
SRHR	sexual and reproductive health rights
STC	Save the Children
UHC	universal health coverage
ULA	Ugandan Land Alliance
UNDP	United Nations Development Programme
UNICEF	United Nations Children's Fund
USAID	United States Agency for International Development
WHO	World Health Organization
WTO	World Trade Organization

GLOBAL DEVELOPMENT AND HUMAN RIGHTS

Introduction

There are two kinds of people, wrote Brazilian sociologist Clodomir Santos de Morais: Those who do not eat, and those who do not sleep.[1] Santos meant that some don't sleep because they live in fear of the poor, who don't eat. But I think the aphorism carries another truth, that many of the wealthy "do not sleep" because most people in rich societies have at least a vague, uneasy sense that there is something terribly wrong with a world order that allows mass poverty, extreme inequalities, and hunger. We don't like to think about what "global poverty" means to our fellow people, but to shape a world where their numbers are dramatically smaller, we have to think clearly about the conditions, opportunities, and constraints they face. This is a book about how human rights can strengthen global development efforts to shape that world.

For most of us living in the relatively rich countries of the global North, what captures our attention and leads us to care about "global development" is not "global" at all; it is the human drama of poverty, injustice, opportunity, and courage. The change we care about, because we are human, is local and human. We respond to stories like these:

- the AIDS widow in Zimbabwe who is denied her modest inheritance when in-laws evict her and local authorities refuse to protect her rights;
- the child in rural India whose physical and intellectual potential are compromised by early childhood malnutrition, when high

seasonal food prices reduce families to one meal a day, with little
variety or nutrition;
- community organizers and human rights activists who are silenced
  or killed in Honduras when they speak up for their neighbors' land
  rights, or their right to be paid fairly for their labor;
- the community that organizes and manages a small-scale irrigation
  system or credit and insurance scheme that brings new opportunity
  and prosperity against all odds.

These injustices, opportunities, and human stories motivate us to
care. Humanitarian agencies know this, and they communicate
their work to us in these terms. Human rights agencies profile the
individual prisoner of conscience or single refugee families, know-
ing that our empathy can lead to solidarity and action. Community-
development NGOs profile individual micro-entrepreneurs using
small loans to increase their earnings and send their children to
school. We know that these are the realities people respond to, yet
development professionals, international organizations, the media,
and academics like me focus a great deal of attention on "world
hunger," "global development," national policy, and abstract principles of human rights. Some of us are policy wonks and enjoy these
abstractions for their own sake. But I suspect that most of us who
pick up – or write – a book like this one are looking for connection
to the lives of individuals, people we may never meet but whose
lives we care about at some level.

This book does deal with global abstractions of development
and human rights. It is about the global effort to craft and implement long-term goals that make a difference to the health, hap-
piness, and freedoms of individuals in countless villages and
neighborhoods. I want to make the connection clear between the
empathy that motivates us to care about our fellow humans and
the global economic and political machinations that open or close
opportunities for them. So, the book engages with two big sets of
issues: the global Sustainable Development Goals (SDGs) that the
United Nations and its member governments have embraced for
the period 2016 to 2030; and the interaction between two fields of
global engagement – human rights and development.

The world is in the middle years of a thirty-year experience with setting ambitious global development goals. The first part, under the Millennium Development Goals (MDGs) from 2000 to 2015, was a focused effort to mobilize external aid and finance life-changing services in the poor countries of the global South. I will show that the MDGs, despite their accomplishments, avoided the more difficult challenges of sustainable development.

The SDGs, beginning in 2016, take on those challenges, calling for the eradication of extreme poverty and malnutrition while also addressing some of the deeper causes of poverty: challenging income inequality, improving access to land and good jobs, and building health systems that move toward universal health coverage and protect people from falling into poverty because of health-care costs. I examine these themes – income inequality, access to productive assets, and health systems – and test three claims about the SDGs.

First, unlike the MDGs, the SDGs do address these, and the fact that they do so, even imperfectly, is important. The goals were negotiated by governments, some of which opposed stronger ties to human rights, but the SDG goals that emerged align more strongly with human rights than did the MDGs.

Second, in each of these critical fields – inequality, access to land and jobs, and health coverage – low- and middle-income societies have been tackling the challenges and have pioneered strategies, institutions, and policies that can be advanced further under the SDGs.

Third, human rights advocates and the global women's movement are actively and critically engaged with promoting and monitoring the SDGs. That engagement, which was largely absent during the MDGs, creates the potential that a diffuse, diverse set of advocates can bring to bear the data, principles, and political energy to motivate action.

My career in international development and in academia has led me to focus on these issues. That career has been in two phases, first as a policy researcher and advocate for US-based humanitarian and development NGOs, and now as a professor in a graduate program that trains students to work in international development.

Twenty-five years of research on development goals, human rights, and the organizations that promote them has convinced me of two things that are central to this book. First, although external development aid is important, transformative change comes from national and local movements and initiatives, not external aid agencies. Second, human rights – including economic and social rights such as the rights to food, housing, and health – offer leverage and political support that help drive transformative national initiatives.

The implication of these principles is that the Sustainable Development Goals can make an important difference to the path humanity is on if they are strongly tied to the standards and principles of human rights, and if governments are persuaded to take up the challenges outlined here. But goals can also be largely empty rhetoric, and this book asks whether and how their impact can be maximized.

The field of international development has long relied on goals, quantitative indicators, and material investment from aid donors. Human rights rest on a set of principles, legal standards, and formal commitments from governments who sign onto conventions that have the force of international law. But the two sectors pursue many of the same objectives, and chapter 1 unpacks what they have in common, and why the differences between goals and human rights are important.

Chapter 2 explores human rights, in principle and practice. After a short primer on what economic and social rights call for in principle, most of the chapter lays out four approaches to advancing economic and social human rights and reviews the work of a handful of local and international agencies using human rights methods in Asia and Africa. The wide variety of methods they employ to advance people's rights to health and water – from litigation to community-based training for community health practitioners and advocates – shows in practice how the idea of human rights is deployed, to inspire and mobilize movements as well as to apply the force of law to social problems.

Chapters 3, 4, 5, and 6 take up three key weaknesses in the previous set of global development goals, the MDGs, and analyze how the SDGs attempt to come to grips with them. Chapter 3 addresses economic inequality, virtually ignored in the MDGs but given a stand-alone goal in the SDGs. Inequality within low- and middle-income countries is a critical factor affecting efforts at reducing poverty, creating opportunity, and building sustainable economies. The SDGs' approach to inequality is far from perfect, but it can help focus attention and create incentives to tackle the problem. Much of the chapter highlights the successes of a handful of governments in addressing inequality, showing some of the policy options available to governments.

Chapter 4 argues for concerted attention to building national health systems that provide universal health coverage and respond to the health-care needs of all groups in society. Goals focused on specific conditions and diseases (the MDG approach) can have important impacts, and the progress on HIV/AIDS, malaria, infant mortality, and maternal mortality in many countries during the MDG period are successes that governments can build on. But disease-specific goals also diverted attention from building health-care systems that can grow to meet the whole range of health needs in society. There is nothing sexy about building and financing strong, inclusive health-care systems, but it is absolutely essential, and countries as diverse as Rwanda, Thailand, Bangladesh, and Kyrgyzstan suggest some of the paths toward those systems.

In chapters 5 and 6, I call for development practice to wake up and tackle the real causes rather than the symptoms of poverty by expanding people's access to land, energy, and decent work at living wages. Development assistance agencies have shown that they are willing to invest in important quick-impact strategies: anti-malaria bed nets, school nutrition programs, immunization campaigns, and better cookstoves, among others. But *sustainable* development, with lasting prosperity and opportunity, requires that all people be able to make a decent living. To do this they need access to the means of production: land, jobs, energy, and capital. This is the stuff that real political and economic competition is about, and the fact that the SDGs include goals related to land, jobs, energy, and credit won't make these challenges easy. But in chapter 5 (labor) and chapter 6 (land) I examine some evidence that governments can and do adopt strategies that work: recognizing and respecting legal rights of domestic workers, trash-pickers, and others in the "informal economy"; increasing and enforcing minimum wages; and expanding women's secure rights to land.

Chapter 7 considers the problem that bedevils all international agreements and cooperative action: accountability. Sixty years of human rights activism and the experience of the MDG period give us some insight into what works, what needs to be done, and what are the prospects for a new, ambitious set of international goals. There is good reason to be wary of these development goals, as governments watered down most of the most important and challenging goals, and any process of monitoring and accountability for a sprawling set of standards is daunting. But the SDGs, linked as they are to human rights principles, have drawn a wide and dynamic coalition of supporters and monitors, including global human rights organizations and a worldwide coalition of women's organizations. The record of implementation in the SDGs' early years has been uneven at best, and if governments and donor agencies are to be held to account for their performance on any of these goals, it will involve political work and careful monitoring at local, national, and international levels.

All development, like all politics, is ultimately local. When we say that rural health care improves in (for example) Central America, we ultimately mean that particular women, men, and children in particular villages and urban neighborhoods got better care at clinics and hospitals, received more affordable medicines, and heard clearer explanations of what would help to keep them healthy. If we say that education improved in West Africa, we ultimately mean that individual children got to school, stayed in school, and experienced real learning in classrooms supervised by effective and creative teachers. Most often these things happen because of what local communities and local governments do, but they are also a function of national and global policies and practices, from trade agreements that govern patent rights over essential medicines to national incentives to encourage high-performing teachers and excellent curricula.

I take a largely positive and hopeful view of the SDGs. I am generally a hopeful but not an optimistic person, and I am convinced of the power of well-organized people determined to claim their rights. I have also seen that bureaucracies and even large organizations full of well-intended people can become dysfunctional and become the butt of well-deserved cynical jokes from experienced international aid workers. But I am taking a long view of the last generation of work in the global development field, interpreting a thirty-year process of global development goal setting and implementation.

Because the SDGs avoid some of the most serious flaws of the MDGs, and because human rights, environmental, and women's organizations have been powerfully engaged with the SDG process from the beginning, there is a real chance to build the kind of political support that is needed to persuade governments to undertake many of the key, poverty-related goals. Strong, independent monitoring of progress at the country level requires energy and analytic firepower, and these have been present from the early years of the SDGs. Success for many of the important goals is dependent not primarily on generosity from aid donors but on real commitments from governments. So, the tone of much of what follows is fairly positive toward the SDGs.

But there are real, serious obstacles to their success.

The SDGs' breadth, with seventeen wide-ranging goals and 169 specific targets, creates the danger that governments' attention and priorities will be spread thin. It is essential that donors and advocates be realistic, recognize that governments will have priorities among the goals, tilting toward health or education, ocean protection or forests, and targeting specific diseases or building national health systems. Governments will choose priorities, their citizens will press for attention and spending on many fronts, and even with the best possible outcome there will not be lock-step consistent progress across all the goals in any country. Much has been written about the importance of not taking a "one-size-fits-all" view of the goals, and those voices are right.[2]

But two obstacles loom largest in 2020, one political, the other biological. An upsurge of nationalist, authoritarian, populist political movements in many societies challenges human rights, international cooperation, and commitments to sustainability and anti-poverty objectives. The political trend is highly visible in the United States and Europe and has some traction around the world, in the Philippines, Turkey, Hungary, and Brazil. In many of these countries this features skepticism about the value of human rights, reluctance to join in multilateral (especially United Nations-led) initiatives, and hostility toward immigration, foreign assistance, and trade agreements. In the Philippines, for example, President Rodrigo Duterte's violent, deadly crackdown on the drug trade, gangs, and Muslim rebel groups, featuring attacks on civilian targets, creates a political environment that makes decade-long concerted effort to fulfill the SDGs hard to imagine.

The right-wing populist swing may be temporary or lasting, but it will be wise for human rights advocates and promoters of the SDGs to keep it in sight. The SDGs may turn out to be well-equipped for a populist era, because the most important elements of the SDGs are less heavily aid driven than were the MDGs. If my premise about the genesis of transformative change in societies is correct – that external donors can make important changes happen from time to time, but domestic movements drive most lasting change – then supporters of the SDGs should do all in their power to win support from women's movements, unions, environmentalists, and human rights activists, to build the broadest and strongest coalitions possible in support of the goals and the vision of sustainability they represent.

Human Rights and the SDGs in the COVID-19 Era

The second obstacle is, of course, the COVID-19 pandemic. The pandemic's impacts on health, education, employment, taxation, and financing through development assistance will be massive but are as yet unknown. Even as the coordinating agencies of the United Nations scramble in 2020 to rearticulate the SDG agenda in light of the pandemic's effects, many human rights and development advocates argue that the pandemic also presents unforeseen opportunities to reset national policies and institutions, "an opportunity to learn the lessons of the past, and present a new vision and a new narrative about the values underpinning our economies and the role and accountability of the State."[3] This vision includes calls for renewed commitment to social spending priorities, progressive taxation, labor rights, and a range of economic and social policy measures discussed in these chapters.

A July 2020 report to the Human Rights Council by Philip Alston, the outgoing United Nations special rapporteur on extreme poverty, has framed the discussion for human rights advocates and other participants in the SDG process who are committed to reducing inequality and eradicating poverty.[4] The report outlines one authoritative take on how the goals will need to be reinvigorated and recalibrated in light of the COVID-19 pandemic.

Alston's parting report is a devastating critique of coordinated global efforts to address poverty. He argues, as this book does, against the very low "extreme poverty" line maintained by the World Bank and widely used to report and celebrate gains in poverty reduction. He notes, on the one hand, that the SDG process has made important contributions to framing the debate around global poverty and calling for further action. But in strong language he calls for steps to reinvigorate the SDG process and "recalibrate" the goals in light of the pandemic and to "avoid sleepwalking toward failure."[5]

The managers of the SDG process have taken some steps to adjust the process to the pandemic, announcing that 20 percent of SDG-related external funding can be used for immediate pandemic response, and reaffirming the need to build recovery policies around the goals and spirit of the SDGs.[6] This is an important acknowledgment that the planned 2020s "Decade of Action" must become a "Decade of Recovery" oriented to policies that protect and uplift poor and marginalized populations and make communities more resilient against future shocks. And UN Secretary General António Gutteres argued forcefully that the pandemic's "devastating impact" is due to "past and present failures in: taking the SDGs seriously; addressing inequalities; investing in resilience; empowering women and girls; heeding warnings about the damage to the natural environment; addressing climate change; and valuing international cooperation and solidarity."[7] But the July 2020 High-level Political Forum on the SDGs, held virtually, while acknowledging that progress in the first decade has been too slow, and reaffirming the SDGs as the framework for recovery that "builds back better," took no fundamental steps to reorient or reinvigorate the process.[8]

The most important refocusing of the SDGs, at least in the near term, will be driven by domestic politics in the low- and middle-income countries, by advocates and movements advancing human rights-consistent anti-poverty agendas, and perhaps by some official (governmental) donor agencies, as in the case of the European Community's green recovery initiatives.

Much of this agenda – as articulated by the Alston Report – is consistent with the themes of this book. The chapters that follow are critical of the MDGs and of self-congratulatory reporting on global poverty; are concerned about slow progress in the early years of the SDGs; and call for an approach to the SDGs that links them more strongly to important standards and principles of human rights. I emphasize reforms in taxation over the stale debate over external aid, and argue that goals and policies to increase access to decent work and land, and to improve social protections, should be de-linked from economic growth prospects.

Where my argument differs from the Alston Report's is clearest in the final chapter, on how accountability can be made effective in the SDG period. I argue that accountability may be supported by global reporting processes, including human rights reporting in the United Nations, but that domestic pressure for better land-tenure security, labor protections, health coverage, and social protections will drive positive change, and will be the most important source of accountability.

chapter one

Human Rights and Global Development Goals

Consider the life of a girl born in Rwanda in the early 1990s, around the same time as my two children were born in the United States. In rural Rwanda, her life had scarcely begun when the ghastly genocidal violence of 1994 broke out, the catastrophic events for which the country is still widely known. Her prospects, if she escaped the murderous violence of 1994, weren't good. Life expectancy at birth was forty-six years, between 19 and 20 percent of children died before their fifth birthday, and only 37 percent of adult women were literate. If she lived through her childbearing years, she could expect to bear eight children.

Some twenty-five years later, a girl's prospects in Rwanda are dramatically better. Life expectancy is sixty-three years, and child mortality is now 5.5 percent. Literacy for women ages fifteen to twenty-four is 78 percent, total fertility rate is 4.6, and women are on average 1.5 years older when they bear their first child (on average, twenty-three years old, the oldest in sub-Saharan Africa). Rwanda's progress has been particularly rapid, and these achievements and similar improvements in nutrition, incomes, and other measures are relatively easy to explain: in addition to respectable rates of investment and economic growth, the Rwandan government began in the late 1990s to implement commitments to education, created a modest universal health-care system, and strengthened women's economic and social rights, including access to land and employment.

The point is not that Rwanda is a model; it is that societies of modest means can and do implement policies that dramatically improve the quality of life and scope of opportunity for millions of people. If you believe as I do that every person – each of our children – has the right to a better life than that faced by a child in 1990s Rwanda, then the story of two generations in that country is one of many stories in many places in the world that is pointing the way. That is why global efforts at promoting human rights and sustainable development hold our attention, and it is why I have written this book to show that the current global campaign around development goals – the Sustainable Development Goals – can have a transformative impact, if we can harness the political energy of people's aspirations and the power of human rights.

With the adoption of the Sustainable Development Goals (SDGs) in September 2015, world leaders and aid donors launched a second sustained period of goal setting for development. The first, under the Millennium Development Goals (MDGs, 2000–2015), set eight global goals related to poverty, hunger, disease, child and maternal mortality, and education, and they produced some remarkable results. The SDGs were adopted alongside the Paris Framework Convention on Climate Change, and the SDGs are both the extension of the poverty-focused Millennium Development Goals and a broader new agreement paired with the Paris agreement, detailing a global sustainability agenda to the year 2030. The SDGs offer a chance for leverage by human rights and environmental advocates on issues largely neglected by the MDGs.

Developed after extended rounds of negotiations and consultations, the SDGs have been more widely debated and more closely monitored than were the MDGs. The goals are better known at their launch by human rights and development practitioners, and the seventeen goals apply to all governments, not only low- and middle-income countries, addressing global issues such as ocean and forest health, as well as the health, nutrition, education, and poverty goals of the MDGs. They were adopted with fanfare: then-UN Secretary General Ban Ki-moon described them as "a plan of action for ending poverty in all its dimensions, irreversibly, everywhere, and leaving no one behind." But they have also drawn criticism. Some, including development analyst William

Easterly, argue that they are too broad to be effective, dismissing them with the quip that SDG should stand for "Senseless, Dreamy, Garbled."[1]

The pandemic may force a stronger refocusing on a narrower range of goals, either coordinated or by individual societies. Just as some governments have embraced a narrower set of priority goals, some commentators are now calling for a process of focusing on 30 or so targets among the SDGs' 169. Naidoo and Fisher argue in a comment in *Nature* that a subset of goals can be identified that have the strongest linkages to the entire SDG agenda and will advance progress on most of the declared goals while strengthening protections against future pandemics and related trauma.[2]

I believe that even in the context of the pandemic, it is time to affirm all people's rights to a decent level of food, health, education, water, housing, and fair and equal treatment, and to mobilize in support of these rights. When people have asserted these rights effectively, they have won rapid advances in health and nutrition, made by diverse policies in highly varied societies. I have written this book to show that such human rights-based demands, policies, and initiatives can have a major impact, that in the MDG era we failed to support and build on these demands, and that the SDGs offer a much stronger opportunity to do so. In this chapter I will lay the groundwork by introducing the MDGs and the SDGs; illustrating the important differences between human rights and development goals; introducing my critique of the MDGs; and arguing that both human rights and the SDGs can succeed where the MDGs did not, mobilizing and supporting domestic movements pressing for pro-poor policies in the countries of the global South.

Human rights and development goals each bring assets to the effort to eradicate poverty and improve health, nutrition, education, and sustainability. Global development efforts have several tools for charting and motivating progress: human rights standards in international law, formal goals set by governments, sophisticated measures of outputs and impact, and pledges of funding and cooperation. Development goals and human rights were too often at odds during the MDG period, but the two can have a powerful synergy. Goals have advantages: they permit the use of quantitative benchmarks in a way that human rights generally have not; and they hold the attention of official aid donors and mobilize funding in a way that human rights have not consistently done.

But if governments in many regions are entering a new period of authoritarian, populist, inward-looking politics and rule, then the SDG period will need the motivating power of human rights claims to make more rapid, sustainable progress. Human rights offer three vital assets that the MDGs failed to take advantage of, and that are central to the success of the SDGs: a system of accountability that, while stronger in theory than in practice, can be an important asset; a source of leverage, anchored in international law and often in domestic constitutions and legislation, that can help to mobilize domestic political energy; and attention to patterns of inequality and to institution building. Underlying all of these is the inspiring claim that every one of us has these rights simply because of the dignity of being human.

From a human rights perspective, the MDGs were seriously flawed. The SDGs are closer in many respects to human rights principles. Although they fall short of human rights standards at important points – a debate that is discussed in this chapter – they offer an opportunity to integrate and take advantage of the two sectors' powers. The MDGs depended on the ability of governments, donors, and advocates to focus attention on a few key problems. The SDGs' longer menu of problems and goals will require a broader coalition, and no single society is likely to focus systematically on all of them. Monitoring – formal and informal, national and transnational – is key.

The remainder of this chapter introduces the MDGs and SDGs and reviews the MDGs' achievements, their failings, and the distinctive content of the SDGs. It concludes with some evidence that the most important driver of significant, sustainable social change has been domestic political pressure, and that the SDGs are positioned to help provide leverage for such movements.

Development and Global Development Goals

International development – the process of economic, social, and political change in low-income countries and communities – has become a profession, a credentialed field (I teach in a master's degree program in international development), and as a field it addresses some of the most acute challenges to the sustainability of twenty-first-century life on earth. The MDGs were adopted by 192 world leaders in 2000 to focus attention and effort on extreme poverty and some of its worst symptoms. They used targets and quantitative indicators to encourage progress on poverty, health, nutrition, education, water, sanitation, and other issues. The Millennium Development Goals and targets appear in figure 1.1.

The MDG years – 1990 to 2015 – saw significant reductions in the number of people living in abject, absolute poverty and suffering some of its worst effects. Many governments and most donors committed themselves to meeting the MDGs, and many key indicators improved. Across the low- and middle-income countries of Asia, Africa, Latin America, and the Middle East, the mortality rate for children under age five fell from 90 per 1,000 live births in 1990 to 48 per 1,000 in 2012, and the percentage of people with access to improved sources of drinking water worldwide rose from 76 percent to 89 percent.[3] Although there is debate over global poverty and malnutrition statistics, these targets of MDG Goal 1 were also reduced substantially. Much of the progress on poverty reduction is the result of very rapid economic growth, especially in China and India, and the rapid progress of the 1990s and 2000s, often attributed to the MDGs, may not be replicable.

Some 836 million people continue to live in extreme poverty after the successes of the MDG era.[4] Because we become inured to such numbers, it is well to remember that "extreme poverty" is extreme in almost every way. For very many it is chronic and persistent, and for those whose poverty is "transient," we must not imagine that they move from extreme deprivation into some form of global middle class. People with few assets and with incomes

Figure 1.1. Millennium Development Goals and Targets

Goal 1: Eradicate extreme poverty and hunger
Target 1A: Halve … the proportion of people living on less than $1.25
    a day
Target 1B: Achieve Decent Employment for Women, Men, and Young
    People (added 2008)
Target 1C: Halve … the proportion of people who suffer from hunger

Goal 2: Achieve universal primary education
Target 2A: [Ensure that] all children can complete a full course
    of primary schooling, girls and boys

Goal 3: Promote gender equality and empower women
Target 3A: Eliminate gender disparity in primary and secondary
    education … by 2015

Goal 4: Reduce child mortality rates
Target 4A: Reduce by two-thirds, between 1990 and 2015, the under-
    five mortality rate

Goal 5: Improve maternal health
Target 5A: Reduce by three-quarters, between 1990 and 2015,
    the maternal mortality ratio
Target 5B: Achieve, by 2015, universal access to reproductive health
    (added 2005)

Goal 6: Combat HIV/AIDS, malaria, and other diseases
Target 6A: Have halted by 2015 and begun to reverse the spread of
    HIV/AIDS
Target 6B: Achieve, by 2010, universal access to treatment for HIV/AIDS …
Target 6C: Halt and begin to reverse the incidence of malaria and
    other major diseases

Goal 7: Ensure environmental sustainability
Target 7A: Integrate sustainable development principles into country
    policies and programs; reverse loss of environmental resources
Target 7B: Reduce [the rate of] biodiversity loss significantly by 2010
Target 7C: Halve the proportion of people without … safe drinking
    water and basic sanitation
Target 7D: [Achieve] significant improvement in the lives of at least 100
    million slum-dwellers

Goal 8: Develop a global partnership for development
Target 8A: [Implement] an open, rule-based, predictable, non-discriminatory trading and financial system
Target 8B: Address the special needs of the Least Developed Countries (LDCs)
Target 8C: [Address] needs of landlocked developing countries and small island developing States
Target 8D: Deal comprehensively with the debt problems of developing countries …
Target 8E: [P]rovide access to affordable, essential drugs in developing countries
Target 8F: [Provide access to] the benefits of new technologies, especially information and communications

Source: United Nations. Some targets are edited for brevity.

close to the extreme poverty range face not only extremely limited opportunity but physical deprivation that taxes their physical systems and vital organs, and often ends with death at an early age.

Living in such deprivation means experiencing near-starvation conditions often; every seasonal downturn in income or rise in food prices can be a life-threatening experience. Stephen Devereux refers to "those with cold hands" in depicting the conditions of deep seasonal poverty in rural areas in Asia and Africa, and "cold hands" symbolize the damaging physical effects on the health, vigor, metabolism, and vital signs of people who are forced to live on very little.[5] The World Bank's "Voices of the Poor" project recorded interviews in the late 1990s with thousands of people living in poverty. Beyond the material deprivation, people spoke of the indignities of being treated badly by store clerks and in government offices; the inability ever to get enough sleep; the lack of any recourse against an employer who refuses to pay for a day or week of work; and, especially for women, the fear of physical attack when venturing out to collect firewood or water.[6]

This suffering does not occur only in societies where poverty is widely shared. The "New Bottom Billion" project has shown that most extreme poverty is now concentrated in middle-income countries with growing economies.[7] Some 72 percent of the world's poor live not in fragile, low-income countries but in middle-income countries, including India, China, Pakistan, Nigeria, Indonesia, Angola, and Cameroon.[8] Especially as poverty has become concentrated in societies with considerable wealth, we need effective policies that address the distribution of income, wealth, and opportunity, and this means giving high priority to human rights.

This has important implications for how we understand "global poverty" and what can be done about it. For more than a decade, Collier's 2007 study, *The Bottom Billion,* has influenced views of poverty: it holds that entrenched, long-lasting poverty is concentrated in countries in Africa and Central Asia, and that failed states, prolonged civil conflict, overdependence on natural resources, poor governance, and weak infrastructure are the central causes.[9]

Many people do live in desperate poverty in such societies, and their plight requires urgent action. But for almost three-quarters of the world's extremely poor people who live in societies enjoying strong economic growth and rising average incomes, the problem is very high levels of inequality in which extreme poverty exists side by side with new industry, modern urban lifestyles, and a prosperous middle class. The implication: "Tackling inequality, not just absolute poverty, must be prioritised in future aid and development strategies."[10]

MDG Achievements

Much of this book is a critique of the MDGs' failings and an effort to learn from them, but the MDGs' record is also impressive in many ways. Former UN Secretary General Ban Ki-moon called them the "most successful anti-poverty movement in history," and it is important to acknowledge the record of the MDG period in targeting poverty and hunger (MDG 1), health (MDGs 4, 5, and 6), water (MDG 7, target 10), and sanitation.[11]

Table 1.1. Progress on health-related indicators in the MDG period

	Maternal mortality rate, developing regions	Under-age-five child mortality	Improved drinking water sources	Access to improved sanitation	HIV incidence rate, new infections per 100 people aged 15–49
1990	380 per 100,000 live births	90 deaths/1,000 live births	76% of world population	49%	Southern Africa 1.98 Central Africa 0.43
2014	210 per 100,000 live births	48 deaths/1,000 live births	89% of world population	64%	Southern Africa 1.02 Central Africa 0.29

Source: United Nations (2014).

Development assistance in each of these health areas increased rapidly in the 2000s: maternal, newborn, and child health assistance by 78 percent between 2000 and 2010; total health assistance by 164 percent; and aid targeted to HIV, malaria, and tuberculosis by 819 percent, 709 percent, and 618 percent, respectively.[12] As aid commitments grew and many governments committed themselves to meeting the MDGs, several key indicators improved. Aspects of this progress are summarized in table 1.1.

Rapid economic growth in India and China played a major role in reducing poverty under the MDGs. In fact, as Thomas Pogge points out, the goals were adopted in 2000 but "back-dated" the starting point for measuring progress to 1990, in effect taking advantage of huge reductions in poverty in China during the 1990s.[13] The UN's 2015 report on poverty reduction shows that a significant part of the global reduction of extreme poverty came during that decade before the MDGs were adopted: roughly 300 million of the 1.1 billion reportedly lifted out of poverty.[14]

Across the global South, the mortality rate for children under age five fell from 90 per 1,000 live births in 1990 to 48 per 1,000 in 2012, and the percentage of people with access to improved sources of drinking water worldwide rose from 76 percent to

89 percent. Although almost 800 million people continue to use unsafe and unimproved water sources, the progress is still impressive. Improvements like the halving of child mortality are historic. Worldwide, cutting child mortality in half took 150 years between 1800 and 1950.[15]

While efforts under the MDGs improved many people's well-being, they did not tackle the inequalities and institutions that systematically exclude hundreds of millions of women and men from job opportunities and the ability to own land and to accumulate assets and wealth that drive growth and income gains. These are among the reasons why human rights are a key to accomplishing the SDGs' lofty goals.

Human Rights versus Global Goals: A Critique of the MDGs

The modern "development" enterprise and modern era of human rights were both born out of post-World War II commitments to reconstructing a peaceful, stable, global order. These twin sectors have remained largely separate for seventy years. Development as a field has grown up around the delivery of material assistance: emergency food and humanitarian aid; community-based and national programming aimed at improving agriculture, education, transport, and other sectors; and policy leverage largely grounded in neoliberal economic theory.

Human rights advocates by contrast have decades of experience in drafting and winning assent to international standards and principles, then documenting governments' performance. While human rights advocacy has overwhelmingly focused on civil and political rights, advocacy on economic, social, and cultural rights has grown rapidly since the 1990s.[16] There are some signs of reunion and partial reintegration of development and human rights since the mid-1990s as human rights NGOs have adopted active agendas that include advocating for economic and social rights, and donor organizations and NGOs in development embrace human rights-based approaches. During the same period, local and national social movements have articulated demands for health, land reform, and water policies that are grounded in human rights claims. Still, human rights and development remain largely separate, and their curious separation, despite shared goals and commitments and the enormity of global poverty and related problems, is a historical artifact that must be overcome if the SDG process is to make a real dent in poverty.

The differences between goals and rights, the preferred standard-setting approaches of the development and human rights fields, have important implications for how goals and rights can be deployed against poverty. Human rights belong to individuals, who can use them as political tools to constrain and guide governments' behavior. Rights make a normative claim, that human dignity entitles each person to certain kinds of treatment and to protection from others. Goals, on the other hand, belong to governments. Most goals are utilitarian, calculated to maximize welfare gains. These differences resurface throughout this discussion, and they revolve around two themes: agency (to whom do the rights/goals belong?), and the nature of accountability they try to impose.

Some human rights adhere to groups such as children, women, Indigenous peoples, and people with disabilities, but most rights contained in the Universal Declaration of Human Rights, and in the International Covenants on Economic, Social, and Cultural Rights (ICESCR) and Civil and Political Rights (ICCPR), are rights of individuals. Goals, on the other hand, *refer* to the people who suffer the indignities of poverty, but those individuals are the objects of the goals, not their agents. The fact that governments adopted the goal of halving the number of people living in extreme poverty did not give any particular destitute person a right or a claim on her government. The MDGs and SDGs are not any individual citizen's goals in the same sense that the right to food or to information is that individual's right.

Rights, unlike goals, inherently create duties for governments, and these duties give human rights their political significance. The claim, for example, that every person has the right to adequate food, even in time of famine, has meaning for policy because it is associated with duties and obligations, and the definition of those duties is discussed in chapter 2. These duties do apply to international actors, other governments, and firms, but human rights standards and law are clear that governments hold the principal responsibility to ensure that resources are marshaled to protect their people.

Development goals always include some form of monitoring or reporting, and the UN produced numerous country-specific, regional, and global reports on the MDGs. But monitoring does not equal accountability, and accountability "outward" to a donor agency is rarely enough to promote the kind of social change envisioned in the MDGs. Such change requires local and national institutions and politics that make governments accountable to organized citizens, and to an electorate as a whole. Human rights standards offer a stronger accountability mechanism, in theory, through periodic self-reporting by governments to UN committees. But these committees have limited powers to investigate and to publicize results, and in practice, especially for economic and social rights, much of human rights' leverage comes through organized citizen efforts to use them as political leverage.

The Millennium Declaration did link the MDGs to human rights in broad terms. The declaration referred to the "collective responsibility to uphold the principles of human dignity, equality and equity at the global level," and the importance of "respect for human rights and fundamental freedoms" and of "the equal rights of all without distinction as to race, sex, language or religion and international cooperation in solving international problems …"[17] But while the declaration and the Secretary General's 2001 "Road Map" document embraced human rights,[18] the goals themselves and the targets and indicators by which they were tracked had significantly different emphases from those of the related human rights standards.

The MDGs ignored or sidestepped key principles of human rights, including the right to participate in shaping policy that affects one's well-being, the principle that all human rights are interrelated and inseparable, and the principle of accountability.

Participation in shaping the goals, we will see, was minimal. Economic and social issues were completely separated from civil and political human rights, which had no direct appearance in the MDGs. And the principle of universality, which holds that all people equally should be protected by human rights, was violated by an approach that targeted some groups for benefits but not others.

These broad principles are woven throughout the three critical issues that are the subjects of chapters 3 to 6: inequality, health systems with coverage for all people, and access to productive resources (land and decent work) for poor people. These are summarized here.

Inequality, discrimination, and disparities were largely ignored in the MDGs. Goals and targets that encouraged quick numerical progress and raising numbers of people above a poverty or other threshold gave governments and donors every reason to concentrate their resources where they could readily move large numbers of individuals over the threshold with respect to income, nutrition, or incidence of HIV, TB, or malaria; or most increase skilled medical attendance at childbirths and reduce the incidence of maternal mortality. Population-wide targets and indicators that ignored disparities created incentives that aggravated discriminatory patterns.

As early as 2005, Lennox raised this concern: "In Vietnam, the national poverty rate is 37% and for ethnic minorities, 67%; in Peru, the national poverty rate is 43% and for indigenous peoples, 65%; in Bulgaria, the national poverty rate is 15% and for Roma, it is 85%. But the decision to call for a 'reduction by half' leaves open the possibility that minorities will constitute the majority of those persons still living in poverty and still suffering from hunger in 2015."[19]

Unfortunately, these predictions were correct, and late in the MDG process official MDG reports began to call attention to patterns of inequality. The 2009 global report showed, for example, that primary school attendance rates varied widely within countries across racial, ethnic, regional, and religious lines. For nine countries the report shows that attendance rates vary as widely as 59:100 for Laos and as moderately as 78:100 for Serbia between the ethnic groups with highest and lowest attendance rates.[20] Human rights analysts treat disparities of this kind as evidence of systematic discrimination in delivery of services, and document them in studies like the Physicians for Human Rights 2007 report on maternal mortality in Peru.[21] Not only do such disparities violate human rights principles, they aggravate inequalities that have corrosive effects on societies.

A second major flaw in the MDGs was the effect of one of their greatest strengths, their approach to global health. Focusing on reducing the incidence of specific illnesses or conditions, including child and maternal mortality, HIV/AIDS, malaria, and tuberculosis, the goals shifted global health spending away from building health systems and financing coverage for entire societies. Health systems worldwide are limited and strained, and their weaknesses have been aggravated by the focus of MDG targets.

Weak health systems cost lives in ways that rarely make the headlines, by limiting people's options to receive an adequate level of care – for example, during pregnancy and childbirth. The success of the MDGs created programmatic silos focused on diseases or initiatives such as measles immunizations. Donors reinforced this tendency by funding specific interventions in preference to "horizontal" measures that build the capacity of the health system. Governments focused on health achievements that could be reported as meeting goals and indicators. So "health systems – hospitals and clinics, procurement structures, clinical professionals, [information and communications technology, and] ... equipment and supplies" – received less attention.[22]

Third and finally, the structural factors underlying poverty and wealth in poor countries – access to land, labor, wages, and energy – were almost completely ignored by the MDGs. The MDGs instead created incentives to find what the Millennium Campaign's 2005 report called "high potential, short-term impact" initiatives.[23] These "quick wins" can have important human impacts, but MDG goals and campaigns gave governments and donors incentives to emphasize the short-term, quick-impact strategies.

Human rights-based approaches tend to call for attention to the *causes and multiple dimensions* of poverty, and to the linkages between poverty and civil and political freedoms; the MDGs aimed primarily for progress in some of the worst *symptoms* of poverty. Human rights-based approaches to social and economic policy involve tracing the social, economic, political, and other causes of rights deprivation. In theory, this is true because human rights principles call for attention to patterns of discrimination in law, institutions, and policy, and because they emphasize the need to establish effective legal and institutional protections for groups that are subject to discriminatory treatment.[24]

The SDGs: Human Rights-Friendly Development Goals?

The MDGs were, as Fukuda-Parr writes, a "North-South aid agenda" focused on issues most relevant to low- and middle-income countries and coordinated largely by donor-government aid officials.[25] The SDGs are different both in their contents and in the process by which they were elaborated. They fall short of human rights principles and standards and they have received important criticism from human rights scholars, but their differences from the MDGs are important to the range of actors and interest groups that are engaged. Unlike the MDGs' fairly focused 8 goals and 21 targets, there are 17 Sustainable Development Goals and 169 targets. The goals are summarized in figure 1.2.

The choice of targets and measurable indicators is vitally important, and I will examine a few of these in later chapters. Here, I focus on the goals themselves. Many of the SDGs continue the MDGs' focus: SDGs 1 to 4 addressing poverty, health, and education; Goal 5 on gender inequality; and Goal 6 on water and sanitation all echo MDG goals in their broad content. SDG 8, on sustained inclusive economic growth and decent work for all, is new as a stand-alone goal, and amplifies a target from MDG 1 addressing employment. SDG 17, like MDG 8, calls for strengthening global partnerships.

But several SDGs represent new themes, or highlight issues that were less prominent in the MDGs: goals on energy access (SDG 7), resilient infrastructure (SDG 9), and cities and human settlements (SDG 11) each give higher profile to these issues. Goal 10

Figure 1.2. Sustainable Development Goals

1. End poverty in all its forms everywhere
2. End hunger, achieve food security and improved nutrition and promote sustainable agriculture
3. Ensure healthy lives and promote well-being for all at all ages
4. Ensure inclusive and equitable quality education and promote lifelong learning opportunities for all
5. Achieve gender equality and empower all women and girls
6. Ensure availability and sustainable management of water and sanitation for all
7. Ensure access to affordable, reliable, sustainable and modern energy for all
8. Promote sustained, inclusive and sustainable economic growth, full and productive employment and decent work for all
9. Build resilient infrastructure, promote inclusive and sustainable industrialization and foster innovation
10. Reduce inequality within and among countries
11. Make cities and human settlements inclusive, safe, resilient and sustainable
12. Ensure sustainable consumption and production patterns
13. Take urgent action to combat climate change and its impacts*
14. Conserve and sustainably use the oceans, seas and marine resources for sustainable development
15. Protect, restore and promote sustainable use of terrestrial ecosystems, sustainably manage forests, combat desertification, and halt and reverse land degradation and halt biodiversity loss
16. Promote peaceful and inclusive societies for sustainable development, provide access to justice for all and build effective, accountable and inclusive institutions at all levels
17. Strengthen the means of implementation and revitalize the Global Partnership for Sustainable Development

* Acknowledging that the United Nations Framework Convention on Climate Change is the primary international, intergovernmental forum for negotiating the global response to climate change.

Source: UN General Assembly (2015).

addresses inequalities, a significant absence from the MDGs. It calls for reduction of inequalities (primarily income) within and among countries, and is the focus of chapter 3. SDGs 12 to 15, all addressing aspects of natural resource use and sustainability, are the major new dimension of the SDGs. All of the SDGs apply in principle to all societies, but the natural resource-use and conservation goals are the themes where shared, common interest and responsibility among rich and poor countries are most explicit. Goal 16, "Peaceful societies," with its emphasis on access to justice and effective institutions is cross-cutting and relevant to all the others.

Among the MDGs' omissions was the conspicuous lack of explicit reference to civil and political human rights in the goals. The SDGs responded to this omission by including goals, targets, and indicators focused on women's full and equal political participation (target 5.5) and on forced labor (target 7.8), and Goal 16 targets address prohibition of torture, equal access to justice, transparent institutions, participatory decision making, the right to birth registration, and the right to information.

The MDGs' strategy was clear, and largely successful on its own terms: identify a set of goals that were achievable in many societies, track those goals using numerical benchmarks and indicators, and use them to concentrate attention and finance from aid donors and governments. The SDGs' broad agenda presents challenges for mobilizing external funding, especially if major donor countries' politics continue to shift to the right. But many of the SDGs are less dependent on external aid than were the MDGs, and the broader agenda has important advantages for building strong domestic and international coalitions. By responding to demands that they address women's sexual and reproductive health rights, Indigenous peoples' rights, or conservation of ocean resources (to take three examples), the SDGs broadened the range of actors with a stake in their success. The benefits of this mobilization are clear when we examine the SDG process and engagement in more detail.

The Process: Engaging Civil Society

The SDGs, unlike their predecessors, were developed in a lengthy process that was unusually open to state and nonstate input. Donor agencies, aid-recipient countries, industry representatives, environmental advocates and human rights NGOs, women's organizations, and many more have staked out positions and formed networks to monitor and influence the goals. While such a process has costs – in time, effort, and perhaps in clarity of focus – it also has broadened interest and support for the goals.

That process contrasts with the MDGs' announcement, which was widely criticized as technocratic and top-down. The MDGs were "based largely on the formulation recommended in [the OECD's] *Shaping the 21st Century* and in a World Bank/IMF 2000 strategy paper, so the MDGs evolved "from being disparate findings in various United Nations conferences to becoming a unified set of DAC recommendations ..."[26] As a result, many NGO activists saw the MDGs as a product of the OECD governments and the international financial institutions.[27] There was little engagement by human rights NGOs.

The SDGs, in contrast, emerged from an extended process of organized public input. Two coordinated formal processes and many informal advocacy campaigns and reports fed into the declaration adopted in September 2015. Internal to the United Nations, a high-level task force organized the debate and deliberations, with a UN task team overseeing the process. Outside voices of individuals, NGOs, and associations provided vehicles for input through the "World We Want" process. This process – an online platform through which individuals with Internet access could vote to express their priorities for the post-2015 development agenda – is said to have engaged a million voices in the SDG design process.[28]

The hopeful assertion in UN documents that "broad ownership of the 2030 Agenda must translate into a strong commitment by all stakeholders to ... achieve the Goals" surely puts a positive spin on the process, but civil society participants, too, acknowledge the openness of the SDG planning process.[29] Honniball and Spijkers' study of civil society participation in defining the SDGs found that the UN agencies made determined efforts to involve civil society.[30] The online platform WorldWeWant2015.org invited "people from every corner of the world" to register their priorities and opinions; but despite outreach efforts, the response was not overwhelming, and national consultations with civil society generally brought in modest numbers of organizations. While the voices that made themselves heard were generally those that also mount lobby efforts in national and world capitals, the SDG effort to encourage input was "a vast improvement on the MDGs process."[31]

Independent informal networks also emerged to influence the SDGs. The Center for Economic and Social Rights, Amnesty International, and the Association for Women in Development co-convened some eighty organizations in a Post-2015 Human Rights Caucus.[32] The network "Beyond 2015" mobilized individuals and organizations (1,500 from 142 countries) around several themes, including human rights; and the Campaign for People's Goals for Sustainable Development played a similar role.[33]

Women's rights organizations formed a similar network that worked to influence the SDG goals and targets and remain engaged in their implementation. Major nodes in that network include the Gender and Development Network, Women's Environment and Development Organization (WEDO), Women in Development Europe, and the Post-2015 Women's Coalition. That coalition, the broadest of the networks, includes NGOs, women's organizations, individuals, and international agencies committed to influencing national and international policy priorities.

Advocates of a human rights-based agenda during the SDG negotiation process used a "Litmus Test" advanced by the Post-2015 Human Rights Caucus in 2014. The Litmus Test called for eight steps, including that goals should apply to people in all countries, emphasize transparency and "meaningful participation," ensure accountability and access to justice, "combat inequality and discrimination," set targets of zero for poverty and other goals, and support women's and girls' rights.[34]

The most important outcome of this participatory process may be in participants' continued engagement. That high level of participation could be seen already in 2016, as comments and documents flooded in from civil society organizations in preparation for the July 2016 meeting of the High-level Political Forum on Sustainable Development.[35] The first meeting of the HLPF reviewed twenty-two countries' voluntary reviews, and discussed monitoring of thematic progress on the goals and other topics. Further progress reports and HLPF sessions have drawn sustained criticism from human rights observers, discussed in chapter 7.

The Contents: The SDGs and Human Rights

The SDGs adhere more closely than the MDGs to human rights standards and principles, but they differ in important respects, and this has led to sharp debates among human rights scholars and practitioners. One important discussion about human rights and the SDGs is represented by two broad approaches. One, exemplified by Stephen Marks's 2014 essay on "Prospects for Human Rights in the Post-2015 Development Agenda," argues that conceptual, disciplinary, and political factors prevent the full integration of human rights principles into these global goals.[36] The partial (at best) integration of human rights principles, in this view, diminishes the value of the goals. Brolan and colleagues illustrate this in a 2015 study of how explicit reference to the human right to health failed to gain direct expression in the SDGs.[37] Some critics argue that this not only weakens the SDGs but means that the goals actually undercut and weaken human rights.[38]

An alternative approach is exemplified by Sandra Fredman's 2018 paper on the SDGs, human rights, and gender equality.[39] Fredman sees the SDGs and human rights as complementary and potentially more powerful in combination, and poses in effect this question: Given the complementarities of the SDGs and human rights, and acknowledging their differences, can the goals be linked closely enough to human rights principles and standards to enable the two approaches to reinforce each other in practice? She argues that while the SDGs set national goals in the aggregate and feature an essentially political monitoring and accountability process, human rights focus on rights of the individual and feature an essentially legal accountability approach. The two can be made to be mutually supportive, she argues, if there is strong, energetic support from civil society.

Some human rights and women's advocates along with other progressive movements are understandably frustrated with the SDGs' limitations. The Post-2015 Women's Coalition, for example, charges that the SDGs offer "only a fragmented plan to empowering half the world's population," and leave other gaps with respect to sexual rights, mandating effective sexuality education in schools, and related issues.[40] The Campaign for People's Goals for Sustainable Development, led by IBON International in the Philippines and involving NGOs from around the world, argued that global development policy is dominated by corporate interests, and that the SDGs could not address this fundamental problem.[41] Esquivel argues that while the goals set "progressive gender equality targets," the targets and implicit strategies for women's economic empowerment are limiting, and Sen's 2019 review finds that the SDGs show "significant advances relative to the MDGs" but may not provide a "bold enough framework" to advance gender-justice agendas.[42]

But I take a pragmatic view that the SDGs and the growing campaign for economic and social human rights can strengthen rather than undercut each other. Many of the SDGs and their targets closely parallel economic and social rights standards. The "Human Rights Guide to the SDGs" of the Danish Institute for Human Rights links each SDG goal, target, and indicator to associated human rights standards, and suggests strategies by which human rights advocates can gain additional leverage from the SDGs. The guide argues that because "156 of the 169 targets (more than 92%) are linked with human rights instruments and labour standards," advocates and development agencies can readily construct advocacy strategies and human rights-based approaches to advancing the SDGs.[43] Although the SDGs are far from perfectly aligned with human rights standards and principles, they are closer to these standards than were the MDGs, and they are viewed by many human rights activists as a resource rather than a problem.[44]

Relatively few in the human rights community took an active interest when the MDGs were launched in 2000. But by 2015 all the major human rights NGOs, the UN high commissioner's office, and many human rights scholars had joined the discussion about the SDGs, and human rights advocates were much better positioned to shape and help drive the SDGs' implementation.[45] Economic and social rights advocates are finding ways to link their monitoring of standards in the Economic, Social and Cultural Rights Covenant to corresponding goals and targets in the SDGs. Jensen, using a database created by the Danish Institute for Human Rights, shows that a high percentage of all recommendations made by UN human rights bodies in 2016 and 2017 make explicit reference to one or more SDG goals or targets, showing "relatively widespread engagement by UN human rights mechanisms with the SDGs ..."[46]

The New York-based Center for Economic and Social Rights (CESR) has shaped human rights strategies on the SDGs. CESR takes a critical but engaged view of the SDGs, participating in and reporting on consultative meetings and highlighting inequality, tax policy, and accountability issues as priorities for human rights advocacy. CESR spoke out on the SDGs' deficiencies when the draft SDGs were weakened in several key respects in the final hours of negotiations, and has continued to do so even when annual HLPFs have given only very limited room to independent voices.[47] Some governments, for example, insisted on a weaker formulation of the targets on water and sanitation, and succeeded in removing the widely used phrase "other status," which would have allowed for a later broadening of the list of social groups protected from specific human rights violations.[48] Nonetheless, wrote CESR's Kate Donald, "despite its compromises and shortfalls, this 2030 Agenda for Sustainable Development gives the human rights movement much to work with over the next 15 years." In particular its universal application, language on inequalities, "leave no one behind" theme, and rhetorical referencing of human rights agreements are improvements over the MDGs.[49]

Early scholarship on civil society mobilization around the SDGs confirms that there is a high level of engagement.[50] An analysis by the NYU Law School's International Organizations Clinic gives a high profile to civic participation and highlights four elements of accountability that civic actors can advance: transparency, inclusiveness, deliberation, and responsiveness.[51] There are caveats: Hege and Demailly's study of French and German NGOs observed that some found little value in the SDGs, noting that standards were spelled out more thoroughly in international human rights covenants.[52]

The SDGs are also succeeding in maintaining donors' attention and support. They are helped in this by the fact that they are heirs to the MDGs and use specific quantitative targets familiar in development agencies. The SDGs address specific objectives – end open defecation, increase recycling and safe reuse of water, double the rate of improvement in energy efficiency – in ways that are not laid out in human rights instruments and could not be derived from existing human rights agreements.

What Drives Progress in Global Development?

What gives human rights and development goals their political force, and what incentives for action do they create? Both human rights and development goals derive their political force from two kinds of sources: international pressure and programmatic support on the one hand, and domestic pressure by social movements and other political forces on the other. Both the MDGs and the SDGs rely to some extent on both sets of factors, international and domestic. But whereas the MDGs relied on strategies driven by external aid (and rapid economic growth), the SDGs are more dependent on domestic policy and movements-driven approaches. International and national NGOs have responded differently to the MDGs, human rights, and SDGs; the SDGs are gaining more "traction" among NGOs in the global South.

International Pressure: Goals, Opportunities, and Leverage by Donors

One route to change in international development policy is top down: donor agencies hold some influence and can drive certain kinds of development initiatives by offering funding, incentives and other material support. The World Bank, United States, and British donor agencies led the push in the 1980s for market liberalization through Structural Adjustment policies and the aid that supported them. Other aid initiatives have been connected to various global goals and commitments, and one could describe the history of development practice in the 1980s and 1990s, in part, as a series of international commitments to soft goals and objectives. Whether their record inspires cynicism and despair or measured optimism may depend on one's point of view.

In 1974, participants in the World Food Conference pledged support for a global effort to eradicate hunger in ten years' time. Other global meetings and pledges intervened, including the 1982 UN Conference on Environment and Development (UNCED) in Rio de Janeiro and multiple UN conferences during the 1990s. While each of these produced resolutions and pledges, the MDGs were the best-articulated, widest-ranging, and most sustained campaign, backed by a UN promotion and advocacy campaign.

Longtime senior UN official Richard Jolly provides a spirited defense of goal setting in development practice. Jolly responds to the "conventional wisdom" on the subject, which holds that UN-sponsored goals are "easy for governments to agree to" and "have rarely been taken seriously and have seldom been achieved."[53] That view, Jolly argues, derives from unrealistic expectations that goals be fully achieved in all countries in order for a campaign to be considered successful. A "more nuanced and disaggregated analysis" of their impact shows that some have been achieved by "a large majority of relevant countries," such as smallpox eradication, child immunization, polio eradication, reductions of infant mortality and diarrheal disease; others reached or nearly reached by more than one-half of countries; "real progress" has been made in one-quarter to one-third of countries.[54] Jolly's analysis of goal setting is largely convincing: goals to expand immunization coverage or increase school enrollments have helped development agencies accomplish what they arguably do best: finance and help to deliver discrete services by providing technical expertise and capital.

The MDGs were donor driven, and the MDG experience is a classic example of how international attention can help generate resources for interventions such as growth monitoring, immunizations, and mosquito bed nets, and sometimes for initiatives that require institutional changes, such as expanding girls' access to education. Many discussions of the goals focus on how well they can mobilize external funding, but for human rights advocates their ability to link to the standards and to mobilize domestic political voices is at least equally important. Global goals and incentives alone are seldom enough to spark real, lasting change. Organized, concerted political pressure from within is essential.

Domestic Politics: Mobilization to Win Services and Reforms

Domestic, internal mechanisms are the key to effective political leverage in support of either the SDGs or human rights. There is considerable evidence that social movements and domestic citizen initiatives can spur changes in social policy.[55] This is apparent in the experience of the Treatment Action Campaign in South Africa, which won a government commitment to guarantee treatment to HIV-positive South Africans;[56] Movement of Landless Rural Workers in Brazil, which has settled more than 250,000 households on under-used agricultural land;[57] MKSS network in India, which has won freedom-of-information laws in Rajasthan and several other states;[58] and the Girl Child Network, founded in Zimbabwe and now organizing through a Girl Child Global Network.[59]

But my research shows that the MDGs did little to help mobilize such domestic movements, and the SDGs are better positioned to do so. The MDGs' lack of traction with domestic movements and NGOs became apparent in 2007 when I studied two samples of NGOs active in development: one of national NGOs based in low- and middle-income countries, across regions; and one of international NGOs. I revisited the same forty organizations in 2017, with the same question: how relevant were the SDGs and human rights standards to their work? I examined the relevant sections of the organizations' websites and publications and used a search function, where available, to find references to either the MDGs/SDGs or to human rights.

The twenty Southern-based NGOs and social movement organizations and twenty international NGOs (INGOs) based in the industrial countries[60] were selected to be regionally representative, and to represent work in various sectors. The results are summarized in table 1.2, which reports whether each organization's publications

Table 1.2. International and Southern NGOs: Links to human rights, MDGs, and SDGs

NGO's name and country	Refers to MDG	SDG	Refers to HR 2007	2017	Refers to neither 2007	2017
Ashwinikumar Medical Relief Society (India)					x	
Asia Pacific Network on Food Sovereignty			x	x		
African Medical and Research Foundation (Kenya)	x	x		x		
BRAC Bangladesh		x		x	x	
Children in Need India (CINI)		x		x	x	
Cambodian Human Rights Association			x	x		
Center for Science and the Environment (India)		x		x	x	
CONADES (Peru)			x	x		
Feminist Dalit Organisation (Nepal)			x	x		
Greenbelt Movement (Kenya)		x	x	x		
Forum for Forest Workers (India)		x	x	x		
Llamado Nacional a la Accion Contra Pobreza (Peru)	x					
MST (Brazil)			x	x		
Rwanda Women's Network			x	x		
People's Health Movement (Bangladesh)		x	x	x		
Philippines Rural Reconstruction Movement					x	x
Self-Employed Women's Association (India)			x	x		
Social Watch	x	x				
Treatment Action Campaign (South Africa)			x	x		
Uganda Coalition for Sustainable Development	x	x				
Southern NGOs and Social Movements	4	9	11	15	5	1
Accion International (US)				x	x	
Action Aid (South Africa/UK)	x	x	x	x		
CARE (US)	x	x	x	x		
Caritas (Italy)	x	x		x		
Catholic Relief Services (US)	x	x		x		
CIDSE	x	x		x		
Doctors Without Borders	x	x	x	x		
Global Campaign for Education	x	x	x	x		

NGO's name and country	Refers to MDG SDG		Refers to HR 2007 2017		Refers to neither 2007 2017	
Halifax Initiative (Canada)/Aboveground	x	x	x			
Healthlink Worldwide (disbanded 2010)	x					
International Women's Health Coalition (US)	x	x	x	x		
Lutheran World Federation (Switzerland)	x	x	x	x		
Mercy Corps (US)	x	x		x		
Oxfam (UK)	x	x	x	x		
Physicians for Human Rights (US)	x		x	x		
Project Hope (US)		x		x	x	
Save the Children (US)	x	x	x	x		
Tearfund (Ireland)	x	x		x		
Water Aid (UK)	x	x	x	x		
World Vision (US)	x	x		x		
Northern NGOs	18	17	11	18	2	0

Sources: Organizations' Annual Reports and websites

and advocacy strategies referred in 2007 and in 2017 to the MDGs/SDGs, to human rights, to both, or to neither. Three results stand out.

First, the contrast between international NGOs and the Southern NGOs and social movements is striking. While eighteen of the twenty international NGOs mentioned the MDGs prominently in 2007, only four of the Southern NGOs made any reference at all. By 2017 that gap between North and South had closed somewhat, as NGOs in the global South appear to be more tied into the SDGs (only two years into their existence) than they had been to the MDGs. But the North-South gap remains pronounced.

Second, Southern NGOs refer much more often to human rights than to the global goals. Compared to the MDGs, Southern NGOs refer to human rights (11 of 20) more frequently than to the MDGs (4 of 20). In 2017, Southern NGOs still appear more oriented to human rights (15 of 20) than to the SDGs (9 of 20).

Third, in 2017, international NGOs remain strongly connected to the SDGs, but the interest among INGOs in human rights is reflected in the sharp increase in INGO references to human rights. The discourse of almost all INGOs in this sample now includes references both to the SDGs and to human rights. I will look closely at the significance of INGOs' interest in rights-based approaches to development in chapter 2.

Conclusion

Human rights and development goals are not the same, in theory or in practice, and in many ways the MDGs undercut stronger human rights standards related to health, nutrition, and other economic and social rights. But goals and rights can complement each other, and that should be the objective in implementing the Sustainable Development Goals.

The MDGs depended on the ability of governments, donors, and advocates to focus attention on a few key problems. The SDGs' longer menu of goals and targets requires a broader coalition and close monitoring, both formal and informal. We should expect governments to make choices, and make the political and conceptual shift from the one-size-fits-all approach of the MDGs to one where accountability will be even more challenging, and where societies will choose areas of focus. Governments who choose priority goals and pursue them with domestic political support will be putting in place initiatives that are likely to be durable and effective.

So, advocacy by domestic political movements, a kind of mobilization that the MDGs never succeeded in sparking, will be centrally important to the SDGs, and human rights can be an asset in this. In chapter 2 I examine how human rights standards and principles apply to health, water, and food policy, and how human rights have been used to advance those rights.

chapter two

Principles and Practice, Human Rights and Development

In 2015 and 2016, Iain Levine, deputy executive director for program at Human Rights Watch (HRW), wrote several blog posts on the HRW website discussing the Sustainable Development Goals. The theme was "righting development," making development and the SDGs work better by enforcing and promoting human rights more vigorously.[1] The growing interest in development policy from HRW and other mainstream human rights organizations is matched, at least rhetorically, by their counterparts among development NGOs. Oxfam International sums up its view of human rights in this way: "We believe that respect for human rights will help lift people out of poverty and injustice, allow them to assert their dignity and guarantee sustainable development. When we speak about having a rights-based approach, this is what we mean."[2]

Human rights' growing salience for development policy is good news for global efforts to address poverty and inequality. Human rights have helped to motivate policies that make water and health services free for the poorest citizens, challenge discriminatory limitations on women's land ownership and inheritance, and reduce regional inequalities in access to health care. The surge of interest in how human rights can inform development policy and practice dates to the 1990s, and while it has been embraced more rhetorically than in practice by most development agencies, it has influenced development as a field for a generation. I contend that this human rights-development engagement enters a new period and confronts new tests with the SDGs. The goals incorporate many human rights principles imperfectly and incompletely, and they are criticized by many for undercutting the rigor of human rights standards. But the SDGs show the influence of human rights in ways that the MDGs did not, and they open the door for greater human rights engagement and influence in global development.

What are the implications of human rights, in principle and in practice, for the policies and practices of international development? Human rights are both a legal system encoded in international covenants and a political set of ideas, articulating rights and responsibilities that are grounded in the idea of human dignity. While theorists engage in important debates over which of these views – legal-formal or political – should prevail, in practice human rights have to be understood as both law and politics.

Accordingly, this chapter is organized around *Principles* and *Practice*. *Principles* examines what human rights standards and principles mean for development policy, focusing on the cases of the human right to health and to water. Then *Practice* observes the variety of ways human rights leverage has been used to promote improved health care and access to clean drinking water. With human rights principles clarified, and examples of the social practice of human rights in hand, we will be prepared to analyze the SDGs, and to understand what human rights can offer to their implementation between now and 2030.

Principles: What Human Rights Offer to Development

Development goals and economic and social rights standards often pursue objectives that are closely in parallel. But as I suggested in chapter 1, the logics of the two approaches are quite different. Development goals set targets and indicators that promote relieving suffering for a proportion or number of the population, while human rights standards propose a minimum standard beneath which no person must be allowed to fall, and to which governments that are party to an agreement must move with all possible haste.

Human rights standards such as the human rights to adequate food and to health, and principles such as equality and nondiscrimination, offer important assets to the development field, assets that also differentiate human rights from global development goals and that have profound implications for development policy and practice. Their coverage is universal; they are "owned" by the people; they establish participation and transparency as rights; they create defined obligations for governments; they require continuous improvement; and they demand equal and nondiscriminatory treatment.

Universal Coverage

Human-rights guarantees apply to all members of society and offer them a source of legal and political power with respect to their governments, while establishing standards that governments must meet in the treatment of every person. This principle of universality is an important contrast to the MDGs, whose goals in effect covered some but not all members of society. In contrast, the SDG principle of "no one left behind," with many goals and targets set at reducing extreme poverty (for example) to zero, aligns the SDGs more closely with human rights principles. The SDGs and human rights are universal also in the sense that they apply to all countries, not solely to the low- and middle-income countries.

Ownership

Human rights, as I argued in chapter 1, belong to individuals, while goals belong to states and the international organizations that oversee them. This is more than a theoretical difference, and the successful South African campaign for HIV-positive individuals' right to receive treatment, led by the Treatment Action Campaign (TAC), illustrates the importance of citizens' ability to claim and assert such rights. Launched in 1998, the TAC leaned heavily on the human rights principles incorporated into the 1994 South African Constitution, in order to win policy concessions and judicial victories in a difficult political context.[3] Through litigation, street protests, civil disobedience, and cooperative tactics, TAC won orders from the Constitutional Court in 2002 to begin treating pregnant women who were HIV-positive, to prevent mother-to-child transmission. The government began providing treatment for HIV-positive citizens in 2004, and by 2010 South Africa had the largest HIV treatment program in the world.[4] Its coverage is still far from complete, but the progress was driven by a movement that asserted the rights of HIV-positive South Africans.

Participation and Transparency

Popular participation has become standard boilerplate language in documents for development projects and agencies, and its acceptance has opened up planning processes that once were managed solely by "the experts." But the right to influence decisions that affect one's life is a strong version of "participation," a term that in development circles is used to mean anything from informing people of plans that have already been made, to creative, dynamic joint decision-making processes.[5] Human rights advocates and Indigenous peoples' organizations have won adoption of the right to "Free, Prior and Informed Consent" for Indigenous peoples, defining standards of information, deliberation, and consent that are required for a government to take actions that affect Indigenous-controlled lands.[6] Human rights reinforce participation as a right, not merely good practice for development agencies.

Obligations: Respect, Protect, and Fulfill

Human rights create binding obligations that governments accept when they sign and ratify a human rights covenant. For all human rights these are defined by three key concepts: *respect, protect,* and *fulfill. Respect* refers to the government's responsibility not to take actions that deny their people any specific right – for example, to summarily evict people from their housing, or close a health center without assuring that affordable, accessible services are available. *Protect* refers to the duty to ensure that other actors don't deny people the right to food or health, whether by confiscating farm land, exposing people to harmful emissions, or taking actions in the marketplace that raise the prices of food or medicines beyond people's ability to pay.

Fulfill refers to the ultimate goal, and requires states to work as rapidly as possible toward the realization of all rights for all people in their territory. This commitment to fulfill is closest to the strategy of development goals such as the MDGs or SDGs. The MDGs called for reductions by half of the proportion of people living in poverty or suffering malnutrition, and the SDGs set "zero" goals in many cases. But the "respect, protect, and fulfill" framework calls on governments not only to sponsor programs and policies that expand the number of people with access to health care or food but also to guard against changes that may compromise other populations' access or ability to afford care. In Uganda, for example, the incidence of malnutrition among children under five was reduced from 26 percent to 14 percent between 1995 and 2013, nearly achieving the MDG goal of cutting malnutrition by half. But populations in several areas lost access to farming and grazing lands with the sale or rental of large swaths of land to timber firms and oil palm producers.[7] These transactions compromised the livelihoods and food security of tens of thousands of people, so they violated the government's duties to respect and protect the human right to adequate food.

A human rights-informed approach is important in such a case. Development goals have tended to rely on population-wide statistical measures of progress, while human rights standards, in principle, mandate that no individual's right to food (for example) be compromised or allowed to backslide. Of course, the principle does not forbid every temporary dislocation or job loss caused by a change in land use or markets. But it does require that governments adopt a high standard, ensuring that such losses are minimized, that relocation from lands occurs only with communities' free and informed consent, and that populations suffering them have a voice in decision making and are offered alternative livelihood options, acceptable land, and the necessary short-term assistance.[8]

States can use many different mechanisms to fulfill the right to adequate food. Consumption-oriented programs such as food vouchers, food reserves, micronutrient fortification of staple foods, school meal programs, and programs for pregnant and lactating women are vital. But the right to food also requires a sustainable, resilient system of food production, markets, and incomes that enables people to buy food, coupled with social protections for those without adequate incomes. The human right to food, as George Kent argues, is not just the right to a minimum number of calories.[9] It requires that people have choices about their food and the dignity of earning or producing it. The right to food entails availability, accessibility (including affordability), and acceptability (including cultural appropriateness).[10]

Despite work within the UN human rights bodies to develop and encourage ESC indicators and benchmarks, economic and social rights generally have seldom employed numerical targets and indicators, although the sector's relatively recent initiatives are discussed later in this chapter. Their complexity no doubt partly accounts for de Beco's observation that "such indicators seem more popular in academic circles than with practitioners. While academics have shown great interest in them and have been developing human rights indicator sets, practitioners are less enthusiastic about using them ..."[11] Economic and social rights have historically suffered from the lack of authoritative and universally accepted measures for their fulfillment.

Two principles are intended to give force to the standards and encourage rapid progress: progressive realization, and non-retrogression. *Progressive realization* defines governments' obligation to move as rapidly as possible toward full realization of their peoples' rights. It recognizes that budgetary and other constraints may make it impossible to fulfill all rights immediately, but it establishes the legal obligation to act "to the maximum of its available resources" to move toward full realization (ICESCR Article 2.1). Progressive realization requires both that governments make efforts, for example by increasing budgetary allocations, and that there be continuous improvement in conditions.[12]

The principle of *non-retrogression* further stipulates that no backsliding or slippage is permitted in the face of budgetary pressure or under a new regime. States may have limited capacities to fund specific health services for all citizens, but they are not permitted to reduce coverage once a service is made available. Like progressive realization, the principle lacks strong enforcement mechanisms, but it upholds the ethical principle that it is as important to protect the gains won by a household living just above the poverty line as it is to raise another household out of poverty.[13]

These principles requiring continuous progress and maximum effort by governments are vague compared to numerical goals and benchmarks. The absence of credible, widely accepted metrics has been a weakness for ESC rights in influencing development policy. Indeed, the High Commissioner for Human Rights wrote hopefully in the preface to a guide to human rights indicators that indicators were "a potential bridge between the human rights and the development policy discourses."[14] In an effort to devise methods that allow credible monitoring of governments' efforts as well as outcomes over time, human rights practitioners have recently launched two new approaches. One, the OPERA framework (Outcomes, Policy Efforts, Resources, and Assessment), is a straightforward framework that guides a review of each of these aspects of a country's ESC rights implementation.[15]

The Index of Social and Economic Rights Fulfillment (SERF) is a more fully elaborated framework to measure and rank national governments' fulfillment of their ESC human rights obligations. Outcome measures such as rates of malnutrition don't capture a government's "effort," its duty to move as rapidly as possible to fully realize the rights of its people "to the maximum of its available resources." The SERF index measures effort by focusing on the relationship between how fully a population enjoys fundamental economic and social rights and the state's "resource capacity" to fulfill its obligations.[16] The index provides objective measures to assess both outcomes and government effort by tracking budget allocations and other indicators. SERF is now linked to the Human Rights Measurement Initiative (HRMI), an initiative whose implications for monitoring progress on the SDGs is discussed in chapter 7.

It remains to be seen how influential these human rights measurement initiatives will become. But they offer a valuable complement to SDG indicators, a way to link the measurable outcomes tracked by most SDG indicators with the principle that governments must make maximum effort to advance economic and social rights.

Equality and Nondiscrimination

Equality and nondiscrimination are central to ESC rights and critically important to the impact human rights can have on development policy. States will move over time toward full realization of economic and social human rights, but they have an immediate and absolute legal obligation to eliminate discriminatory treatment. This means that individuals have an equally absolute right to treatment that is equal and nondiscriminatory.

Exactly what constitutes discrimination can be debated in specific circumstances, and the UN Committee on Economic, Social and Cultural Rights clarified the scope of what is prohibited under nondiscrimination in the 2009 General Comment Number 20.[17] Discrimination, under General Comment 20, can be formal or substantive, and direct or indirect, and these distinctions help to clarify the implications of nondiscrimination for development policy. Direct discrimination is spelled out in law or regulation, while indirect discrimination occurs when a law or policy that appears neutral in fact has a disproportionate impact on a group. Requiring birth certificates for school enrolment, for example, may constitute indirect discrimination if members of social, ethnic, or economic groups are unlikely to have such documents. Discriminatory treatment may include expenditure, staffing, or other patterns of resource allocation that have the effect of treating defined social groups differently in ways that are not justified by "reasonable and objective" social purposes.[18]

Formal discrimination is encoded in law or regulation (a law prohibiting women's inheritance of property, for example), while substantive discrimination may be the result of persistent patterns of prejudice or cultural practice. Women may have equal land ownership rights under the law, for example, but be largely excluded by the widespread practice of informal land transactions among men, as in Nicaragua, or by the enforcement of "customary law" by tribal authorities, as in many African societies.[19] The remedies vary in practice, but the two forms of discrimination are both considered to violate core principles of economic and social human rights.

States are expected to abolish laws, regulations, and practices that create a pattern of discrimination and to avoid practices that tend to create patterns of discrimination in implementing programs or laws. Obviously, not all forms of inequality are evidence of discrimination, and not all forms of discrimination are immediately recognizable from a review of human development indicators or budget allocations. Still, the strong prohibition of discriminatory treatment in human rights law offers an important tool for analyzing and addressing persistent inequalities in development policy and practice.

Equality and nondiscrimination are enormously important for the impact of human rights on development policy. Chapter 3 is devoted to inequality, and will show how goals like the MDGs that aim simply to reduce the number of people suffering poverty or malnutrition can largely exclude some groups – ethnic minorities or women, for example – while overall measures for the population improve. Insisting on policies that remedy this kind of discrimination is one of the most important contributions human rights can make to development in practice.

Human Rights and Development Policy: Health and Water

How do these economic and social human rights standards and principles help to shape development policy? The human rights to health and to water have contrasting histories, and examining their content and interpretation will allow an analysis of how they are employed to change policies and conditions in practice. Each establishes a set of standards that define the right operationally; applies the principles of equality and nondiscrimination, universality, nonretrogression (and others); and provides a language and mindset that grounds progress in people's rights rather than in charity.

Human Right to Health

The standards – concrete definitions of what constitutes the right to health, food, or water – are essential. Article 12 of the ICESCR declares "the right of everyone to the enjoyment of the highest attainable standard of physical and mental health," and spells out the basic obligations of states, giving special attention to the health of children; the health of natural and workplace environments; disease prevention, treatment, and control; and the provision of health-care services. As with many human rights treaties, governments are required to report to the supervising committee every five years.[20]

The authoritative General Comment of the UN Committee on Economic, Social and Cultural Rights lays out the "AAAQ standard": health facilities, goods, and services must meet standards of availability, accessibility, acceptability, and quality. States must concern themselves with the accessibility (including affordability) of health facilities, goods, and services for every individual, protect each person's right to participate in decisions regarding their health, and provide a minimum of access to potable water, sanitation, health care, and related goods at costs that are affordable to all, on a nondiscriminatory basis.[21] In poor countries and especially in rural areas, this standard of health access has been elusive.

Health includes a wide range of issues, not solely health-care delivery, and this is reflected in the agenda of the UN's special rapporteur on the right to health. The active agenda includes an expected set of high-profile issues where human rights are often invoked, including HIV/AIDS, access to essential medicines, mental health, and sexual and reproductive rights. It includes a second set of issues that may be less visible to those outside the health professions, such as drug policy and the financing and organization of health systems.[22] Finally, the agenda also engages with the social determinants of health, including the effects of poverty, climate change, violence, and conditions affecting specific groups, including children, LGBT and sexual minorities, and the elderly.[23]

Health-care finance is discussed at length in chapter 4, and the issue of affordability is central to governments' obligations. Human rights law upholds a principle of equity in health-care finance and access, which requires that health-care facilities, goods, and services be "affordable for all," and that poorer households "not be disproportionately burdened."[24] Health as a human right, then, does not mean that health care must be free, but it does require a system that protects low-income households from disproportionate costs and from falling into poverty as a result of health-care costs.

Human Right to Water

Although water is closely tied to the rights to food and to health, a human right to water appears nowhere in the major human rights agreements. It was formally recognized with the 2002 release of General Comment 15, and the 2010 adoption by the General Assembly of a resolution recognizing the human right to water.[25]

Drawing on various international agencies' standards, the UN high commissioner for human rights defines the right to water for practical purposes in terms of quantity, distance and time required to collect it, cost, and purity. "According to WHO, in order to have a basic access to 20 litres per day, the water source has to be within 1,000 metres of the home and collection time should not exceed 30 minutes."[26] Water need not be provided free of charge, but its cost should never be "a barrier to access," and a target expenditure of no more than 3 percent of household budget is sometimes cited.[27] One strategy for upholding this requirement while allowing water utilities to recover costs is the "block tariff," which provides a defined amount of water in each billing period free, and charges for consumption exceeding that defined amount on a scale that increases with consumption.

Water illustrates the life and influence of human rights as ideas not exclusively tied to a body of international law. The absence of a separate standard before 2002 did not prevent advocates from claiming that water was a human right. Advocates asserted that water is a foundation for the right to life and right to health, and constructed arguments linked to other international agreements, such as the Convention on the Rights of the Child and Article 14(2)(h) of the Convention on the Elimination of all forms of Discrimination Against Women (CEDAW), or the Millennium Declaration that accompanied the MDGs.

Advocates worldwide have appealed to the sentiment that water is a human right, using strategies as diverse as a successful campaign for a constitutional amendment in Uruguay; street demonstrations in Bolivian cities that blocked privatization of urban water systems; cooperative campaigns in Manila that expanded access by working with private companies; and legal challenges in South Africa.[28] Legal rulings in South Africa and elsewhere have mandated that a minimum amount of water be free to all consumers.[29]

The Practice: Human Rights in Action

How do human rights and human rights methods advance health and nutrition in practice? The remainder of this chapter examines human rights-based approaches used by development agencies and governments and by historic human rights agencies. Work to advance human dignity and human rights is not confined to the legal system, nor to the professionalized arena of international human rights NGOs and agencies. The work in community development, social movements, educational institutions, and many other arenas is sometimes referred to as the social practice of human rights.[30] The methods, strategies, and actors are many: community development organizations that do human rights education, health-care institutions, social movements, and both international and local NGOs of many kinds. The working definition that I use considers development work to be "human rights based" if it "promotes justice, equality and freedom and tackles the power issues that lie at the root of poverty and exploitation" and "makes use of the standards, principles and methods of human rights, social activism, and of development."[31]

The emergence in the 1990s of human rights-based approaches to development won enthusiastic support from practitioners and observers who saw the potential for greater accountability, stronger ties by development organizations to social movements, and deeper, transformative impact on development policy that had been dominated by neoliberal theories and policies.[32] Development donors in the UN system, some bilateral donors (Swedish Sida and British DfID), and many international NGOs (Care, Oxfam, ActionAid, Save the Children UK and Sweden, PLAN International, and others) affirmed that they were adopting "rights-based" approaches, and scholars suggested that rights-based approaches were taking the development sector by storm. Kindorney, Ron, and Carpenter write that "[w]ithin less than a decade, this new approach had swept through the websites, policy papers, and official rhetoric of multilateral development assistance agencies, bilateral donors, and nongovernmental organizations (NGOs) worldwide."[33] Schmitz asserts that "[h]uman rights-based approaches (HRBAs) to development have become the new and dominant norm among most development organizations over the past decade," and Grugel and Piper write that "[h]uman rights ... are now seen as central to the development process."[34]

But a sober assessment of the impact on development agencies suggests we should examine the development work more carefully. My 2018 study, with Ellen Dorsey, shows that development donors have tended to affirm human rights rhetorically without making major changes in operations, and suggests several reasons.[35] "Rights-based" has no widely accepted definition, and development organizations often use "rights" and "human rights" broadly, as "an all-encompassing reference to people's general sense of equity, justice, entitlement and/or fairness."[36] This "lack of precision," Nyamu-Musembi and Cornwall argue, makes it easy for organizations to "repackage what they have always done in the new language."[37] Destrooper observes the same tendency in a 2016 review of UNICEF's rights-based work.[38]

Organizational routines, practices, and cultures have tended to steer human rights emphases toward familiar, less challenging policies and practices. Development organizations tend to emphasize procedural rights over substantive rights – that is, participation and voice over the right to food, health, or housing. Finally, the MDGs likely played a role in taming the human rights-based trend. Their dominant influence on development aid priorities appeared to shift DfID and several UN agencies away from human rights approaches.[39] More generally, while the MDGs highlighted meeting numerical targets, they encouraged donors to sidestep the human rights priorities that are the focus of the remainder of this book: addressing inequalities;[40] building responsive health systems;[41] and expanding access to land, capital, and good jobs.[42]

But while there has not been widespread, transformative adoption of human rights methods in international development agencies, there is plenty of evidence that human rights values and methods can shape and strengthen campaigns, programs, and policies. That influence is visible in the work of local and international organizations on health and water issues.

Human Rights in Practice: Health and Water

To see how human rights can support and inform the making of social policy, consider how several movements for health and water rights have played out across the global South. A typology of rights-based actions developed by Gauri and Gloppen in 2012 helps us to understand these in more detail.[43] Human rights-based work, whether led by traditional community development organizations or longtime human rights advocates, can be seen as using one or more of these four approaches.

- Global Compliance approaches: These include pressing for ratification, reporting, and compliance with human rights standards, through both legal and political accountability efforts. Examples are "shadow reporting" by NGOs to UN human rights bodies, and calling attention to violations that the governments' reporting does not acknowledge.[44]
- Programming approaches: These include projects and programs that expand the capacities of duty bearers and/or rights-holders and use analysis informed by human rights standards and principles.

- Awareness raising: This includes rhetoric, advocacy, and educational work to strengthen awareness of a group's rights, including through social movements (Gauri and Gloppen use the label "Rights Talk").
- Legal mobilization: Litigation in domestic courts to strengthen the legal basis for claiming particular rights can lead to substantive policy changes, as in India's right-to-food cases and South Africa's rulings on the right to treatment for HIV-positive citizens.[45]

Some of these actions are pursued primarily by historic human rights organizations; most work on global compliance approaches, for example, is done by agencies familiar with the treaty bodies and staffed by human rights lawyers. Human Rights Watch is a leading voice among international NGOs documenting national laws and community practices that prohibit women from owning and inheriting property in many societies. The Global Initiative for Economic, Social and Cultural Rights (GI-ESCR) has done significant work to strengthen UN and regional human rights standards on women's economic rights.

Material aid and community development work are mainly the domain of humanitarian and development organizations, and since the 1990s some of these have adopted human rights-based approaches to the design and implementation of projects.[46] But some human rights NGOs also do training, capacity building, and other support work that uses programming approaches. Organizations in both sectors may engage in human rights education and awareness raising and participate in political advocacy, while human rights organizations and public-interest lawyers are most likely to litigate in domestic courts. The NGO Namati-Global has made important innovations in using justice systems to advance economic rights through a Global Legal Empowerment Network.[47]

These four categories give us a guide for observing how human rights principles translate into action. We can see how these strategies are used and combined and how human rights principles are applied in human rights work on health, water, and food.

In Practice: Health

In practice there are multiple dimensions to the quality of a population's health, from the social determinants of health (air and water quality, nutrition, housing, literacy) to the quality of care available and its cost. Human rights principles have proven helpful in meeting difficult health challenges locally and nationally. To see this in practice, I examine selected rights-driven initiatives in India, Nepal, Mozambique, and Brazil (table 2.1).

In India, human rights advocacy for health confronts extreme inequalities of income and government services, a sharp contrast between sometimes wealthy, modern, post-industrial urban life and the extreme poverty of poor and underserved villages and urban slums. Here, as in most domestic rights-based litigation, the cases don't appeal directly to international standards but to the national statutes or constitutional provisions in which those principles are enshrined.[48] Recent experience shows that such public-interest litigation, linked to active, rights-driven campaigns for better health services, can establish national law and norms and force improved delivery of essential health services.

McBroom documents the record of legal challenges addressing health-related services in India.[49] The long record of such litigation, often coordinated by the New Delhi-based Human Rights Law Network (HRLN), has addressed various issues, including the rights of excluded communities to be served by child nutrition programs, human rights abuses committed in facilities for sterilization of women, the quality of care in maternity and delivery wards, and access to effective treatment for tuberculosis. In Kenya, litigation beginning in 2009 challenged the government's protection of patent rights for anti-retroviral medicines, and victory in 2012 opened access for HIV patients to cheaper generic versions of the drugs.[50] In each case, legal efforts to establish these rights "can only chip away" at massive inequalities.[51]

But the record in India also shows the pivotal contributions that such litigation can make. HRLN researchers have assembled authoritative evaluations of existing TB treatment programs, for example, which provide the basis not only for litigation but for

Table 2.1. Actions to promote the human right to health: five cases

	Form of Human Rights Action	Key Actors, Allies, Impact
India	Litigation in Indian courts	"Chipping away" at inequalities, securing redress for individuals
Nepal	Expanded services under Safe Motherhood & Newborn Health Plan	Improved coverage of emergency obstetric care in rural clinics
Mozambique	Training of volunteer health defenders, confronting local service providers to improve delivery	Strong record of grievance petitions and response
Brazil	Legislation and implementation of national health system	Labor government in alliance with health advocates
Global: Essential Medicines	International pressure for exceptions to patent protections; campaigns for ARV access in South Africa and elsewhere	Global campaign for Essential Medicines; national movements together with HIV/AIDS activism

government and nonprofit service providers to track the quality of services. By taking state governments to court, they have highlighted and corrected appalling conditions at particular health-care facilities and forced states to increase expenditures to fund health services guaranteed under law.

But not all human rights progress involves litigation. In neighboring Nepal, the national government's ten-year commitment (2007–2016) to a Safe Motherhood and Newborn Health Plan is grounded in a commitment to anchoring health initiatives in human rights principles. The initiative includes expanding access to emergency obstetric care, often a critical gap in remote rural areas. A range of family planning and emergency obstetric care services, including in rural primary health clinics, contributed to significant gains in skilled birth attendance, maternal health, child survival, and other key variables.[52]

In Mozambique, advocates are addressing a perennial problem: government agencies' failure to translate good policy into high-quality, equitable services because of failures at the point of delivery. Mozambique's constitution affirms the human right to health, and health policy has been strengthened by a 2006 Charter of Patients' Rights, by 2014 rights guarantees for HIV-positive persons, and by other statutes and patient protocols.[53] But how can health advocates confront the routine problems that undercut the delivery of health services: bribery, staff absenteeism, and the lack of procedures to force local officials to respond to grievances?

Grassroots health advocates (*defensores de saude*) in Mozambique are one part of the answer. Sponsored by the NGO Namati, they use multiple strategies to help communities confront local service providers, strengthen accountability mechanisms, engage in dialogue with local officials, and strengthen patients' understanding of their rights related to health care. They lean on a strong body of statutory and constitutional guarantees, including the 2006 Charter of Patients' Rights and Obligations, and work systematically to "close the gap between policy and reality."[54] The key to the *defensores'* approach is their ability to combine follow-up and advocacy on specific cases where patients received substandard service with an ongoing effort to facilitate dialogue between the community and public officials. A review of 1,307 grievances in several districts between 2013 and 2015 shows that this combined strategy has been highly effective.[55] When coupled with ongoing education to raise "rights awareness," the strategy corrects specific abuses and improves the level of service.

Brazil's experience raises the human right-to-health debate to the national level.[56] Consistent with the affirmation of human rights in its 1988 constitution, Brazil created a national health system in 1990 that is universal, community-based, and tax-funded. The positive effect on women's sexual and reproductive health has been reinforced by a series of policies and initiatives affirming every person's right to family planning information and services (1996), "humanized" care in pregnancy and childbirth (2000), and comprehensive care for women's health (2004). National results are impressive, showing big gains in skilled birth attendance, antenatal care, and prevalence of contraceptive use across all income quintiles between 1996 and 2007.[57]

Finally, at the global level, human rights advocates have pushed for anti-retroviral (ARV) drugs used to treat HIV and other essential medicines to be treated differently under rules governing intellectual property rights. Campaigning by civil society organizations and governments has used the human right to health to make the case for exceptions to intellectual property protections, allowing increased production of cheaper generic versions of essential medicines. Helfer summarizes the global human rights campaign and domestic advocacy in South Africa, Brazil, and elsewhere in Latin America that led to national policy gains and won a "modest weakening" of patent protections for widely used medicines, access to which is a key component of the right to health.[58] The fact that legal pressure for access to essential medicines and particularly to ARV drugs was most successful in Latin America reflects the region's "rights-rich constitutions" as well as the failings of governments to respond quickly and effectively to the AIDS pandemic.[59]

In Practice: Water

The human right to water, though formally recognized only in 2010, has been asserted and claimed for much longer. The claim that water is a resource in nature and not a commodity has been central to debates over private management of water utilities, to competing claims to groundwater between small farmers and beverage bottling plants, and in calls for water service to arid or difficult-to-serve communities such as urban slum settlements.[60] In recent decades the claim of a right to water has often been central to disputes over the privatization of urban water utility schemes, plans to expand rural water access, and the development of models and systems to serve the populations of the rapidly expanding peripheries of many urban areas.

Battles over the privatization of urban water utility management have seen some of the most visible assertions of the human right to water. At the municipal and national levels, coalitions of human rights, environmental, consumer, and labor-union activists have mobilized to oppose the contracting out or (rarely) sale of public utilities to private firms.[61] These movements have sometimes explicitly pressed for recognition of a human right to water, as in Uruguay, where the 2003 outcome was a constitutional amendment

Table 2.2. Actions to promote the human right to water: five cases

Country	Form of Human Rights Action	Key Actors, Allies, Impact
South Africa	Litigation in South African courts	Municipal workers union; rulings in constitutional courts
Uruguay	Campaign for Constitutional Amendment for Right to Water	Neighborhood consumer organizations, public sector unions
Bangladesh	Adoption of model created by NGO DSK for water service in Dhaka slums	DSK, Dhaka public water utility, neighborhood "water points"
Kenya	Adoption of a "pro-poor, rights-based" framework for service to Nairobi slums	International NGO WaterAid, other NGOs, neighborhood groups
Paraguay	2007 law, reorganization of national water services	National Health Ministry

affirming the right to water and the national public obligation to provide it.[62] In South Africa, litigation challenging several cities' privatization schemes rested on the right-to-water language in the country's 1996 constitution.[63] More often, movements have used the language of water rights while pressing for a return to public management.[64]

In these cases and others (table 2.2), the threat or reality of privatization of a municipal water utility was a central factor in mobilizing NGO and social movements. Although the form of mobilization, the composition of the coalitions, and the nature of NGOs' intervention varied greatly, in all cases the anti-privatization advocates could be said to be calling for human rights-inspired initiatives. The disputes are part of a broader trend against privatization contracts and a return to public sector management often referred to as re-municipalization. In the 1990s and early 2000s privatization schemes, often encouraged by the World Bank, provoked opposition and resistance. The political coalitions varied, with unions more significant actors in Uruguay and Argentina, political parties figuring prominently in Uruguay and South Africa, and judicial action based on formal human rights-inspired legal principles in South Africa.

But the right to water – as legal doctrine, political principle, or organizing sentiment – was present in every case, and has been influential in other domains of water policy as well. In the years since formal UN endorsement of the human right to water, public health and human rights authorities have geared up to clarify its implications in practice, and several national governments have adopted new constitutional or statutory water policies resting on the human right. Paraguay's rapid progress in expanding the rural population's access to safe water – access grew from 51 percent to 94 percent between 2000 and 2017 – was driven by the 2007 Water Law's commitment to water access as a human right, and by an effective system of local water management associations (*Juntas de Saneamiento*).[65]

Rights-based interventions have also persuaded governments to provide service to urban slum neighborhoods that often spring up without planned services. Residents often buy water of dubious quality at astronomical prices from private vendors, but initiatives in Kenya and Bangladesh are demonstrating policies and institutions that deliver water. Kenya's 2002 Water Services Act, reinforced by the 2010 constitution, created a "pro-poor, rights-based" framework for water policy, together with institutions to implement and regulate drinking water.[66] The policy framework is solid, but there are significant obstacles to implementing it: slum dwellers and others without legal title to their land have trouble getting water service, and huge informal neighborhoods in Nairobi are logistically difficult to serve.[67] Glaring disparities remain between slum dwellers and the population as a whole, and challenges around regulating water quality and sales by informal vendors and kiosks and regularizing service to all residents.

The government of Bangladesh has implemented its urban water policy in parts of its sprawling capital, Dhaka, by collaborating with the NGO Dushtha Shasthya Kendra (DSK) and embracing their model, which emphasizes forming local community groups and encouraging their interaction and negotiation with local water authorities.[68] The DSK "water point" model is a framework for the Dhaka Water Supply and Sewerage Authority to serve previously unserved neighborhoods. Community organizations of eight women manage price, payment, and other features of a "water point" that serves as many as 500 neighborhood households with two hand pumps, a reservoir to hold water from the Dhaka utility, and a direct connection to the utility pipes.[69] Beginning in 1992, DSK provided guarantees to the utility that community organizations would pay water bills, a step that was needed to overcome the cautious skepticism of utility managers. But by 2008 the utility was providing water service without the NGO guarantee, and by 2017 the Asian Development Bank was praising the system's "turnaround" and vastly improved delivery to the most difficult-to-serve neighborhoods.[70]

In water policy as in health policy, therefore, initiatives to advance rights are widespread and varied, linked to the human right to water by the principle that cost should not be a barrier to access. The initiatives have been advanced through the ballot box, in the streets, in the courts, and through community-based work to organize services and negotiate with water utilities. They have shaped policy and institutions, assigning priority to making services available and affordable without discrimination and with special attention to those whose rights have been overlooked.

Conclusion

Human rights principles have important implications for economic and social policies, and for the practice of international development by NGOs and donor agencies. Rights-based approaches have been widely praised but unevenly adopted and implemented by development agencies. But when human rights principles and standards are rigorously and creatively applied to development policy problems, they can have an important impact on communities and on a larger scale. The movements reviewed in this chapter use human rights principles and advance them by pressing for improved health-care coverage and water services in a range of countries and cities across Africa, Asia, and Latin America. The human rights-based strategies are diverse, from global and national legal advocacy to human rights education and projects that strengthen communities and government agencies. In the next four chapters I argue that these human rights principles also have implications for global development goals, in particular calling for greater emphasis on inequality, health systems with universal coverage, and access to productive assets – land and decent work – for people living in poverty.

chapter three

Challenging Inequalities

High levels of inequalities have corrosive economic, political, and social effects, and in low- and middle-income countries where they exist alongside extreme poverty, addressing inequalities should be an urgent priority. Yet the MDGs' targets and indicators focused attention and incentives on reducing absolute numbers or proportions of people suffering health or nutrition problems, not on addressing enduring inequalities, and inequalities generally did not improve and often grew worse even as MDG targets were met. Moreover, as average incomes grew in populous emerging economies such as India, China, Brazil, Indonesia, and Nigeria, inequalities became the key factor in explaining and addressing continued extreme poverty.

In human rights terms, patterns of inequality based on gender, ethnicity, geography, or other factors are evidence of discrimination and are in violation of human rights principles. They also have powerful practical impacts. For example, Quinn and Kumar's 2014 study of health inequalities and preparation for global influenza epidemics reveals that health inequalities encourage and accelerate the spread of infectious respiratory, malarial, tubercular, and diarrheal diseases.[1] Inter-group inequalities are strongly associated with violent conflict, and high levels of income inequality are associated with a stunning range of social ills in the rich countries, affecting educational outcomes, public health, teen pregnancy, obesity, and even life expectancy.[2]

In short, there are principled and pragmatic reasons to focus more attention on inequalities, and although the SDGs' effort to do so is flawed, it is an opportunity for human rights and other advocates. The goal has reinforced a growing global concern about income inequality that is generating a broad agenda to tackle disparities. This chapter makes the case that inequalities matter and are important to a human rights-based approach to development. It discusses in turn inequality in the MDGs and in the SDGs, and shows how governments have put policies in place to reduce inequalities, and how a broader grassroots movement and agenda against inequality is coming together during the SDG period.

Inequality on the Rise

Over the period of the MDGs, the standard measure of domestic income inequality, the Gini coefficient, rose substantially in almost all high-income countries and in many low- and middle-income countries.[3] The Gini coefficient is a number between 0 and 1 that indicates how far an income distribution is from perfect equality. A Gini score of zero would indicate perfectly equal income distribution, and higher scores indicate greater inequality. In 2019, Canada's Gini is 0.340, that of the United States 0.415, and of Brazil 0.533. Slovenia's 0.255 is the lowest current estimate; South Africa, Sierra Leone, Central African Republic, and Botswana top the list, all above 0.60.[4]

Globally, average incomes of low-/middle-income and high-income countries also became more unequal – that is, the gap widened between rich countries and poorer countries – unless the country data are weighted for population. In that case, because of rapid economic growth in India and China, global average incomes across countries were more equally distributed.[5] Finally, by measures of "global inequality" – the global distribution of income among individuals, ignoring national borders – the world grew dramatically more unequal in recent decades, as wealth and incomes of the top earners grew rapidly.[6]

All of these measures are important, but I will focus primarily on in-country inequalities, because these are the inequalities that national policies are best able to address, and on which human rights principles are clearest. Country by country, the record of income inequality during the 1990s and 2000s is mixed, with roughly equal numbers of countries growing more unequal and less unequal.[7] Many societies in Latin America grew more equal, as did a few in Africa and Asia, particularly Southeast Asia. This is potentially good news if we can identify the conditions and policies that led to greater equality.

But first we need to understand inequalities and their effects. Of the many measures of inequality other than income, wealth is generally the most important, because the ability to accumulate wealth in the form of housing, property, savings, animals, or other goods is key to families' ability to make lasting gains in income and well-being.[8] Wealth is distributed more unequally than income in every country that reports data on both,[9] and it is a predictor of income gains, a source of reserves in times of crisis, and a critical factor in families' ability to invest in children's education.

Inequalities are manifested in other life conditions as well, as recent health-related evidence shows. Urban-rural differentials are often high: in rural India, child mortality and rates of anemia among mothers and children are significantly higher than in urban areas, while infant mortality is dramatically higher (73 versus 40 per 1,000 live births).[10] The incidence of a range of diseases and life-shortening health conditions is many times higher in low-income countries across the Americas than in the United States and Canada; incidence of diseases and life expectancy also vary dramatically across income groups within countries in the region.[11] Disparities appear in the rich countries as well: infant mortality in the mid-2000s was 13.35 per 1,000 live births among African-Americans in the United States, 5.8 among whites.[12] Research has documented inequalities in the implementation of land-tenure rights for men and women;[13] regional inequalities in access to water and sanitation, within countries;[14] and inequalities in access to family planning and sexual and reproductive health services, within countries.[15]

Defenders of inequality, even extreme inequality, argue that increased inequality is a phase in a pattern of economic development; that much inequality reflects merit, hard work, and effective investment that must be rewarded for economies to grow;[16] and that worrying about inequality is a distraction from the real moral task, which is to raise the living standard of the poor majority to acceptable levels.[17] But leading economists and political economists are convinced that inequalities, particularly within societies, are a compelling concern.[18] Our focus is primarily on low- and middle-income countries, where gross inequality and extreme deprivation often create a toxic situation that demands effective action.

Why Inequality Matters

Arguments about the significance of inequality easily become confused, because high concentration of income is often associated with a high rate of poverty. But while high levels of inequality are often associated with extreme poverty, inequality is also a serious problem independent of income poverty. There are three broad reasons for this, tied to inequality's economic, social/political, and human rights impacts.

Economically, multiple studies show that "high or rising inequality" of income and particularly of assets has a negative effect on growth rates.[19] Evidence is even stronger that inequality slows countries' ability to reduce poverty through economic growth.[20] The old debate over whether economic growth itself will reduce poverty is now known to depend largely on the degree of inequality in a society: moderate to high growth rates over extended periods have much larger effects on poverty when inequality is less severe, both in economic models and in the experience of recent decades.[21]

Historically, people have tolerated inequalities more readily when they believe that social mobility gives them and their children a good chance to climb the social ladder. But extreme inequality limits social mobility. The evidence for this comes from places as diverse as rural Ethiopia,[22] OECD countries,[23] and Latin America and the Caribbean, where Ferreira developed an index to estimate how much of a society's inequality is determined by circumstances beyond individuals' control.[24] In practice, across many societies, extreme inequality of wealth or of income also signals extreme inequality of *opportunity*. An economy in which returns to capital are disproportionately higher than returns to labor leads to a trap for poor households, in which almost no amount of effort is enough to accumulate savings and assets to be able to invest in a house, property, education, or any other livelihood strategy.[25]

This is particularly true and costly in cases of horizontal inequalities, when a clearly identified group suffers visible inequalities.[26] This distinction is important, because the evidence shows that poor groups' inability to participate effectively in political life isn't mainly a function of absolute poverty – that is, is not primarily because they can't afford to participate. It is relative: because they can't participate in the ways and with the effect that wealthier groups do, they are left on the margins of political life.[27] John Gaventa calls attention to this link between economic inequality and political marginalization.[28] The two are so intertwined, he argues, that social movements and development practitioners often fail to distinguish between them. Thus, we refer to access to credit as a form of "empowerment," when the language of power used to be reserved for the political realm.

Nancy Birdsall, longtime president of the Washington, DC-based Center for Global Development, shows that inequality makes it more difficult to create and maintain accountable government, and discourages the kind of social and civic interactions that make effective collective decision making possible.[29] A high level of inequality not only makes governance processes less fair by skewing access and power, it colors poorer groups' perceptions of their ability to participate meaningfully, reinforcing social and political institutions that favor wealthier groups' interests.[30] This pattern appears in wealthy societies as well, where upper-middle-class families "hoard" privileged access through social networks to schools, clubs, internships, and other social goods.[31]

Economists debate the fine points, but mainstream economists and donor agencies, including the World Bank in its 2006 *World Development Report* and the IMF in its 2013 Discussion Note on Income Inequality, agree that extreme inequality reproduces itself – and poverty conditions – across generations. This produces what

Bourguignon and colleagues call "inequality traps," and how it happens is no mystery.[32] Extreme relative poverty leads to exclusion from public policy or community decisions, "discrimination in access to state services," unequal treatment in the legal system, "and, ultimately, the reproduction of poverty over time."[33]

Extreme inequality, in short, has economic, political, and social-psychological effects that are bad for poor people, for the economy, and for society.

Human Rights and Inequality

No single human rights standard directly upholds income parity as a right, but nondiscrimination and equality are a powerful theme in human rights doctrine and practice, and human rights approaches to development have become strongly associated with egalitarian development policy.[34] Among human rights scholars and professionals there is growing sentiment that because inequality is so strongly linked to many of the substantive rights and to principles of nondiscrimination that are central to human rights practice, human rights advocacy should take a strong position on extreme inequalities.[35]

The stipulation in the Universal Declaration of Human Rights that "everyone is entitled to a social and international order in which the rights and freedoms set forth in this Declaration can be fully realized" calls for a "social order" that allows people a reasonable opportunity to achieve the rights they hold. Balakrishnan and Heintz argue that this creates "an implicit obligation within the human rights framework" for governments and human rights advocates to work on distribution of income.[36] Doing so allows human rights advocacy to challenge the patterns of economic and social relations that systematically prevent people's realization of their rights.

Inequalities compromise the ability of many people to claim their rights, and this inability is visible both in who exercises their voice effectively in political processes and in the outcomes of government policy and public services. Inequality is not the only factor here, of course, but when wealth, income, and economic power are skewed, governments spend less on redistributive programs, and wealthy elites successfully oppose progressive forms of taxation, limiting domestic capacity to raise resources to pay for health care, education, and social protection.[37]

The requirement that governments move as rapidly as possible toward full enjoyment of economic and social rights ("progressive realization") and the principles of nondiscrimination and equality both reinforce the importance of income equality to human rights. The principle of progressive realization obliges states to use "maximum available resources" to move toward fulfillment and, in a highly unequal society, a government can hardly be said to meet this obligation without some effort at redistribution.[38]

Nondiscrimination holds that "the realization of rights should not differ across individuals based on gender, race, ethnicity, nationality, or other social grouping,"[39] while equality refers to equal treatment before the law. Human rights analysts treat systemic inequalities as evidence of discrimination in delivery of services and document them in studies like a 2007 report on maternal mortality in Peru.[40] The report documents a system of laws, expenditures, staffing, and social relations that result in shocking disparities in maternal mortality between urban, ladino women and rural, Indigenous women. Along with extreme inequalities in maternal mortality rates, the report identifies similar gaps by region in expenditures, staffing, and proportions of women whose births are attended by a skilled birth attendant.

Economic inequality is not the same as poverty, even though the two are closely related. I know of no example of human rights advocacy that argues that extreme wealth violates any human rights standard directly. But human rights advocates do work on income and wealth inequality, and indirectly on income and wealth concentration, largely using three approaches. First, advocates argue that income inequality has indirect effects on human rights, by shrinking the tax base, decreasing social trust or willingness to fund programs for the common good, or creating economic exclusions that marginalize low-income people politically. The Tax Justice Network, for example, calls for greater transparency and measures to block capital flight and revenue loss due to tax havens.[41] Oxfam and CESR both argue directly for tax reform as a human rights measure.[42]

Second, inequality is held up as evidence of governments' failure to act as quickly as possible with the economic resources at their disposal to fulfill economic and social rights. Third, human rights principles point to inequalities that are inter-group disparities, where people of a region, ethnic group, generation, or gender are treated differently, and where that treatment contributes to their relative poverty. All of these argue for policies that promote greater income equality, and the SDGs' stand-alone goal on reducing inequality is broadening the attention to inequalities in policy circles.

The MDGs: Ignoring Inequality

The MDGs set targets to reduce the incidence of disease or move a proportion of people above an income threshold for the most part without addressing inequality, discrimination, or disparities. This gave governments and donors setting social development strategies strong incentive to concentrate their resources where they could move the most individuals over the threshold with respect to income, nutrition, or incidence of a disease or health outcome. By setting population-wide goals and measuring progress without targets and indicators that track disparities, the MDGs created incentives that aggravated disparities.

Put another way, because the MDG goals and targets neglected inequalities, "[i]t would [have been] possible to reach the MDGs while still ignoring the 'worst' 20% of poor people in the world, that is, the poorest and most marginalized (around 500 million people). This is not acceptable in [a rights-based approach], which work[s] to increase equity and improve justice, for all people, without discrimination."[43]

The impacts of these disparities were not well documented until evidence began to surface late in the MDG period. NGOs and others concerned with inequalities called attention to the relative progress of racial, ethnic, and other minorities under the MDGs. Extreme inequalities in some South Asian and Latin American societies were major reasons for limited progress on health and nutrition, as Indigenous populations experienced little improvement on health-related goals.[44] Inequalities and patterns of discrimination in Latin American countries from Brazil to Guatemala are blamed for persistent high rates of maternal death and child malnutrition.[45] Inequalities in income, wealth, housing quality, and legal protections were critical factors in determining access to health services as well as nutrition and health outcomes, across regions and in South Asia particularly.[46]

The MDGs' targets and indicators created incentives that ignored or even exacerbated health inequalities. The MDG campaign to reduce under-five mortality illustrates this. Because its targets and indicators rewarded governments for saving the greatest number of young lives possible, governments had little incentive to try to reach remote or marginalized populations. In the absence of a concerted effort to improve services to the most disadvantaged groups, severe inequalities persisted even when overall child mortality levels fell. The 2010 UNICEF Progress for Children Report showed that even in countries that had reduced under-five mortality by 10 percent or more, inequalities in the rates for the poorest and richest households had not improved or had worsened, sometimes significantly.

Consider that statement: in the UNICEF studies, twenty-nine countries experienced reduced national rates of child mortality, five experienced increases, and two were essentially unchanged. But of the twenty-nine successful cases, eighteen saw an increase in the ratio of the rate for the poorest fifth to the rate for the richest fifth.[47] Progress was concentrated among better-off groups, leaving the poorest populations behind at best. When we applaud the progress made to lower national rates of infant mortality and other scourges, we tend to assume that the poor are the beneficiaries. But the data show otherwise.

Inequalities in access to water and sanitation are even greater. The UN's special rapporteur on the human right to water and sanitation examined progress under the MDGs in a series of country studies and found that disparities along urban/rural, regional, ethnic, and other lines remained constant. In the process, Indigenous peoples, those with disabilities, and other historically marginalized groups were left behind. A 2010 UNICEF report showed that the bottom wealth quintile in the world (the poorest 1.38 billion people on earth) did not benefit measurably from expanded water and sanitation access.[48]

These disparities undercut the widely held, celebratory view that many MDG goals were met at global and national levels. Brazil had met the MDG Goal 1 targets as early as 2010, but 45 million Brazilians lived in poverty, and Afro-Brazilians and Indigenous peoples were vastly over-represented among the country's poorest.[49] Rapid progress concentrated in Brazil's "already richer non-Amazonian States of the South East, in effect [left] the Amazonian States ... further behind."[50] This despite the fact that Brazil and Mexico, both with stark inequalities along regional and ethnic divides, have used cash-transfer programs to make progress toward reducing inequalities.[51]

UNDP national reports highlighted these disparities by 2010 in Thailand[52] and in India, arguing that India's central problems were "[p]ersistent inequalities, ineffective delivery of public services, weak accountability systems and gaps in the implementation of pro-poor policies."[53] UNICEF's India office echoed this frustration, citing "two prominent trends in India: impressive economic growth and wealth creation; and stagnation in key social indicators, particularly among disadvantaged populations (i.e. geographically, by caste, gender)."[54] Extreme inequalities weren't being addressed by MDG "successes," and after the High-level Plenary Meeting on the MDGs in 2010, UN documents reported more regularly on these concerns.[55] But by then only five years of the MDG period remained, and the UN 2015 report on the MDGs made this sweeping assessment: "Millions of people are being left behind, especially the poorest and those disadvantaged because of their sex, age, disability, ethnicity or geographic location."[56]

MDG Outcomes: Inequality in the MDG Period

If we applied the SDG-10 target calling for faster income growth in the bottom four income deciles to the experience of the MDG period, how would governments fare, in countries that met the MDG poverty target? Data are incomplete, but had the SDG inequality target been in place, analysts and UN agencies would be writing that the outcome was mixed and disappointing.

I used a list of thirty-six countries that are rated as the top achievers in reducing absolute poverty (MDG-1), or in progress on the combined MDG targets addressing poverty – nutrition, health, education, water, and sanitation – in a study by the Overseas Development Institute.[57] Of the thirty-six countries, thirty-four also had enough data on income distribution to allow an analysis of how MDG progress squared with inequality trends. I applied the SDG standard, the share of national income or consumption held by the bottom 40 percent in 1990 and in 2007/8, to data from these thirty-four MDG success stories. (2007/2008 was the most recent year for which I found consistent data for most of the countries.) These figures are reported in table 3.1.

Of the thirty-four "top achievers" on either poverty reduction or the combined MDG targets listed in table 3.1, twenty-two also increased the proportion of national income flowing to the bottom 40 percent, moving in the direction of the SDG 10 target. There is some association between income redistribution and MDG success: countries that reduced inequalities during the period are over-represented among the MDG leaders, making up 64.7 percent of the MDG leaders (22 of 34); however, exactly half (29 of 58) of all low- and middle-income countries with complete data show reduced inequalities. For these countries, where income growth raised the share of the bottom 40 percent, the addition of an inequality goal in the SDGs can serve to reinforce an existing trend.

But there are important exceptions, indicated in boldface type in table 3.1, where inequality increased, even measured by the share of income to the lowest 40 percent. This occurred in twelve of the thirty-four countries, notably in populous countries that enjoyed high rates of economic growth during the period, including China, India, Indonesia, Vietnam, and Bangladesh. Clearly China, India, and other societies managed to reduce the poverty headcount in a period of rapid economic growth, even while the lowest two quintiles' share of income dropped. This phenomenon is more common

Table 3.1. MDG income inequality trends, 34 top achieving countries

Country	MDG Record*	Bottom 40% share 1990	Bottom 40% share 2007/8
Armenia	Targets	14.9	21.6
Azerbaijan	Poverty	18.8	29.5
Bangladesh	**Targets**	**23.9**	**22.0**
Belize	Targets	7.5	17.5
Brazil	Targets	7.7	10.9
Burkina Faso	Targets	13.5	17.6
Cambodia	**Targets**	**19.0**	**16.2**
Central African Rep.	Poverty	6.6	14.6
Chile	Targets	10.3	11.8
China	**Targets, Poverty**	**17.7**	**15.5**
Costa Rica	**Poverty**	**13.0**	**12.9**
Ecuador	**Targets and Poverty**	**11.1**	**10.6**
Egypt	Targets	21.0	21.6
El Salvador	Targets	10.9	13.5
Ethiopia	Targets	18.1	22.5
Gambia	Targets	4.5	13.4
Ghana	**Targets**	**18.2**	**15.0**
Guatemala	**Targets**	**19.6**	**18.4**
Guinea	Poverty	11.3	15.4
Honduras	Targets	9.1	9.2
India	**Targets**	**22.2**	**19.4**
Indonesia	**Targets**	**19.6**	**18.4**
Kazakhstan	**Targets**	**22.0**	**21.5**
Malawi	Targets	13.4	17.8
Mali	Targets and Poverty	17.2	17.2
Mauritania	Poverty	13.7	16.7
Mexico	Targets	11.3	12.5
Nepal	**Targets**	**18.7**	**15.0**
Nicaragua	Targets	9.7	11.5
Pakistan	Poverty	7.9	9.1
Senegal	Poverty	10.5	16.8
Thailand	Targets and Poverty	14.9	15.9
Uganda	Targets	14.9	15.9
Vietnam	**Targets**	**19.3**	**17.9**

Sources: UNDP 2013, Annex 2; Overseas Development Institute, 2010.

* Countries are among leaders either in reducing the extreme poverty headcount ("poverty") or in progress on all MDG numerical targets ("targets").

Bold type indicates leading performers on MDG poverty reduction where the bottom 40 percent share of national income decreased, 1990–2007.

in middle-income countries of Asia and Latin America than in sub-Saharan Africa, where Ghana is the only society ranked among the MDG leaders that saw the bottom 40 percent share shrink

One lesson is clear: countries whose poverty reduction strategies were driven by rapid economic growth – China, India, Indonesia, Vietnam – tended to experience increases in inequality. Poverty strategies that shift income toward the bottom 40 percent will benefit from growth, but will require labor, tax, social protection, and other redistributive policies.

Looking more closely at several of the MDGs' biggest national success stories (seven countries, 3.7 billion people), we can see some of the reasons for the uneven record on inequality. China, Indonesia, India, Mexico, and Brazil all cut into poverty and contributed statistically to the global success of MDG-1. But their records on income distribution are quite varied. China's rapid economic growth lifted 439 million people out of extreme poverty,[58] but inequality increased, and between 1990 and 2012 the bottom fifth of income earners' share of national income dropped precipitously from 8 percent to 4.7 percent. In India, Indonesia, South Africa, and Bangladesh, the bottom quintile also saw this share of national income fall.[59]

The contrasting experiences of the BRICs countries show the power of national social policy to reduce inequality. Using Gini coefficient measures of household income and data from the early 1990s and late 2000s, Ivins shows that while inequality increased in South Africa and Russia at rates comparable to the average of wealthy OECD countries, and in China and India much more rapidly, Brazil had the reverse experience, reducing its Gini coefficient for household income from 0.61 to 0.55. The bottom four deciles' income share grew from 7.7 percent to 10.9 percent.[60]

Three sets of factors figure most prominently in the record of poverty and inequality reduction: rapid economic growth; strategies that improve livelihood opportunities and incomes for the poor specifically; and social programs, including cash-transfer payments. In most cases, of course, more than one strategy is involved. But rapid growth dominated in the Asian countries just discussed, and most analysts of poverty and inequality agree that maintaining an "adequate and sustainable rate of growth" – Morley recommends 3 percent per year – is fundamental to almost all poverty and inequality strategies.[61]

Cash transfers and related social programs have had major impacts in Brazil, Mexico, Bangladesh, and several other countries.[62] Brazil's government long maintained its commitment to targeted social programs during the last two decades, and both contributory (social security) and noncontributory (Bolsa Familia) payments are widely seen as impacting both poverty and inequality. Similar family support programs, often conditional on school attendance, have had positive effects on inequality elsewhere in Latin America. Labor market policies helped, too, as countries throughout Latin America adopted new minimum-wage policies and levels during the 2000s, helping account for the strong record of reduced inequality in the region.[63]

No set of development goals and no international agency or donor can (or should) mandate any society's development strategy. The SDGs' addition of a goal and targets to reduce domestic inequalities may be able to add some incentive and provide some additional leverage for domestic forces that call for more pro-poor tax, employment, or social policies. Recent successes show that there are multiple alternative policies, all of which address in some combination four "driving forces" of inequality: labor force inequalities, urban-rural divides, disparities in education, and barriers to women's employment.[64]

The fact that inequality worsened in the MDG period is worrisome, and the experience shows that the MDGs' poverty-reduction goals could be accomplished while societies grew more unequal. From one perspective this is good news: poverty can be reduced even in the presence of high and growing levels of inequality. But we know that high levels of inequality make the challenge of reducing poverty through economic growth more difficult, so it is important to see the data's "bad news" message that even as the poverty headcount went down during the MDG period, some societies became more profoundly unequal, and this worsened the prospects for sustained, rapid improvements for the poor.

The SDGs: Tackling Inequalities and Disparities?

Widespread concern about growing inequalities motivated much greater attention to inequalities in the SDGs. The goal, targets, and indicators that emerged from the SDG negotiations on inequality are problematic, but the new focus on inequality takes two forms: the framing of universal or "zero" goals – eradicate extreme poverty, as opposed to reduce by half – and the presence of a specific goal focused on inequalities. These will be the main focus of this analysis, but several other goals, especially on gender equality and on labor, also include targets that are clearly designed to address inequalities of opportunities and outcomes.

First, "zero" goals are widely said to help address inequalities.[65] In principle this is true, because "zero" goals avoid the unintended effect of some of the MDGs, which encouraged policies that helped those most easily moved out of poverty, and the SDG catch-phrase "leave none behind" emphasizes this. Their actual effects on inequalities in health, nutrition, education, and income remain to be seen.

Second, SDG 10 is the centerpiece of the goals' approach to inequality. It calls for reduced economic inequalities, and features ten targets (figure 3.1) that address inter-state inequalities as well as inequalities within societies. Some are general policy recommendations to governments, such as adopting fiscal policies to reduce inequalities (10.4) and facilitating orderly, safe, regular, and responsible migration and mobility of people (10.7). Several other targets are the responsibility of international organizations and transnational investment and finance policy.

Among these, four are especially important to our focus on internal national inequalities. Target 10.1 is central, and its call for expanded shares of income to the lowest four deciles is the focus of much of the discussion that follows. Target 10.4 is significant because it brings tax policy into the SDGs; 10.7 is important given the resistance to migration that has gained influence during the 2010s, and 10C would have a significant impact on migrant incomes by cutting the cost of sending remittances home. Finally,

Figure 3.1. Targets for SDG 10, Reduce inequality within and among countries

10.1 By 2030, progressively achieve and sustain income growth of the bottom 40 per cent of the population at a rate higher than the national average

10.2 By 2030, empower and promote the social, economic and political inclusion of all, irrespective of age, sex, disability, race, ethnicity, origin, religion or economic or other status

10.3 Ensure equal opportunity and reduce inequalities of outcome, including by eliminating discriminatory laws, policies and practices and promoting appropriate legislation, policies and action in this regard

10.4 Adopt policies, especially fiscal, wage and social protection policies, and progressively achieve greater equality

10.5 Improve the regulation and monitoring of global financial markets and institutions and strengthen the implementation of such regulations

10.6 Ensure enhanced representation and voice for developing countries in decision-making in global international economic and financial institutions ...

10.7 Facilitate orderly, safe, regular and responsible migration and mobility of people, including through the implementation of planned and well-managed migration policies

10.A Implement the principle of special and differential treatment for developing countries, in particular least developed countries, in accordance with World Trade Organization agreements

10.B Encourage official development assistance and financial flows, including foreign direct investment, to States where the need is greatest ...

10.C By 2030, reduce to less than 3 per cent the transaction costs of migrant remittances and eliminate remittance corridors with costs higher than 5 per cent

Source: UN SDGs, http://www.un.org/sustainabledevelopment/inequality/.

Target 10.3, calling for elimination of discriminatory regulations and laws, puts SDG 10 in line with human rights principles, which emphasize creating a constitutional and legal framework that brings national laws in line with human rights standards and creates a source of political leverage for policy change.

But the first is the core indicator, and calls for the bottom 40 percent to make income gains *relative to the rest of the population.*

The target offers incentive for governments to pursue policies that differ from widely accepted "poverty-focused growth" strategies, and that shift income, assets, or both toward the bottom 40 percent of the population. It is a truncated version of the measure some experts recommended,[66] known as the Palma ratio. Palma measures the ratio of the total income of the top 10 percent of the income distribution to the total income of the bottom 40 percent. Some national Palma ratios illustrate the range of current income distributions: Germany 1.0, Canada 1.2, the United States 1.9, Chile 3.5, Qatar 9.2.[67] Compared to other measures of inequality it is relatively easy to understand and to measure. It takes advantage of the fact that across most countries the middle strata of the income distribution, deciles five through nine, tend to earn approximately half of national income,[68] and focuses attention on income and wealth shifts affecting the top 10 percent to the bottom 40 percent.

But the SDGs' 40 percent target, without reference to the top income decile, ignores the increasing concentration of wealth.[69] As MacNaughton observes, a country could accomplish the target while continuing to heighten income inequality, if incomes of the wealthiest continue to grow most rapidly.[70] Fukuda-Parr argues that opponents of a true income inequality target succeeded in reducing it to a measure of shared prosperity.[71] And no target addresses the even more stubborn problem of inequality of wealth. Moreover, it does not provide a target for an adequate level of income growth, nor a target for the income share of the bottom four deciles.

In the SDG negotiations it proved to be difficult to win consensus on inequality. For example, the target that most directly addresses macro-economic policies, 10.4, calls for egalitarian "fiscal, wage and social protection policies" without specific benchmarks or indicators. Advocates worry that SDG 10 is particularly vulnerable to neglect or to political backlash because it does not have a powerful government as a champion.[72] Yet an income inequality goal was adopted, and its inclusion in the SDGs gives advocates of egalitarian economic and social policies a new source of leverage. Advocates gained support in July 2016 when the governments of Chile and Finland in July 2016 sponsored a thematic workshop on the topic at the first High-level Political Forum on Sustainable Development. An independent experts group provides ongoing analysis, and the Pathfinders initiative on Inequality and Inclusion brings together governments, NGOs, and others to "identify practical and politically-viable solutions to meet the targets on equitable and inclusive societies."[73]

The 2017 Progress Report on the SDGs, for example, reviews the inequality goal, noting the mixed record of the MDG period when it comes to the relative share of national income accruing to the bottom 40 percent.[74] The UN 2018 Report on the SDGs contains a hopeful report on SDG 10 that is both good news and illustrative of the UN approach. In sixty of the ninety-four countries with data, it reports that the income share of the lowest 40 percent grew faster than the national income.[75]

Mobilizing to Support SDG 10

The inequality goal needs active support from outside the UN system, and it has prompted multiple initiatives to monitor its impact. The World Bank's annual inequality report tracks conventional Gini coefficient data and the limited data available on income distribution by income decile. Human rights and development NGOs monitor key policy changes that support redistributing the shares of national income. ActionAid produces an annual report monitoring legislation on social protection and equal pay, to track countries' readiness to reduce inequalities.[76] Oxfam monitors a broader set of tax, social spending, and labor policies to compile a Commitment to Reducing Inequality Index.[77] And CESR has publicized its human rights-based country assessments of governments' voluntary national reports on SDG progress. The 2019 fact sheet on South Africa, for example, documents the government's failure to adopt policies to reduce inequalities.[78]

Save the Children-UK proposed the use of "stepping-stone" inequality goals and benchmarks, goals that focus on the groups farthest behind for a given target, and set five-year benchmarks for the compensatory progress required to close the disparity gap entirely.[79] To overcome disproportionately high child mortality among a minority ethnic group in Benin, for example, the government would set benchmarks that aim for a steeper decline among that group than the population at large. The intermediate "stepping-stone" approach appears in the strategies of the Global Partnership for Education[80] and the plans of the SDG Steering Committee for Education (SDG 4) for addressing educational inequalities.[81] But the approach has not been applied to the income inequality target itself. The income inequality goal illustrates the importance of having diverse stakeholders take an informed interest in the goals and press for a responsive, human rights-consistent framing of the problems. Don't expect to see this kind of intensive focus on overcoming inequalities in the annual UN-wide reports, but if human rights and development agencies such as STC, CESR, ActionAid, Oxfam, and UNICEF adopt this approach in their dialogue with governments and their public monitoring, it is possible that their under-the-radar monitoring will help produce progress.

Much of this monitoring focuses on specific policy changes that would encourage greater income equality. There are multiple ways to deviate from the "business as usual model of economic growth" and promote greater equality of opportunity and outcomes.[82] Short of transforming growth-oriented economic strategies, significant gains can also be won by changes to employment incentives, labor standards, minimum wage laws, tax policy, or social support programs. The SDG-10 targets suggest these options, including wage and social protection, lowering the cost of remittances, and improving tax and fiscal policy. But the agenda of global networks against inequality reminds us that inequality is closely linked to several of the issues behind other SDG goals. Four of the key linkages are to gender equality and the care economy; wages and labor rights, especially in the informal sector; protecting poor people's assets, especially their land; and health coverage and the financial protection it provides. These combine with tax policy (discussed below) and the Goal 10 targets on migration and lowering the costs of remittance payments to set much of the practical agenda on inequality.

Oxfam's 2020 report on inequality, timed to coincide with the World Economic Forum in Davos, focuses on the link to gender equality and the care economy, showing how the unpaid care work of women, especially poor women, alongside other huge disparities in incomes and assets, creates the global income gaps that Oxfam's annual reports highlight.[83] Women are more likely than men to live on incomes below the median. In addition to its global advocacy on inequality, Oxfam maintains a multi-country campaign, with local advocates, for Fiscal Accountability for Inequality Reduction.[84]

The global Fight Inequality Alliance, with more than 200 organizations worldwide, reports active agendas focused on living wages for garment industry workers in Bangladesh, wages and labor rights in extractive industries in Zambia, and protecting Indigenous communities' land rights in multiple countries.[85] Governments and other advocates working on inequality and inclusion through the Pathfinder network emphasize the role of social service coverage, in particular financial protection from the devastating and impoverishing effects of catastrophic health costs.[86]

Reducing the costs of remittance payments to 3 percent and eliminating transmissions more expensive than 5 percent illustrate the options that are available to improve the share of income accruing to low-income groups. The high cost of sending money home reduces the value of remittances by more than 6 percent. Remittances to low- and middle-income countries amounted to some $550 billion in 2019, more than foreign direct investment and official development assistance to those countries.[87] Lowering average costs by five percentage points (from over 8 percent in 2015) is estimated to add $16 billion in value to the $529 billion in remittances sent by workers to families and communities in low- and middle-income countries.[88] Even in a period of political hostility to migrants in the United States and some European countries, these costs have continued to fall. Tracked quarterly by the World Bank, average costs have fallen from roughly

8.2 percent in 2015 to 6.8 percent in 2019. As lower-cost "corridors" for fund transfers become available in more countries, and become better known and more accessible, average costs continue to fall gradually.[89]

Tax policy and tax administration are also central to the inequality goal. Many low- and middle-income countries have weak tax systems. Their tax revenue as a portion of GDP (this is referred to as "tax effort") is low, and wealthy residents avoid taxes through a variety of loopholes, including off-shore tax havens and evasion. While high-income countries' total tax collection amounts to roughly 40 percent of GDP, most low-income countries are in the 10 to 20 percent range.[90] Taxes play two roles in addressing inequality. They produce revenue to fund programs such as cash transfers, and – if tax systems are progressive – they transfer wealth from upper- to lower-income groups. Many governments lose vast amounts of revenue because of weak tax administration and widespread tax evasion.[91] Effective taxation is associated with democratic and responsive governance,[92] and off-shore tax havens and ineffective tax administration weaken governments' ability to set their own development agendas.[93]

There is plenty of experience to show the benefits of improved tax policies and administration: Bolivia's tax reforms in the 2000s, including new taxes and royalties on fossil fuel extraction, yielded revenue that funded cash transfers, pension programs, and education improvements.[94] New or higher taxes on tobacco products in several Southeast Asian countries have raised significant revenues, in addition to their public health benefits.[95] Governments generally use tax revenue over aid to fund teachers' salaries, so improvements in taxation in (for example) Kenya have been essential to making progress toward the government's 2005 commitment to universal free primary education.[96] Development NGOs such as Oxfam, Christian Aid, and ActionAid, and human rights advocates, including CESR and numerous national tax justice organizations, are all active in global networks pressing for improved taxation.[97]

The global interest by aid donors and low-income countries in tax policy, including through the Addis Ababa Tax Initiative in 2019, is encouraging, and a review of seven cases of successful reform (Afghanistan, Bangladesh, Vietnam, Bosnia and Herzegovina, Georgia, Paraguay, and Rwanda) emphasizes the gains they have made in revenue collection, efficiency, and spending for social programs.[98] But it will be important to press for reforms that not only raise revenue (domestic revenue mobilization) but also promote equity. Greater emphasis on personal income taxes and property taxes can shift the impact of taxes on equity. The first four years of the SDG period have not seen decisive steps on the tax front, but movements pressing for tax reforms have been building for more than a decade. The Global Tax Network and Global Alliance for Tax Justice both coordinate national and regional organizations pressing for effective tax systems and improved capturing of tax revenues from extractive industries, other corporate actors, and tax havens.

The agendas of the Global Alliance and its five regional tax justice networks are focused on diverse forms of tax avoidance and on using tax policy to reduce inequalities. The Tax Justice Network-Africa's 2019 report, for example, makes the case for tax reforms to fund additional access to education for excluded groups in Uganda, Tanzania, and Zambia,[99] estimating that 1 trillion Tanzanian shillings (roughly 440 million US dollars) in foregone tax revenue in Tanzania from 2010 to 2017 could fund four additional years of free education for all Tanzanian children. Other recent regional efforts target tax policy toward extractive industries and other international firms.

This kind of citizen campaign, often with donor government support, has helped to spark a modest series of national tax policy changes. Oxfam and ActionAid have produced reviews of campaigns for equity-oriented policy changes in Vietnam and Nigeria.[100] Interestingly, these two episodes were supported by contrasting advocacy strategies: a bottom-up community approach in Nigeria, and a top-down effort building support in key government ministries in Vietnam.[101]

It would be unrealistic to expect many governments to launch new development strategies that change policies on all of these fronts. But a more flexible view, that governments could be persuaded to make one or more of these changes and contribute to measurable improvements in income distribution and economic opportunities, is entirely realistic in a climate where many donor agencies are already actively concerned about inequality. This implies that, while global advocates will aim to raise and maintain the profile of SDG-10 and to encourage effective monitoring across the board, in-country advocates will likely be engaged in campaigns to build support for one or more strategies and donor agencies working to encourage and help finance them.

Pandemic and Inequalities

Advocates of SDG-10 will, however, likely be battling against the effects of the COVID-19 pandemic. The pandemic's disproportionate health and employment effects on informal-sector and low-income workers means that while upper-decile incomes may suffer some losses, low-income workers will likely slip more. In the longer term, the impact of school closures may exacerbate inequalities by compromising the development of young children. Several of these factors also threaten to worsen gender inequalities, or at least compromise progress. Women are over-represented among frontline workers; they are most acutely affected by school closures and children's distance-learning strategies; and their economic status, including through land ownership, is at risk as well.[102]

Governments and donor agencies have expanded social support payments in many cases – these actions and their limitations are discussed in chapter 5. International NGOs are taking coordinated action as well. A group of influential international NGOs has launched one response: Namati and four co-sponsors announced the creation of a COVID Justice Fund to raise $1 million in support of grassroots organizations and movements that expand marginalized peoples' access to justice. The pandemic has "exacerbated the problems of inequality and injustice and made it harder for grassroots organizations to provide much needed support," according to former UN High Commissioner for Human Rights Mary

Robinson, and the fund aims to address the funding shortfall of those grassroots groups.[103]

There will be exceptions, and at least a few economists predict possible equalizing effects from the pandemic. Some observe historical patterns, in which extreme events disrupt economic and political patterns and reduce inequalities. Piketty's much-discussed *Capital in the Twenty-first Century* makes this argument, claiming that the two world wars and the Great Depression had a levelling effect in the United States. In addition to the benefits to lower-income groups of expanded social protections, it is also true that after the pandemic governments needing to repay debts incurred during the pandemic response may have little choice but to tax higher-income groups more heavily.[104] Historian Walter Scheidel argues more broadly that since the Roman Empire, wars, revolutions, state failures, and pandemics are the events that have produced egalitarian changes.[105]

But any hopeful prediction about inequality in the aftermath of the pandemic hangs on political pressure and decisive government action. The pandemic makes the need for better social protections vivid, but that priority will compete with multiple other demands on governments' resources. The pandemic can change political equations, as we are seeing in the United States in 2020: a government whose management of the pandemic results in visible increases in inequalities may face political repercussions.[106]

Conclusions

The MDGs ignored most aspects of inequality, and inequalities increased even in many of the MDGs' anti-poverty success stories. Can we hope for better from the SDG era? Although the SDGs' inequality goal did not win strong governmental support, advocates and some governments are calling attention to the possibility and benefits of reducing inequalities. This is an unprecedented level of attention for disparities in international goals and agreements, and although the SDG 10 targets and indicators are flawed, SDG 10 affords an opportunity to focus global attention on reducing disparities as a core development goal. Human rights-based advocacy played a central role in winning the stand-alone goal, and in critical oversight of its implementation.

The populist trends in national politics – even authoritarian populist trends – should not diminish this opportunity. Demands for tax reforms, employment gains, and labor rights – changes consistent with more egalitarian development policies – are established populist themes. Effective movements of working people and others can advance an agenda that promotes broad participation in the gains of economic growth. The continuing effects of the coronavirus pandemic are a serious threat to progress against inequality, and will require vigilance and persistent advocacy by human rights advocates and others in favor of economically progressive tax and fiscal policies.

Putting the current efforts to monitor and implement inequality issues in context, there is good news: while at the beginning of the MDG period there was almost no thought being given (in official development circles) to issues of inequality, already in 2020 there are sustained efforts to work out the conceptual, data, and political issues involved in monitoring and implementing inequality concerns for water, income and wealth, child welfare, and others.[107]

Alongside the established target for SDG 10 – that growth rates for incomes of the bottom four deciles grow more rapidly than the national average – governments should be encouraged to monitor the indicator widely agreed to be the best single index of inequality: the ratio of the post-tax income of the top decile to the post-transfer income of the bottom four deciles. The SDGs' inequality strategy calls attention to the benefits of reducing this ratio: the handful of societies in northern Europe and Canada with a ratio close to 1:1 enjoy other desirable social outcomes. Alongside the highlighting of inequalities by advocates and scholars, the presence of inequality on the SDG agenda may allow us to establish more firmly in public discussion that good development, human rights, and good society require limits on inequality.

chapter four

Health Systems

In 2014 the MDGs had been in place for fourteen years and were showing important progress in reducing the incidence of targeted diseases – malaria, tuberculosis, and HIV/AIDS. But in March 2014 terrifying reports of a virulent new disease surfaced in Sierra Leone, Liberia, and Guinea. Ebola gripped the attention of public health authorities and of the news media in much of the world, and it exposed the weakness of national health systems. Multiple reports from the field chronicle the difficulty of identifying and treating Ebola patients in districts where there were no trained public health personnel, where laboratory tests could not be evaluated quickly, and where hospitals were poorly equipped and lacked basics such as running water.[1] The weaknesses of health systems – including in personnel, equipment, referral processes, and training – are compounded by limited infrastructure, especially roads and Internet connectivity. Containing an Ebola outbreak, of course, requires special procedures and measures in any setting, but the difficulty is compounded when basic health systems are absent. Health systems are being tested again in 2020 by the COVID-19 pandemic.

Ebola was controlled by determined and heroic local and international efforts in all three countries. But the weaknesses it revealed – of communication systems, transport and laboratory equipment, sanitation, and other dimensions – are still present, and targeted assaults on individual diseases will not correct them. This is the problem of health systems. Improving personnel, communications, referral systems, and health coverage has none of the sex appeal of conquering a dread disease, but it should be the centerpiece of health-related goals. Health systems and universal health coverage goals are written into the SDGs, and the coming years offer opportunities to expand rapidly the access to health services.

The four messages of this chapter amount to a critique of the approach that prevailed in the MDG period, and a case for a human rights-consistent approach to building health systems. First, vertical (disease and problem-specific) and more systemic horizontal approaches to health problems are often at odds, and the MDGs promoted vertical approaches with little attention to health systems. Second, the goal of universal health coverage and other elements of a strong health system – such as health finance, equity, human resources, and essential medicines – are complex challenges, but some low- and middle-income countries are devising systems that work, and that advance the human right to health. Third, the SDGs, with goals that encourage progress toward universal health coverage and strong health systems, can help spur widespread progress. Finally, human rights principles and public health experience will be important for resisting the tendency to prioritize the health-care demands of the growing urban middle classes, and will help to steer resources toward primary health-care systems that can dramatically improve health outcomes for the most vulnerable and the poor majority.

Health Systems and Finance

What is a health system, and why are health systems so important? Many definitions of "health system" are broad and include many of the factors that influence health and wellness, such as community and household factors, macroeconomic policies, and civil service rules. Including all the factors that decisively influence health makes sense conceptually because health outcomes are determined in important ways by social factors such as poverty, nutrition, and housing. But for present purposes I will focus more specifically on

Figure 4.1. Three dimensions of universal health coverage

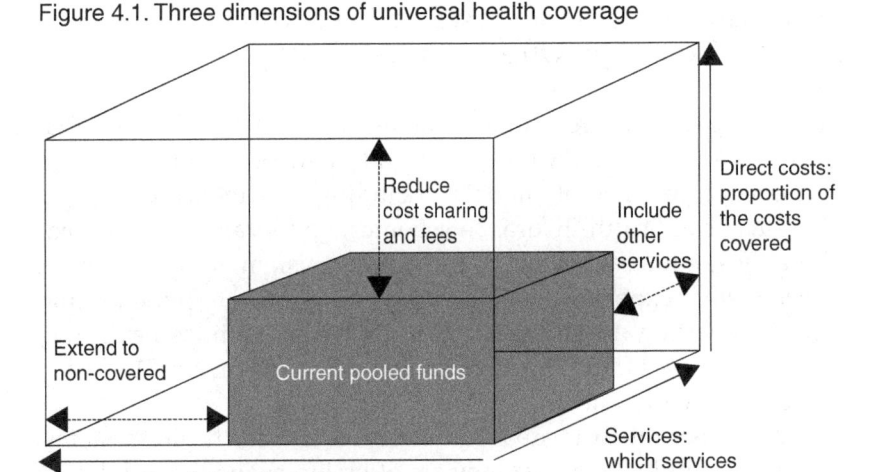

Source: World Health Organization (2010, 13).

the health-care, health-finance, and health-maintenance system – the systems that provide "promotive, preventive, curative and rehabilitative interventions."[2] This includes the people who provide care; the institutions, equipment, medicines, and other goods they use; the training they receive; the facilities (hospitals, clinics, mobile facilities) where they provide care; and the policies, budgets, and administrative structures that finance, oversee, and facilitate the care, including the financing of patient costs.

Most countries – including most low- and middle-income countries – now have some form of health coverage, for some of their people. The extent, effectiveness, and cost of that coverage are the three variables at the center of discussions and of the SDG agenda: How many people are covered? How much of health-care costs is borne by the patient? And what services (including medicines) are covered? Figure 4.1 represents the situation graphically: societies can move toward universal coverage by expanding any one or more of the three dimensions of coverage.

Financing Sustainable Systems That Protect People from High Out-of-Pocket Costs

Financing health care is one of the most complex challenges that any government faces. Low- and middle-income countries have adopted a number of models, including tax-financed, payroll-based, social health-insurance schemes, and strategies that combine these sources. Whatever the finance system, it must in effect decide what expenses will be out-of-pocket costs to patients, and in every society these out-of-pocket costs sometimes have devastating impacts, forcing households below even the $1.90/day extreme poverty line.

Out-of-pocket costs are a complex problem for health systems, but for individual patients they are often life-changing and devastating. In the forty-six countries of sub-Saharan Africa, the World Bank estimated in 2016 that 35 million Africans (total population approximately 960 million) experience catastrophic medical expenses annually, incurring expenses equal to at least 15 percent of their total consumption. Because health insurance and other forms of financial protection are relatively weak, most pay out-of-pocket, and the regional annual average payment grew from $15 per capita in 1995 to $38 in 2014. "As a result, 11 million Africans are falling into poverty every year due to high out-of-pocket payments."[3]

Out-of-pocket spending (OOPS) – health expenses that patients bear directly – varies enormously. Table 4.1 suggests the variation among countries and regions. Most societies rely on a mix of private and public funding, but out-of-pocket payments as high as 36.7 percent in sub-Saharan Africa or 64.5 percent in South Asia are unsustainable. Countries as diverse as Cuba, South Africa, Botswana, Oman, France, Timor-Leste, and Mozambique hold OOPS at or under 10 percent of total spending.[4]

Although the percentage of total health costs paid by patients has been falling globally for some years, those patient payments are a growing percentage of household incomes.[5] National averages obscure the effects on low-income households, whose health expenditures may be small in absolute terms but have powerful

Table 4.1. Out-of-pocket, public, and external health-care finance, selected countries and world regions

	Health spending per capita ($PPP)	Public funding as % of total	External aid as % of total	Out of pocket as % of total
Rwanda	130.4	33.9	50.6	6.4
Bangladesh	90.6	18.0	7.6	71.9
South Africa	1,071.3	53.7	0.9	7.8
Colombia	829.8	62.3	2.1	20.2
Ukraine	534.2	42.4	0.8	54.3
Latin America	1,277.2	47.3	0.4	36.7
Africa (sub-Saharan)	198.0	35.1	11.7	36.7
South Asia	217.3	25.5	2.1	64.5
Europe/ Central Asia	2,698.0	77.7	–	17.8
North America	9,351.9	81.4	–	11.3

Source: World Bank, World Development Indicators, 2018 (2016 data).

impacts on their finances and well-being. Out-of-pocket health costs, especially catastrophic health-care costs, are a significant cause of impoverishment, and high out-of-pocket costs can discourage patients from using health-care services.

Anirudh Krishna's 2010 book, *One Illness Away,* documents this, with wide-ranging research in poor countries and in the United States.[6] Even very poor people will pay high health costs when they can, Krishna shows, averaging twice the proportion of income that nonpoor households spend on health care. Why? Their bodies are "often poor people's main productive asset" (87), and ill health can turn that asset into a liability quickly. Studies from low-income countries in every region show high health-care expenses as a major factor in "the creation and persistence of poverty" (77). When clinics or other facilities are far away, poor households studied in Gujarat, India, pay higher fees to private providers.

When countries improve health coverage and reduce costs, this link between health expenses and extreme poverty is weakened. In Sri Lanka, Oxfam reports that publicly funded health finance and services have provided large-scale protection from the financial impact of catastrophic health costs, reducing the number of households pushed into poverty each year.[7] During the implementation of Thailand's universal coverage plan, in the early 2000s, the proportion of low-income households that faced catastrophic health-care costs was reduced by three-quarters, from 4 percent to 0.9 percent.[8] Another study estimated that the percentage of households made poor by health costs dropped with the adoption of universal coverage, from 11.9 percent in 2000 to 4.3 percent in 2002, to 2.6 percent in 2004. Most of this is concentrated among people needing hospitalization and choosing private hospitals.[9]

In Cambodia, 70 percent of health expenditures are out of pocket, and 14 percent of the population lives in absolute poverty, with many others having incomes just above that extreme poverty line. For a large part of the population, health expenditures can drive a household into deeper debt, force the sale of assets, and force compromises on other expenditures, such as for food or education. The government's Health Equity Fund finances free access cards for poor households, selected by local leaders, and in 2014 it covered 3.1 million Cambodians, 21 percent of the population.[10] The Health Equity Fund is not a universal coverage scheme but a targeted program, funded largely by external donors to support low-income families. Services are limited to those provided by public health clinics, but Cambodia's fund shows the impact that targeted spending can have in the short and medium term, while longer-term proposals for universal coverage and health finance are worked out.

The Indian state Karnataka, whose population of 61 million would make it the seventeenth largest of the 137 LMICs,[11] implemented social health insurance through the Vajpayee Arogyashree Scheme (VAS) in 2010 to increase poor households' access to hospital care. Approximately one-third of the state's population who are classified as poor are participants, and the health and financial outcomes are impressive. Use of hospital services rose among covered households, mortality from conditions covered by the plan decreased by nearly two-thirds compared to outcomes for poor nonparticipants, and out-of-pocket costs were dramatically reduced.[12]

As Karnataka's experience shows, catastrophic health payments only tell half the story, because many financially strapped people avoid these costs by choosing low-cost options such as self-medicating.[13] This under-utilization of available health care, alongside limited supply of quality health care in many sites, is why the objectives for improving health systems must include increasing expenditures, holding down out-of-pocket spending, and moving toward providing the full range of services equitably and at reasonable cost.

Human Rights, Health Systems, and Universal Health Coverage

Universal health coverage (UHC) has huge implications, and the prospect of significant progress toward UHC is of historic importance. Rodin and de Ferranti argue convincingly that UHC can be the third global health transition – after public health and hygiene changes and the epidemiological progress that reduced the impact of communicable diseases.[14] Chapman notes, moreover, that UHC can be closely identified with the human right to health.[15]

The human right to the highest attainable standard of health sets a high standard with important implications for the social institutions that deliver health care. Alicia Yamin articulates the basic principle: "When health is understood as a right, it implies that health systems function as 'core social institutions' that bind together or exclude segments of society through common values and principles, and define people's life chances as well as ability to participate fully in society."[16]

One implication is for spending priorities: the immediate ethical and legal obligation of governments to "mitigate the erosion of dignity caused by extreme poverty and lack of economic and social rights."[17] This obligation, made explicit in the Committee on Economic, Social and Cultural Rights' General Comment 3 (1990), implies that with limited financial and other resources, priority must be given to making high-priority basic services available, over high-cost services that benefit only a few. This does not mean that health systems should not develop the capacity to provide (for example) kidney dialysis, but it does hold that expenditures "should not disproportionately favour expensive curative health services" (General Comment 14, paragraph 19), meaning in effect that access to some expensive curative services may be limited. These are hard choices for governments, and one of the purposes of ratifying human rights covenants is to bind a society to politically difficult commitments that advance the common good. Foreign assistance for health must play a role by holding rigorously to priorities that make high-quality basic services available and affordable for all.

The human right to health has a second implication for spending: it requires substantive equality for individuals and groups who are disadvantaged by socioeconomic, geographic, or biological factors. Courts in many societies have clarified policy implications, as in cases requiring the availability of sign language interpretation in Canada and Colombian decisions that exempt persons with physical or mental disabilities from paying fees for health-care services.[18] Finally, governments must move toward universal health coverage as rapidly as possible, and their choices of how to do this, by expanding coverage, broadening the health-care procedures covered, and/or reducing patient costs, are in turn guided by fundamental human rights principles. Before turning to how low- and middle-income countries have tackled UHC, consider the very different approach that the MDGs took to health priorities.

The MDGs: Attacking Health Problems, Ignoring Health Systems

Formidable health challenges confront every society, most seriously in low- and middle-income countries. The need for continuing efforts to improve child survival, maternal health, and care for people in remote rural locations, and to meet the health needs of refugee and migrant populations, is compounded by new and rapidly growing threats. The Zika virus, health needs associated with rapid urbanization and compounded by the effects of climate change, the growing incidence of chronic noncommunicable conditions such as diabetes and heart disease, and the serious mental health needs of traumatized populations are a few of the health challenges facing communities, governments, and health professionals.[19] Add to those a global coronavirus pandemic that threatens to overwhelm even the world's best-funded health systems in 2020, and the list of challenges is daunting.

Since the late 1990s donors have invested heavily in health initiatives in low-income countries. The expanded health aid in the 1990s and 2000s emphasized disease-specific initiatives and the targets and indicators of the MDGs, and created bilateral and multilateral initiatives that target HIV/AIDS, malaria, tuberculosis, and other health needs. Health policy discussions distinguish vertical approaches that tackle a specific disease or problem such as tuberculosis, malaria, or maternal health from horizontal, system-wide approaches that work to strengthen elements of the system, such as building networks of community health-care providers, communication and information systems, or health-care financing and coverage of costs to patients. It is easy to see why the architects of the MDGs chose the vertical strategy: energy and resources are more readily mobilized around reducing the incidence of dread diseases such as HIV/AIDS, tuberculosis, and malaria than by most of the systemic factors that underlie the effectiveness of the entire health system. Systemic approaches are at least one step removed from the human outcomes that motivate aid agencies and governments, and funders gravitate toward disease-specific goals and initiatives.

But pumping money and resources into campaigns to reduce a specific disease may not strengthen overall health care; it may even weaken or at least distract resources from building a sustainable system for a healthy society. Reducing mortality and specific disease incidence will be Pyrrhic victories if they are not supported by a health system that can maintain these gains. Summing up assessments of fragile and Ebola-affected societies, Salama and Alwan write in the medical journal *Lancet* that "unless we find ways to build functional health systems in fragile and failed states, it will be harder to make further progress on key global goals, such as the reduction of maternal and child mortality, as well as to protect the world from new infectious disease outbreaks."[20]

The two approaches aren't mutually exclusive, of course, and there are counter-arguments. Building a system in and of itself is not the goal; improved health outcomes are. A vertical strategy – a campaign for improved treatment of HIV-positive patients, for example – can and should also aim to strengthen elements of the health system. When this does happen, it produces a set of parallel efforts to improve (for example) pharmaceutical procurement and management for HIV treatment, and communication and referral systems for managing antenatal care and deliveries that need emergency care. But scholars and health-care providers have argued since early in the MDG period that working in this way, on parallel tracks, is inefficient and doesn't build a lasting, resilient health system.[21]

Moreover, identifying health needs that elicit support this year, or this decade – AIDS, malaria, tuberculosis, maternal and child health – fails to take into account the growing health needs that will dominate in many countries in the next decades. These are chronic, noncommunicable diseases, including heart disease, cancers, and diabetes. The bottom line: vertical, disease- and need-specific strategies tend to lead to neglect of systemic needs.

The shift toward bilateral agencies and toward measures and organizations focused on disease-specific targets has been reinforced by the rising influence of US government initiatives and of the Bill and Melinda Gates Foundation. In the wake of the financial crisis beginning in 2008, and as European aid shrank for several years, the Gates Foundation became the dominant private donor and the third-largest health aid donor of any kind, behind only the United States and the United Kingdom. US government programs likewise grew, coming to represent more than half of official health assistance. The Global Fund to Fight AIDS, Tuberculosis and Malaria and the World Health Organization, during the same years, suffered lagging contributions and budget shortfalls.[22] In the same period, the flow of global health funding de-emphasized the World Health Organization's role in building national health systems.

The MDGs encouraged this trend toward disease- and problem-specific interventions. An important series of papers on the "Power of Numbers," later published in the *Journal of Human Development and Capabilities*, examined the mixed effects of MDG goals, targets, and indicators, showing that the choice of quantitative indicators can attract new spending and shift existing priorities. Yamin and Boulanger, for example, dissect the effects of the targets for reducing maternal mortality.[23] The centerpiece of their critique is that the maternal mortality goal de-emphasized well-established norms and rights of access to full reproductive health services, instead "refocusing … [sexual and reproductive health rights] to maternal, newborn and child health" and treating "women as instruments of reproduction." Responding belatedly to these concerns, a new Target 5B calling for "universal access to reproductive health" was added in 2005, and indicators were in place in 2007.

Still, the MDG period has seen a dramatic de-emphasis on family-planning funding and little focus on broader, systemic requirements, such as referral systems and the expansion of effective and equitable access to emergency obstetric care. Family-planning funding has languished for twenty years, largely due to the George W. Bush administration's restrictions on abortion counseling and on funds to the United Nations Population Fund (UNFPA). The effects are clear: stalled funding contributed to extremely limited access to family-planning resources in some of the societies most in need. A study of contraceptive prevalence from 1990 to 2013 found that in the twenty-six countries with contraceptive prevalence below 10 percent in 1990, prevalence and estimated unmet needs were virtually unchanged between 1990 and 2010.[24]

A strong, resilient health system can provide quality preventive care to whole populations and respond to the same critical health needs identified in the MDGs. But health systems worldwide are limited and strained, and their weaknesses have been aggravated by the focus on MDG targets. In a 2014 paper, Sophie Harman explains that funding for specific initiatives and needs, such as HIV in Africa, causes some health systems to become "organised around HIV/AIDS programmes."[25] These goals create programmatic "silos" focused on specific diseases or initiatives such as measles immunizations. Donors reinforce this tendency by funding specific interventions in preference to "horizontal" measures that would build the capacity of the health system and health services generally. Consequently, the same feature that has made the MDGs effective – intensive focus on measurable goals and targets – leads to a focus on achievements that can be reported in these terms. These achievements are important, but the unintended consequence is that "health systems – hospitals and clinics, procurement structures, clinical professionals, [information and communications technology, and] ... equipment and supplies" – are given less attention.[26]

These effects on health systems are visible in the impact of MDG goals and targets. Critics argue that targeting reductions in maternal mortality rates accelerated the trend toward narrow, vertical interventions calculated to move the MDG targets without sufficient attention to systems that provide the forms of health care critical for maternal health. In maternal health, four components of an effective health-care system are among the essential needs: family planning, skilled birth attendance, emergency obstetric care, and a functioning referral system.[27] The MDGs monitored two indicators – maternal mortality rates and rates of skilled birth attendance – and these choices are defensible, tracking outcomes and one important indicator of care provision.

Improving the coverage by skilled birth attendants (SBA) contributed to improvements in maternal health, but practitioners argue that to lower the maternal death rates further would require reliable, timely access to emergency obstetric care for pregnancies and deliveries with complications, and this is where the health system is critically important. So, although the indicator measuring birth attended by an SBA encouraged progress on one important aspect of maternal health, it excluded others. The SBA variable was easy to measure, but "focusing on SBA alone may likely have also had the unintended consequence of contributing to narrow approaches to maternal health. SBA focuses specifically on a subset of delivery care without improving or assessing the quality of the health system" or meeting other reproductive health needs.[28]

Access to high-quality emergency obstetric care, considered by many the key to reducing maternal deaths, depends on such a system. If a woman in labor suddenly requires emergency care, a system must be in place with effective primary health-care facilities even in remote areas, good information and referral systems to clinics and first-level regional hospitals, and good care that is understood to be free or affordable, so that cost does not delay a patient's effort to gain access to care. This strong system must also be understood and seen as accessible and affordable by the patient population. The absence of such a system results in what Physicians for Human Rights calls the "deadly delays" in seeking care.[29] An excessive focus on vertical health care intervention de-emphasized the health-care system that is essential to delivering emergency obstetric care.

Similarly, the MDG Goal 4 to reduce child mortality adopted the rate of measles immunization as one of its three indicators. Measles accounts for 10 percent of under-five deaths, but measles immunization is effective with a single administration, and high immunization rates can be reached with a single campaign. More complex child health indicators would arguably be a better indicator of a health system able to maintain healthy conditions for the population. This gap, along with other limitations in the MDG Goal 4 strategy, led the United Nations to take a welcome corrective measure by launching a "Global Strategy for Women's and Children's Health" in 2010. This new model specifically emphasized the need for country-led health initiatives and indicators addressing pneumonia and diarrhea as well as measles.

The SDGs brought a new approach to setting health goals. The remainder of this chapter lays out this approach and explores what health-care coverage and financing look like in low- and middle-income societies. The SDGs and human rights pose a set of challenges, demanding that every person has access to an acceptable level of health services, and that financing arrangements ensure that no one will be impoverished by health-care costs. These issues of coverage and finance are intricately linked to the complex issues of equity, health personnel, and access to essential medicines.

SDGs and Universal Health Coverage (UHC)

The SDGs' attention to UHC and health systems sets them apart from the MDGs, but the UHC target (3.8) is alongside a broad and ambitious set of health-related targets. These include disease- and condition-specific targets for maternal and child mortality, AIDS, tuberculosis, malaria, and other diseases, as well as issues not addressed in the MDGs, including traffic deaths, vaccine development, and early warning for national and global health risks. The targets are listed in abbreviated form in figure 4.2.

The universal health coverage target (SDG 3.8) illustrates the importance of developing effective indicators. The first two indicators track two core objectives: expanding coverage and increasing financial protection. They do so using data that now enable governments and observers to track progress in 133 countries.[30] Indicator 3.8.1 tracks the extent of health coverage with an index constructed from the average of coverage of sixteen total services, four each drawn from four distinct health-care categories: reproductive, maternal, newborn, and child health; infectious diseases; noncommunicable diseases; and service capacity and access. For example, coverage in the communicable diseases category is tracked through these four measures:

1. Tuberculosis treatment: TB effective treatment coverage
2. HIV treatment: People living with HIV receiving ART
3. Malaria prevention: Population at risk sleeping under insecticide treated bednets
4. Water and sanitation: Households with access to at least basic sanitation.[31]

The average of sixteen such "tracer indicators" (four in each of the four categories) produces a composite index of health care coverage for Indicator 3.8.1.

The financial protection target – to protect individuals from high out-of-pocket costs – is tracked by Indicator 3.8.2: how many people in the population spend more than 10 percent of income on health

Figure 4.2. SDG 3: Ensure healthy lives and promote well-being for all at all ages

Health targets for SDG 3 address:

3.1 maternal mortality ratio

3.2 preventable deaths of newborns and children under 5 years of age

3.3 the epidemics of AIDS, tuberculosis, malaria and neglected tropical diseases

3.4 premature mortality from non-communicable diseases

3.5 substance abuse, including narcotic drug abuse and harmful use of alcohol

3.6 global deaths and injuries from road traffic accidents

3.7 universal access to sexual and reproductive health-care services

3.8 universal health coverage … financial risk protection, access to quality essential health-care services, … safe, effective, quality and affordable essential medicines and vaccines for all

3.9 hazardous chemicals and air, water and soil pollution and contamination

3.a implementation of the WHO Framework Convention on Tobacco Control in all countries

3.b research and development of vaccines and medicines for the communicable and non-communicable diseases that primarily affect developing countries

3.c health financing and the … health workforce in developing countries

3.d … early warning, risk reduction and management of national and global health risks

Source: United Nations Sustainable Development Goals (https://www.un.org /sustainabledevelopment/health/).

care, including medicines. The 10 percent threshold is widely used as an indicator of "catastrophic" health-care costs,[32] and these data are widely collected, from sources including household surveys and monitoring of health-care facilities, and are disaggregated by income, sex, age, and geographic location. Because the SDGs do not use a measure of impoverishment due to health spending as an indicator, the 10 percent threshold is a proxy.

This and the other SDG health goals call for huge achievements laid out in carefully negotiated UN-speak. Even among the low- and middle-income SDG countries, as we have seen, societies start from very different levels of health-care access. How will these improvements be financed? Donor support will be important, and donors, including USAID, are stepping into line with expanded emphases on health systems support.[33] But there is an important new movement among health-care advocates to put greater emphasis on "domestic revenue mobilization." External aid covers only 28 percent of health spending in the very poorest countries, such as Niger, Mali, and Sierra Leone; and just 3 percent of costs in middle-low countries such as Kenya and Ghana.[34] So health care even in the poorest countries is essentially domestically funded, and better health systems will be, as well. The memorable remark of Thailand's minister of public health, Piyakasol Sakolsataydorn, became a slogan in the universal-health-care movement: "Because we are poor, we cannot afford *not* to have universal health coverage."[35]

The SDGs' focus on UHC has helped to grow a broad coalition of support from governments, foundations, and international organizations under the banner of UHC2030. The coalition, renamed from the International Health Partnership that supported the MDG health goals, works to mobilize political and financial support for broader adoption of UHC strategies.[36]

Universal Health Coverage in Low- and Middle-Income Countries

What does it mean to call for universal health coverage in societies where per capita income is less than $1,025 and in middle-income countries where there is more wealth but society's resources are still severely constrained? Low incomes and modest government revenues, weak infrastructure, and limited supplies of trained medical professionals all constrain the ability of health systems in low- and middle-income countries to approach universal coverage. But among the 31 low-income countries (all but three in

Africa) and 108 countries classified as either lower-middle income (USD1,026–3,995) or upper-middle income (USD3,996–12,375), many now have substantial records of providing broader health coverage and working toward universal coverage.

For decades, primary health care (PHC) has been the agreed strategy for expanding health-care coverage in low-income countries, established in the 1978 statement of a global health conference in the Soviet city Alma-Ata: "a well-functioning PHC system emphasizes provision of preventive and curative ambulatory services by frontline health workers in close proximity to where the poor live; disease-oriented interventions in the service of ... public health goals; community oriented interventions [for] ... improved sanitation and safe drinking water; and health promotion."[37] Precisely what services and treatments are included is subject to debate, but PHC personnel and clinics function as the front line of health systems that also include regional hospitals and other health-care institutions. A number of governments use PHC and community-based health care as the foundation for systems of universal coverage.

Primary-health-care strategies rely on teams of medical professionals and volunteers to deliver health education and services to broad populations, and they have proven effective in monitoring nutrition, encouraging immunization and breastfeeding, and improving maternal and child health. Similar models have addressed daunting challenges such as multi-drug-resistant tuberculosis in Peru,[38] and expanding care, including for mental illnesses, in rural Chiapas, Mexico. In Chiapas, the Boston-based NGO Partners in Health works with the Ministry of Health to place first-year doctors (*pasantes*) in remote rural communities. By providing extra training opportunities and supervision, Partners in Health makes the rural clinics more attractive to top medical school graduates, and physicians in ten clinics provided 28,000 patient visits in 2015.[39]

For many low-income countries, the strategy will be to expand and improve primary-health-care coverage, stressing low-cost delivery of community-based health services to their least-served rural populations. In Kenya, for example, forty-seven new administrative units (counties) were created in 2013, and many of those counties have devoted relatively high levels of resources to health services. Stephen Muchiri, East Africa director for the Health Policy Plus network, argues that Kenya has the basis for effective universal coverage but will have to continue to commit funding to health while finding ways to reduce the very high percentage of the health budget (70 percent) devoted to personnel costs.[40] In many counties, he argues, private and nonprofit-sector services can help to reduce patients' out-of-pocket costs, but most universal-coverage advocates call for a central government commitment to financing some level of financial protection from catastrophic health costs.

There is now a wealth of research demonstrating the impact of community-based primary-health-care systems on multiple health priorities: maternal, neonatal, and child health in Brazil; malaria control in Ethiopia; antenatal care in Nepal; child health in Colombia; and a wide range of diseases across low-income countries.[41] The record demonstrates both that primary-care systems can have a major impact on the quality of care and that each country and sometimes each health condition requires tailoring of the community-based model.

Universal Health Coverage

Rwanda's and Thailand's health-care and health-financing systems offer a view of the possibilities, the limitations, and what systems of universal coverage might look like as other low- and middle-income country governments pursue the goal. Rwanda's USD802 per-capita income places it squarely in the low-income group, and Thailand's booming economy and USD7,808 middle-income status masks significant inequalities.

Rwanda adopted a health-driven development plan in 2000, a new vision for the country's development that saw improved health not as a product but as an animating development strategy. It has produced what Emery calls "the most dramatic improvements of health in history."[42] These gains are reflected in the country's progress on the MDGs' health-related goals: deaths from malaria, tuberculosis, and HIV reduced by more than 80 percent, and maternal mortality – the most elusive of the health-related MDGs for many countries – cut by 60 percent. These dramatic changes were accomplished with modest expenditures, as spending on health remained in the middle of the pack of forty-three sub-Saharan countries.

How did a country with a per-capita income of USD802 manage this health transformation? Like other aid-recipient countries, Rwanda's external aid for health programs came largely through initiatives targeting diseases and services. But Rwanda deployed that financial assistance to build the elements of a health-care system with a focus, in particular, on three key features: a strong, well-staffed network of community health workers and clinics; an improved network of district and provincial health facilities; and a locally managed bare-bones health-insurance system.

Steady increases in national health spending have contributed to the modest increases in the supply of physicians, nurses, and midwives. The ranks of these professions had to recover from the tremendous losses of life and skilled workers in 1994, and Rwanda improved the ratios of physicians and nurses to population through the 2000s.[43] In addition 45,000 community health workers, chosen by their communities, were recruited and trained to serve in three-person teams, each including one female volunteer focused on maternal and newborn health.[44] Their pay includes an incentive system that rewards progress on key indicators in their locality.[45] Health facilities' geographic distribution remains a serious problem, as 15 percent of the population lives more than ninety minutes from a clinic. A largely successful experiment with performance-based pay for government maternal and child health-care providers shows that the quality of care can also be improved with the right policies and incentives.[46]

Health workers, clinics, and hospitals offer the services, but the best-designed health system still requires that the population trusts the care and has the means to access it. Rwanda's answer is an innovative, locally controlled system of health insurance, the *mutuelle de santé*. Managed by community committees, the scheme creates local insurance and risk pools, requires modest premium payments from all but the poorest community members, and covers a wide range of medical expenses, with co-payments. The insurance, which covers relatively few services but is nearly universal, helps to explain the enormous increase in patient use of clinic and hospital services. "[In 2008], when giving birth in a health center cost around $25, only 20 percent of women did so. Now that it is 33 cents, 70 percent do – a big reason that deaths of mothers and children have dropped so precipitously."[47] National data show similar increases for patients seeking care for malaria and childhood illnesses and accessing family-planning services.[48]

The expansion of coverage in Rwanda is impressive, but this model of voluntary social insurance has limitations and can't be a viable route to universal coverage in many societies. Voluntary contributions limit the system's effectiveness, although Rwanda has provided incentives to participate that have led to unusually high participation rates. Risk pools that are locally based are generally too small to spread the risk adequately and allow for broad coverage of health needs and services, and the package of services covered remains quite basic.[49] National tax revenue, many argue, is required to make health coverage sustainable and to spread the risk adequately, and insurance schemes often charge a flat premium, resulting in a regressive system. But Rwanda has adjusted this, using a sliding scale since 2012, and other governments have subsidized the insurance pool with tax revenues to finance free services for people below a poverty threshold. So, while it may be true that voluntary insurance schemes are a less favored mechanism for moving toward universal coverage, this approach can expand access to health services and help to meet expanding demand.[50]

Other national plans have had mixed results. Ghana's National Health Insurance Scheme, launched in 2003, is a tax-funded national system that covers a broad range of medical services (excluding many expensive treatment options), said to include 95 percent of medical services used by Ghanaians.[51] The system is criticized for uneven quality of services, but a 2016 review of studies shows sharp increases in prenatal care visits and the percentage of births delivered in health-care facilities, as well as sharp reductions in maternal and infant mortality.[52] Equity remains a fundamental challenge, and a program ostensibly designed to address health equity issues continues to experience the lowest registration and participation rates among poor Ghanaians.[53] Averill and Marriott found in 2014 that 64 percent of the population still relied on out-of-pocket payment for health costs, and Chapman argues that the program's financial structure – it requires continuing contributions from participants – will make it difficult to include workers outside of the formal sector.[54]

Thailand's Universal Coverage Scheme, introduced in 2001, is a centralized system funded from general revenues, and has the advantages and challenges of scale: the system pools funds for 50 million people and is supported by national commitments to expenditures for health-care training and for essential medicines.[55] Patients must use the public district health system rather than private providers, and they pay a nominal fee of thirty baht (roughly one US dollar) per visit. They receive extensive inpatient and outpatient coverage.[56] Sri Lanka uses a similar strategy, financing a national system from general revenues and relying on strong administration and efficiency improvements to hold down costs.[57] The Thai system has been strengthened in stages since 2001, with coverage expanded and deepened to pay for more health services. Thailand's strong health-professional education system (training both doctors and nurses) reinforces the system, and contributes to gains in life expectancy and other health outcomes.

Universal Health Coverage and Equity

Universal health coverage provokes an important concern among advocates of health equity. Will the attention to expanding health-care coverage and addressing financial burdens result in more investments in clinical care used mainly by the urban middle class, and pressure to expand the list of costly procedures covered by UHC, reducing investments in primary health care that addresses the needs of the rural poor? The disparities between urban and rural health-care coverage are startling: worldwide, 22 percent of urban dwellers lack health coverage, but 56 percent of rural dwellers.[58]

Reallocation of resources away from public health agencies and pressure from urban middle-class participants for coverage of expensive procedures are both causes for concern.[59] After Thailand and Colombia adopted UHC policies, spending for curative services grew more rapidly than public health budgets, meaning that users of formal clinics and hospitals were the chief beneficiaries at least of the early stages of UHC expansion.[60]

The popularity of voluntary-coverage insurance schemes is another concern. The challenge of successful universal coverage in low- and middle-income societies is even greater than in the United States or Canada, and requires a high rate of participation by prosperous citizens in order to create a large enough risk pool and generate the financing needed.[61] For this reason, many health insurance schemes that are voluntary or cover a part of a population suffer the financing challenges of insurance with a small risk pool. National systems like those in South Korea, Slovenia, and Estonia have less administrative overhead and a bigger pool than those in countries that rely on several smaller schemes.[62] Lagomarsino and colleagues found that the African and Asian countries making the most sustained progress toward UHC had systems financed from tax revenues rather than from alternative mechanisms.[63]

Governments must devote public funds to covering some costs of health care for people who cannot afford to contribute significantly to a fund for health coverage. Various international conferences have set spending targets, but as Jowett and colleagues at the WHO argue, there is no "magic number" that provides good coverage.[64] Spending levels greater than $40 per person tend to be more effective in approaching universal health coverage but may not be enough to reduce people's financial risks from catastrophic health costs. Financial protection only improves significantly when spending rises above $200 per capita, and that is a real burden for governments with few resources. That kind of expenditure is not consistently viewed as an investment that can drive economic development, but Jim Yong Kim, Paul Farmer, and Michael Porter, in an influential 2013 article, make the case that health spending can do exactly that.[65]

Experience shows that societies can expand relatively low-cost, high-quality health care that gives priority to the urgent health needs of low-income citizens but that to do so requires a determined, consistent commitment to health services for the poor. To ensure that increases in health spending disproportionately benefit low-income groups (say, the bottom 40 percent) means, in effect, that goals of expanding coverage or of reducing disease incidence should focus on change among this group.[66] A Rockefeller Foundation-funded study in 1985 examined the experience of China, Costa Rica, Sri Lanka, and the Indian state of Kerala – countries that provided "good health at low cost" – and a recent follow-up study highlighted more countries now accomplishing excellent health outcomes with modest expenditures.[67] The 2013 study analyzed four countries and the Indian state of Tamil Nadu to identify the features of their health systems that lead to continuing good outcomes.

Primary-health-care strategies were key to these successes. Among the features that allowed good health services at low cost were Ethiopia's use of trained health extension workers, Bangladesh's and Tamil Nadu's continuing emphasis on primary-health-care workers, and Thailand's system of posting medical graduates in rural areas.[68] These measures have maintained or increased resources for care of low-income populations, even as demand for urban and higher-cost services grew. Health-care expenditures for the urban middle class still grew faster, in dollar terms, than expenditures for the poor majority.

Human Resources

Training an adequate number of general practitioners, nurses, and physician assistants and retaining them in systems that serve low-income communities is a challenge in virtually every society. Sub-Saharan African countries, with 24 percent of the global burden of disease, have 3 percent of global health workers, and this kind of shortfall is typical of low-income countries.[69] These societies clearly need to train, retain, and deploy more nurses, doctors, and public health professionals, a challenge made more difficult by the demand for health professionals in rich societies.

But in the near term, community health workers serve growing numbers of people at low costs in many countries. How does Brazil, with the largest population in Latin America and the greatest number of people living in poverty, provide health care to its people? Brazil's Family Health Strategy (FHS) uses teams of health providers with diverse skill levels to serve two-thirds of its population with low-cost basic health services that the rural poor in many countries lack. Clusters of six community health workers (CHW), recruited locally and trained to provide primary health services to some 150 families each, are linked to a general practitioner and registered nurse. CHWs register each family; make home visits; monitor living conditions, nutrition, and other social determinants of health; and are paid at rates determined locally.

This team structure has won widespread support, and building and maintaining it has meant that spending on primary health has grown six-fold in the 2000s.[70] Municipalities maintain the system and receive federal funding if their system conforms to the family health strategy and structure. Brazil's national health system is plagued by serious problems, but the family health strategy is a continuing strength, as is the statute, tied to the 1988 constitution, that requires that national health spending not decrease. The FHS in effect serves the poorest two-thirds of the population, since many wealthier people opt for private care. But the FHS's preventive health strategy is credited with decreased mortality, increased immunization and breastfeeding, reduced inequalities in health outcomes, and fewer hospitalizations for some chronic diseases.[71]

Essential Medicines

Access to medicines is an essential and complex aspect of universal health coverage. Since 1977, the WHO has maintained a "model list" of essential medicines that serves as a guide for 156 national lists.[72] But multiple factors limit access to many of these medicines in most low- and lower-middle-income countries, and expanding access is a key step in realizing the human right to health. A 2016 UN report estimates that 400 million people lack access to essential medicines, three-quarters of them in middle-income countries.[73] The medicines on the list are selected and tested for safety, effectiveness, and cost-efficiency, and many governments and health-care providers rely on the list. In one representative Indian hospital, just twenty-one medicines accounted for 50 percent of medicine budgets, led by anti-infective drugs (including anti-retrovirals), insulin, and antibiotics.[74] But expensive new medicines such as drugs for treatment of hepatitis-C and several cancer therapy medications have recently been added to the list, as perceptions of what are "essential" medicines grow.[75]

The Trade Related Intellectual Property Rights (TRIPS) agreement concluded in 1995 established a new regime regulating trade in pharmaceuticals and other products that in effect blocked World Trade Organization (WTO) members from copying expensive medicines by creating less expensive generics, and did so at a time when expensive anti-retrovirals were becoming available to treat HIV-positive patients. The WTO recognized in 2007 that public health can constitute a compelling public interest that justifies exceptions to international patent rules.[76] But TRIPS restrictions have been strengthened in a series of bilateral and regional trade agreements – so-called TRIPS-plus – closing many of the possible exceptions to rules protecting patents.

The UN secretary general's 2016 High-level Panel highlighted these issues, in an effort to encourage governments and international organizations to be strict in designating medicines as new and patentable. This advocacy under the secretary general's auspices picks up the themes of the global movement for access to essential medicines, coordinated by Doctors Without Borders since 1999. The campaign presses for changes in patent laws and rules, as well as encouraging changes to build a research and development agenda for pharmaceuticals driven by patient needs.[77]

A second panel, the 2017 Lancet Commission, was financed in part by the Gates Foundation and sought to broaden the focus to a set of five priority issues for expanding access, including how to finance greater access, ensuring quality of medicines, and developing needed but missing medicines for neglected diseases. The Lancet panel was less willing than the secretary general's panel to challenge the legitimacy of some patents and intellectual property rights, instead promoting approaches that accommodate pharmaceutical patent protections and urging new arrangements with nonprofits and product development partnerships.

Financing the development and dissemination of essential medicines is a complex challenge, both because market-driven research and development dominates research and because of the limited funds available in most low- and middle-income countries. Of USD240 billion invested in pharmaceutical R&D in 2009/2010, 60 percent was from the private sector, 30 percent from governments, and 10 percent from nonprofits.[78] This re-emphasizes the importance of the SDGs' equity-oriented targets, and of the vigilance of health rights advocates.

COVID-19

Is ambitious, hopeful talk about universal health coverage still relevant in the wake of a devastating pandemic? The pandemic could have major impacts because it threatens to interrupt child immunization campaigns; disrupt access to contraception and reproductive health care; discourage patients from seeking care for chronic illnesses, both communicable and noncommunicable; and decimate the ranks of skilled health-care workers. These threats associated with the pandemic heighten the importance of building broad coverage and developing durable egalitarian strategies. The relative success of Thailand and Vietnam in managing the pandemic (as of August 2020) testifies to the value of the health-systems approach.[79] Two of the strategies highlighted in this chapter – UHC and community health workers – appear as centerpieces of proposals to strengthen health systems while responding to the emergency. Kadaki and Thoumi, for example, argue that four strategies that have helped protect some communities and societies from the worst effects of COVID-19 are also the priorities for years ahead.[80] UHC and CHWs are two of these, along with greater attention to the interaction of health and climate change, and innovative financing for health-care innovation, especially the development of pharmaceuticals.

Community health workers' effectiveness in pandemic response has been demonstrated in Ebola-affected countries as well as in Ethiopia on a national scale, and investing in recruiting, training, and compensating CHWs has been shown to be both an effective short-term response and a long-term foundation for expanding coverage and care.[81] Strategies to expand health coverage and social protection schemes, even those that were poorly funded and had limited coverage, have helped extend benefits to vulnerable groups during the pandemic and facilitated public health communication. In health as in other sectors, human rights principles and the SDGs provide a guide to giving real meaning to the slogan "build back better." McDonnell's exhaustive 2019 review of countries' progress toward UHC found that most countries move toward UHC after a time of "disruption," when the status quo of political arrangements is disturbed and new possibilities are opened up.[82] The pandemic, which surely qualifies as a major "disruption," may create the space for such a shift.

Conclusions

The shift from targeting specific diseases to building systems of universal health coverage is dramatic, and it is a key element of the SDGs. Organizing and financing universal coverage in low- and middle-income countries is challenging and will not happen overnight, but it is proceeding, and human rights principles provide important guidance for setting priorities. Even though the SDG Target 3.8, achieving universal health coverage, is not framed in human rights terms, it is a new level of commitment to creating systems that protect the health of all members of society.

The varied experiences of countries such as Thailand, Rwanda, Brazil, and Sri Lanka show that societies with modest resources can move decisively toward making basic quality care available and affordable for all. That goal may be accomplished through a national health system such as Thailand's, with coverage extending to nearly all residents. Or it may be through a model like Brazil's health teams, relying heavily on community health workers organized in teams with health professionals who can provide more complex care when it is needed. The growing support from international organizations and major donors and foundations can accelerate this progress.

chapter five

Access to Productive Assets: Labor

As a graduate student in the late 1980s I had an experience in Guatemala that has shaped my understanding of development ever since. In the course of two summers working in the country's beautiful, temperate highlands and the steamy, tropical Pacific coast, I met men and women who pieced together survival-level livelihoods as farmers and wage workers. They grew food crops on tiny plots, sometimes sent a crop to market, and then migrated to the coast for seasonal work at poverty wages on plantations. Often a family member also worked as a day laborer or housekeeper. Every aspect of those livelihood strategies was insecure: the land tenure, the prices at market, the daily wages, and the working conditions and pay on plantations. The physical quality of their lives, and their ability to invest in their children's education, depended directly on their land and labor rights.

To make sustainable, lasting, economic and social change requires addressing the constraints on this kind of access to productive assets. One fundamental flaw in the MDG strategy was this: while its short-term measures to improve health and incomes sometimes succeeded, they did not address the causes of poverty. As a result, they sometimes distracted governments from trying to improve poor communities' access to the key productive assets: land and the inputs needed to make agriculture productive, decent work, energy, and financial services.

Just as goals and indicators can perpetuate inequalities and reduce the incentive to build stronger health systems, the MDGs focused attention on short-term "quick-fix" strategies, rather than on the hard task of expanding poor populations' access to land, capital, jobs, and energy. Improving access to education and health services does contribute to the ability of poor people to farm, work, and live productively, and the gains made during the MDG period are important. But what was missing was a sustained effort to expand access to those productive assets, and that presents a challenge for the SDGs. The MDGs encouraged governments and development agencies to solve what Michael Edwards calls "thick problems" with "thin" solutions.[1] This is a longstanding reflex in the practice of development, but when problems are rooted in the structures of the economy, when they are thorny and complex and political, the durable solutions will have to address the thorny problems.

Increasing access to land, decent work, capital, and energy can certainly be done: the national experiences I examine here and in chapter 6 show that land reform, improved women's property and inheritance rights, and improved labor rights and opportunities are being accomplished in poor societies, and that they are driven mainly by domestic politics and initiatives. Effective anti-poverty strategies include MDG-style investments in short-term measures to improve health and education and expanded investments in community-based nutrition monitoring and care. But sustainable success will also require that poor people have access to the productive assets that give them opportunities to prosper. Widespread, shared access is a foundation for sustainable, equitable, productive economies, and the SDGs include goals and targets that focus on these productive assets, both in land and labor. This chapter begins with a discussion of the MDGs, then unpacks labor. Chapter 6 addresses land.

Labor, Decent Work, and Poor People's Livelihoods

Fashions come and go in international development, and it is a field full of debates over the relative importance and value of its many strategies. But there is substantial agreement about the importance of access to land and the availability of decent-paying employment, and recent research and experience in the field confirm this: livelihoods are central, and land and labor are essential factors in livelihoods.[2]

Labor conditions and the availability of good-paying jobs are increasingly a central factor. Rapid urbanization means that 40 percent of Africa's population now lives in urban centers, 49 percent of Asia's, and 80 percent of Latin America's. Paid employment is an essential part of the livelihoods of most of the world's poor people, urban and rural, although relatively few of them hold full-time, formal, regulated jobs. Piecing together estimates of the job status of the almost 3 billion people who earn less than the equivalent of $5.50 a day[3] makes it clear that wage and work conditions could have a significant impact:

- 192 million are defined as unemployed;[4]
- 176 million employed people live in "extreme working poverty," with household consumption less than the equivalent of PPP$2.00 a day;[5]
- hundreds of millions work part time in addition to earning their agricultural livelihoods on farms;
- 90 percent of workers in developing countries are in the private sector;[6]
- most of these are either self-employed or casual workers such as domestic workers, waste pickers, or vendors who are without social protections in the so-called informal economy;
- worldwide, the labor force participation rate for women aged between twenty-five and fifty-four is 63 percent; the rate is 94 percent for men.[7]

The bottom line, according to labor economist Gary Fields, is that

> [m]ost of the world's poor people are self-employed, but because there are few opportunities in most developing countries for them to earn enough to escape poverty, they are working hard but working poor. Two key policy planks in the fight against poverty should be: raising the returns to self-employment and creating more

opportunities to move from self-employment into higher paying wage employment.[8]

The MDGs: Quick Impact, Ignoring Root Causes

Human rights-based approaches tend to call for attention to the causes and multiple dimensions of poverty, and to the linkages between poverty and civil and political freedoms; the MDGs were goals that aimed primarily for progress in some of the worst *symptoms* of poverty. Both in principle and in the practice of many agencies, human rights approaches to social and economic policy involve tracing the social, economic, political, and other causes of rights deprivation. In principle, this is true because human rights principles call for attention to patterns of discrimination in law, institutions, and policy; because they emphasize the interrelatedness of political and civil freedoms with economic and social rights; and because they emphasize the need to establish effective legal and institutional protections for groups that suffer discriminatory treatment.[9] In practice, human rights advocates show a strong tendency to challenge policies and practices that exclude or disadvantage any group, and to probe for the root causes of deprivation.

The MDGs and human rights approaches differ in their attention to structural and sociopolitical factors that cause and perpetuate poverty. Of the structural factors underlying poverty and wealth in poor countries – access to land, labor, wages, credit, and (some would add) energy – none was mentioned by the MDGs until a labor target was added to Goal 1 in 2007 (see below). Simon Maxwell's (2003) warning early in the MDG process that targets would have perverse impacts on decision making by donors and governments was well-founded, because the MDGs diverted attention from difficult, structural features of poverty and inequality.[10]

It is true, as MDG proponents argued, that the goals were outcome measures, not strategies, and they did not exclude or directly discourage broader efforts to expand opportunities and address the causes of poverty. But embracing the quick-impact strategy for a global anti-poverty initiative that quickly became the organizing principle for many aid agencies did mean that other possible strategies were often de-emphasized. This was because of the emphasis on what a 2005 Millennium Campaign report called "high potential, short-term impact" initiatives that could yield "breathtaking results within three or fewer years ..." and "start countries on the path to the Goals."[11] These "quick wins" strategies can have important impacts, and I am not arguing that governments should not invest in anti-malarial bed nets or in-school meals. But the two approaches lead to different kinds of strategies: quick fixes versus investment in sustainable development. Except for employment rates covered by the indicators of MDG 1, none of the MDGs mentioned the structural factors underlying poverty and wealth in poor countries – secure access to land and work at good wages.

The MDGs created incentives for donors and governments to favor quick impact over addressing complex social systems. These "quick win" measures included, for example, mosquito bed nets for malaria protection, MDG model villages, immunizations, and school meals. Such investments can quickly drive down key indicators for the goals, and they mobilized donors' aid funds. Most of them involve not catalyzing systemic change but delivering individual health and education benefits. These "quick win" strategies were attractive to donor agencies and their domestic constituencies, and they attracted aid funds and therefore the attention of poor-country governments.

In one pragmatic view, this feature was a strength of the MDGs: they relied on interventions that could be accomplished without even attempting to address the thorny social and political causes of inequality and deprivation. The goals heightened the general tendency in development practice to look for the silver bullet, the single product, service, or reform that will transform lives and economies. The history of development is littered with these: the improved cookstove, the new tree crop with extraordinary nutrition and economic benefits, microfinance loans to unleash hidden entrepreneurial talents, bio-fortification of foods, even the introduction of vaccines.[12] Many of these are in fact helpful, but no single innovation has had the dramatic effects that promoters often predict.

Likewise, progress on the MDGs produced real improvement in quality of life for some of the world's poor. But these incentives also implied a quiet retreat from important trends in development cooperation toward greater recognition of the right of people affected by development policies to participate influentially in shaping them, and the need to guarantee political freedoms in order to make poverty reduction politically sustainable. Most important, the MDG strategy retreated from the politically challenging work of expanding poor peoples' secure access to land and increasing the rewards for their labor.

The MDGs did belatedly add a target on labor to the Goal 1, on poverty reduction. The Target 1B, adopted in 2007, halfway through the MDG period, called for countries to "Achieve full and productive employment and decent work for all, including women and young people." Their decent work target was to be tracked by four indicators; but while the ILO succeeded in adding the employment target, it was an afterthought in the MDGs, and the UN's final MDG report discusses the workforce target primarily by acknowledging that the labor force had grown more rapidly than employment.[13]

These differences are not only matters of strategy: the MDG and human rights-based approaches differ fundamentally. Most MDG strategies invested in measures that benefited individuals and households without creating social or institutional changes that give reason to hope for follow-on benefits for those not reached. Moreover, because the MDGs did not call for an analysis of the causes of poverty and its manifestations, they generally did not directly address the structural factors that human rights analysis points to as root causes.

The effects of these goals and targets can be seen in the shifting focus of development assistance from governments and official aid donors during the period. The Washington, DC-based Center for Global Development reports on global aid policies and finds that official development aid flows increased during the MDG period and shifted modestly toward health and education sectors, consistent with the MDGs' strong emphases.[14] A global framework for development that de-emphasized rural livelihoods and capacity to produce food coincided with a long-term decline in assistance to the agriculture and rural development sector. Official aid to agriculture and rural development declined consistently from 1989 to 2004, with commitments (calculated as five-year averages) falling from $13.5 billion in 1989 to slightly less than $6.5 billion in 2004.[15] Aid to the sector began to increase again in 2005, and aid totals to sub-Saharan Africa show that much of the increase was in assistance for irrigation and for industrial and cash crop development, while support for agrarian reform policies dropped sharply after the 1990s.[16]

Alongside the problems of the MDGs' omitted goals, some of the indicators chosen were also problematic. The MDGs encouraged renewed investment to improve nutritional outcomes, and MDG goals and targets on poverty and hunger, which called for reduction of the number or proportion of people experiencing hunger, measured progress on malnutrition by tracking two outcomes: the incidence of under-age-five malnutrition; and the national measure of prevalence of undernutrition.

These hunger indicators encouraged governments to understand food security solely as a function of the number of calories consumed. This misses two important dimensions of nutrition: the variety and adequacy of diets, and the sacrifices of other expenditures made in order to secure those calories. First, the MDGs included no indicators to encourage progress in low-income households' ability to produce and buy foods that provide a varied and healthy diet throughout the year. Humanitarian agencies and nutritionists recognize the central importance of dietary diversity, and USAID uses a Household Dietary Diversity Index that produces a household score, corresponding closely to overall nutritional status.[17]

Second, even as the MDGs' nutrition measures improved in sub-Saharan Africa, indicators of the vulnerability and the uncertainty of nutritional status were worsening. One key measure, the percentage of income spent on food, is especially telling: the percentage in many low-income countries remains as high as 70 to

80 percent, compared to an estimated average of 40 percent of income spent on food in Brazil.[18] The high percentage is both an indicator of severe poverty and an ominous sign that households have very few ways to adapt to food price hikes or other economic shocks.

These limitations don't diminish the positive impact of the MDGs. But they do highlight the fact that a sustainable, enduring assault on poverty, malnutrition, and ill health is not possible without expanding economic opportunities for poor and marginalized people, and this means access to land and work with dignity. In the next two sections I focus on the essential role of decent work that pays a living wage in reducing poverty, and on recent initiatives in a handful of countries that demonstrate the ability of societies to address these issues.

Effective Labor Policies in Practice

Can governments and aid agencies successfully tackle these labor issues, which deal with the most fundamental economic conflicts over the ownership and control of the means of production and the division of the surplus? Some recent experiences show that they can, and that there is no single prescription. In a handful of countries across Asia, Africa, and Latin America, labor policy, job-creation incentives, minimum wage policies, and measures to help workers in the informal economy have been important forces in driving down poverty. Alongside effective social safety nets, gains in labor income are a principal driver of recent poverty reduction gains in some regions. The fact that these issues are highlighted in SDG Goal 8 (Decent Work and Economic Growth) should encourage greater attention to labor policy as a potent anti-poverty tool.

Economic growth is an important factor, and all the strategies discussed here are most effective in an expanding economy where growth is in labor-intensive sectors. But even with slow or little growth, governments can employ four broad sets of policies that have expanded incomes and opportunity recently in several low- and middle-income countries: government employment guarantees and subsidies; minimum wage policies; initiatives to increase rural off-farm employment; and labor rights reforms benefiting workers in the informal economy.

Employment Subsidies and Guarantees

Many social protection programs include short-term public employment to cushion the effects of economic or weather shocks, or address the effects of seasonal price variations.[19] Some governments have embraced permanent job-creation strategies. Algeria addressed its "formidable unemployment challenge" (30 percent in 2000) by offering subsidies to private sector firms for new hiring, alongside a public employment program. The impact was dramatic: 1.4 million new jobs were created from 2004 to 2009, and the total unemployment rate fell from 30 percent in 2000 to 15.3 percent in 2005 and 10.2 percent in 2009.[20] India's widely discussed National Rural Employment Guarantee Act, enacted in 2005, guarantees 100 days of manual work to those in need, and it employed 126 million individuals for some time during 2018.[21] Despite problems with transparency and corruption in the program's implementation, it has had a significant impact on the seasonal poverty and malnutrition that rural households suffer.[22]

A rural employment scheme launched in 2003 in Ethiopia employs individuals from households at risk of severe food insecurity, paying either cash or food for labor on public works or water and soil conservation initiatives.[23] The Productive Safety Net Programme (PSNP) employed 7.9 million individuals in 2015 and, now in its fourth phase, also operates as a safety-net program for households without an employable member, which receive allotments without a work condition.[24] PSNP aims to cushion life-threatening food price rises and to allow households to navigate these threats without selling off household assets such as cattle or land. The program was joined by an ambitious broader employment plan to create 3 million jobs in 2019–2020.[25]

Ethiopia's PSNP illustrates the value of having social-safety-net programs in place at the time of a shock such as the COVID-19 pandemic. Nguyen reports that the Ethiopian government was able to respond to the crisis by making advance payments through PSNP and making additional benefits available to pregnant and lactating women.[26] Gentilini's tracking of such programs shows that cash transfers to informal sector workers, who are generally not covered by other forms of unemployment insurance, had reached an estimated 136 million workers worldwide.[27]

Minimum Wages: Latin America and Southeast Asia

Governments in Latin America and in Southeast Asia have responded to regional growth by raising and expanding the coverage of minimum wages. The World Bank's 2015 report on labor and poverty in Latin America finds that income gains from the labor market drove poverty reduction in the region, aided by minimum wages and related policies. Rising labor incomes led to reductions in poverty and inequality both in countries that benefited from high commodity prices in the MDG period and in those that did not. The gains were strongest for less-skilled workers, and the World Bank credits a set of policies including "day care and early education to increase female labor force participation, training programs, formality incentives, and minimum-wage legislation."[28] These factors are nonetheless still major causes of gendered wage inequalities in low- and middle-income countries.[29]

The World Bank has historically been skeptical of aggressive minimum wage policies, yet its recent reports take a more favorable view. The 2015 report finds that wages for unskilled labor rose twice as rapidly in percentage terms as for skilled labor, and credits minimum wage policies. The last decade's experience in the region also suggests that national minimum wages, which generally don't apply to very small firms and informal sector employers, nonetheless exert a strong positive effect on wages in those firms.[30] Economic research on the effects of Brazil's minimum wage uncovers a related benefit: the minimum wage has reduced wage inequalities both within and between enterprises, a significant contribution to the effort to reverse rising inequalities discussed in chapter 3.[31]

A 2018 review of the literature on minimum wages finds that they are "back at the top of the policy agenda," and that although they do not target the poorest households effectively, they do have a positive effect on incomes in the lower portion of the income distribution. New, higher or more inclusive minimum wage policies in recent years include those of South Africa, Cambodia, Cape Verde, Costa Rica, Myanmar, and Malaysia.[32]

In Southeast Asia, a 2018 business report shows that minimum wages in the region averaged 63 percent of the global average in 2015 but had risen to almost 82 percent in 2019.[33] While business interest groups worry about rising minimum wages, the floor is helping to ensure that highly skilled workers aren't the only ones benefiting from growth in technology and related industries. Higher wage levels for more skilled workers may also help the cause of movements such as the Asian Floor Wage, a region-wide coalition of labor and anti-poverty groups calling for a region-wide base.[34]

Across Asia, rapid wage growth in many countries has lifted average incomes since 2000, but gaping disparities, including gender inequalities, remain in most countries. Minimum wage increases have helped boost pay in garment industries across the region, but many women – particularly large populations of domestic workers – are either in jobs not covered by minimum wages, or the minimum wages that do apply are not well enforced.[35] Worldwide, more than half of domestic workers are covered by minimum wage laws, but in Asia the figure is 12 percent, suggesting that expanding the coverage and improving the enforcement of existing wage laws should be priorities for governments in the region.[36]

Rural Off-farm Employment

Employment in rural areas is critically important to raising incomes and reducing risks among the rural poor. Smallholder farmers' livelihood strategies typically include seasonal work off the farm: "the rural non-farm economy accounts for about 30% of full-time rural employment in Asia and Latin America, 20% in West Asia and North Africa … and 10% in Africa."[37] In every region, manufacturing makes up less than a quarter of rural off-farm employment, with 75 percent consisting of services, including transport, construction, and other financial and personal services.[38]

Rural nonfarm employment has grown rapidly across poor societies and "non-farm activities account for 35 to 50 percent of rural income," more for landless and very poor households.[39] Expanding rural employment is essential to making small-scale farming economically viable, and rural employment grows most readily when supported by a growing regional economy, incentives to rural manufacturing and service industries, and an educated local workforce with appropriate skills.[40] The record of programs to promote rural nonfarm employment is uneven, but there have been national-level successes in Brazil (the SENAP) and with Namibia's Community Skills Development Centres, and local projects have succeeded elsewhere.[41] Brazil's national rural apprenticeship and skills training program has been evaluated and studied extensively, and findings show that demand-responsive apprenticeship programs increased skilled employment opportunities and wages in rural areas and among rural migrants and urban dwellers, but that there was a strong bias toward male trainees.[42]

In some countries, local and regional initiatives have been effective. Improving rural and feeder roads, for example, can facilitate the development of employment opportunities along transport routes. In other cases, national legislation is needed. The simple step of making citizens' eligibility for social benefits portable when they migrate within-country for work, for example, improves labor mobility, allows workers to respond to economic opportunity, and provides them at least a minimal safety net when they do. China, Vietnam, and several Indian states have taken steps in this direction.[43]

Labor, human rights, and anti-poverty networks have initiated campaigns to promote and monitor the labor rights and decent work agenda of the SDGs. The Trade Union Development Cooperation Network, for example, publishes a periodic review of critical SDGs (1 on Poverty, 5 on Gender, 8 on Decent Work, 10 on Inequality, 13 on Climate, and 16 on Peace, Justice, and Strong

Institutions). The network's 2018 report is a detailed assessment of countries' voluntary national reports on these themes and an important contribution to independent monitoring of labor-related SDGs.[44]

Informal Economy

Whether we call it informal sector employment, self-employment, or casual labor, unregistered work without social protections is a frequent option for poor workers, and improving their wages and conditions should be a top priority. The 2 billion workers in informal employment are 61 percent of the world's workforce.[45] This kind of self-employment is sometimes idealized as entrepreneurship, but very poor people are usually "reluctant entrepreneurs,"[46] working for themselves because of the severe shortage of formal jobs. The numbers of people affected are mind-boggling, and the informal economy is not a side issue or an optional topic for people concerned with labor rights and poverty. It is central.

Who are these informal sector workers? Of some 8 million people residing in Bangkok, Thailand, for example, an estimated 1.8 million work in the informal economy.[47] These manual laborers, domestic workers, vendors, waste collectors, motor-tricycle taxi operators, and others have no job security and no social protections, and often they have little recourse if they are not paid for day labor. Effective policies and interventions to improve their options are among the most important strategies available to create sustainable solutions to poverty, and government policies and development agency initiatives have seen many failures.

Worse, many municipal and national governments give in to the impulse to regulate and hassle self-employed individuals (especially vendors in large cities) even when policy options are readily available to improve their livelihoods and strengthen their contributions to communities. Fields chronicles major city governments' efforts in South Africa to stop "illegal, unlicensed street trading," when the traders are only "illegal" because governments won't issue enough licenses.[48] When policies that encourage and nurture informal enterprises are combined with opportunities to improve workers' skills and labor market policies that expand formal sector jobs, the results are positive.

Recent policy changes in several societies show that models now exist that can significantly improve the economic situation of informal workers who have long lacked legal protections and lived in poverty. In Colombia, Bogotá's network of collectors of waste and recyclables won recognition and a contract as part of the municipal waste management plan. After years of collecting waste to sell to dealers at low prices, some 9,000 waste collectors are now paid twice or more their former earnings and work as part of the city's waste management plan.[49]

In Thailand, an estimated 440,000 workers, mostly female, do sewing, assembly, and other production work out of their homes for small manufacturers and other employers. After years of advocacy by HomeNet Thailand, the Thai parliament passed, first, a Homeworkers Protection Act in 2010 that expanded home workers' legal rights, as well as legislation in 2011 giving home workers access to social security benefits.[50] The results are sweeping, and the law now mandates that

> fair wages – including equal pay for men and women doing the same job – be paid to workers hired to complete work at home for an industrial enterprise. It also obliges the hirer to provide a contract, to ensure occupational health and safety, and to establish a committee that provides access to the courts in labour disputes and gives women a place at the decision-making table.[51]

Similar policy changes are continuing in the early years of the SDG period, as is domestic pressure in many countries for further changes. Reforms to registration, location, and charges to street vendors in Durban, South Africa, and new licensing arrangements for street vendors in Lima, Peru, demonstrate the range of policy changes that can improve wages, working conditions, and prospects for informal workers. The Gauteng regional government in South Africa announced expanded recognition and support to waste recyclers' cooperatives in 2017, and multiple movements and consultations regarding housing rights, taxation and regulation, health care coverage, and other issues are ongoing.[52]

Domestic workers – those working in the home of another person – are perhaps the least well-protected. They work and sometimes live in employers' households, making them difficult to organize collectively, and the traditional privacy of the home and family life has made regulation and enforcement difficult. But the last decade has seen gains in several countries with the formation of domestic workers' unions and associations.

Domestic workers gained a broad set of rights in the Philippines with the 2013 Kasambahay (domestic workers) law. The country's 1.9 million domestic workers won significant new protections: a minimum wage, a mandated weekly day of rest, five days' annual leave, annual thirteenth month pay, and social security benefits.[53] These benefits (along with other educational benefits) were passed under President Aquino's government and have persisted through the first years of the populist Duterte regime. The law implements the ILO Convention 189, which addresses issues specific to domestic workers, and of which the Philippines was an early ratifier.[54]

Recent legislation protecting domestic workers in Bolivia is similar evidence of progress and of challenges. The Law2450/2003 Regulating Paid Household Work laid the legal groundwork for regulations regarding pay, hours, and treatment by employers. But implementation is uneven, and important issues such as access to public pension benefits are not covered.[55] The Bolivian experience highlights the difficulty of defending labor rights for workers who work as individuals in other people's homes, and their association, *Fenatrahob*, continues to press for regulation and enforcement. Some issues are only partly resolved: domestic workers in the capital, La Paz, have coverage for health services for a nominal charge through the National Health Insurance plan under a municipal law, and the requirement that written contracts replace the practice of oral agreements has been poorly implemented.[56]

The challenges of implementation and enforcement are front and center for Bolivia's advocates and internationally. Although collective bargaining with the very large number of individual employers is difficult to organize, it has been done successfully in Uruguay and elsewhere. More often, governments have taken other measures including standardized written contracts (Lebanon, Jordan, and others), weekly or monthly minimum wages (Kenya, Malawi, and many others), and regulations regarding hours, pensions, and time off, in keeping with the ILO's Convention 189 on domestic work.[57]

There is good reason to believe that these trends in labor policy, especially toward the informal economy, can accelerate in the SDG period. Several governments, including Senegal, Gambia, and Bangladesh, have announced new initiatives to expand national "decent work" programs. The Bangladesh initiative, whose initial phase runs from 2017 to 2020, emphasizes job creation in manufacturing and increasing women's access to job skills training, as well as overseeing enforcement of labor conditions standards. (This last objective dovetails with the Better Work Bangladesh initiative, which has targeted work conditions in the garment industry there since 2014.) Canada is among the four international funders of the government's garment industry safety initiative, while USAID has funded a US-based NGO to support Bangladeshi initiatives on child labor.[58]

Other initiatives in the SDG period continue efforts to enable and expand social benefits and workplace protections for informal labor (Peru, Senegal, Malawi, Chile, and others); efforts to simplify and create incentives for worker registration (Brazil, Argentina, Chile, and Peru); and numerous reforms to business registration and taxation intended to encourage formalization of small and medium-sized enterprises.[59] In Latin America, the Avina Foundation and *Red LACRE* (Latin American Recyclers Network) are leading a new regional campaign for "inclusive recycling." Building on successes in Buenos Aires, Bogotá, and other major metropolitan areas, the initiative works to formalize recycler networks in the informal economy, increase the efficiency and profitability of operations and value chains for recycled goods, and advocate for broader adoption of the same principles.[60]

These measures to improve conditions for informal sector workers show that there is some momentum for measures to improve or formalize work conditions for some of the workers most vulnerable to exploitation. Other new measures, including some tied to the development of circular economies, also offer strategies for the decade ahead.

Economic Growth and New Initiatives

Economists at the World Bank and OECD focus attention on growth. If national GDPs grow rapidly, opportunities expand and the challenge of providing decent employment for low-income workers becomes easier. The 2018 reports on global employment all wish for faster growth: GDP growth in the Least Developed Countries was 5 percent in 2017, short of the 7 percent goal in SDG8. (This compares to recent growth rates of 1.9 percent in Canada and 2.9 percent in the United States.)[61] Initiatives to improve skills and expand opportunities for low-income workers will of course be helped if economies grow rapidly. But well-designed policies and interventions – especially for underemployed young workers – can succeed in cooler economies, too. In the wake of the COVID-19 pandemic, it may be essential to emphasize social sector and labor policies that can be delinked from the prospect of economic growth, potentially a transformative change.[62]

Colombia's Youth Entrepreneurship Programs, launched nationwide in 2009, have targeted vulnerable rural youth with skills development and business management training. To date, program participants have shown a high rate of success in starting new businesses, income gains, and business successes. The entrepreneurs were supported by seed grants, but an impact evaluation found that the training and skills development model used by Colombia's National Training Service was a key factor in participants' success.[63]

Apprenticeships have been highly successful in some high-income countries such as Germany, and initiatives to create apprenticeship-style opportunities for women in several southern African countries have had some success. For more than two decades the Dutch-founded NGO Young Africa has matched young women in Zimbabwe, including orphaned female youth, with entrepreneurs and businesses that provide training. The program provides life-skills training and other forms of support, and has expanded to four other countries in the region. An evaluation finds that 83 percent of graduates transition successfully to employment.[64] Ismail's 2018 review of studies on youth employment programs reveals that their record is mixed, and finds that public sector programs have been better able to scale up than either private sector or NGO efforts.[65]

A significant opportunity for some informal workers is opening up with growing interest in the materials- and energy-efficient "circular economy." Reworking sectors of an economy to make more efficient use of materials (recycling, reusing) and energy in what has come to be known as the "circular economy" is more strongly associated with northern Europe than with the global South. But the Irish NGO Tearfund is documenting and promoting the value of these methods on a large scale in low- and middle-income countries.[66] Visitors to poor communities often observe the ways that people earn income or save by recycling and reusing materials. I have seen people washing out plastic beverage cups in an alleyway in Manila, gathering and sorting recyclables from trash dumps in Nicaragua, and disassembling old electronics for parts and repair in workshops in Accra.

A circular economy organizes and systematizes these activities, builds similar reuse initiatives into large- and small-scale production processes, and rewards the labor of those who make it work. In sectors throughout the global South, aspects of a circular economy are being built into small and medium enterprises through (for example) collection and reuse of acids from metal finishing businesses in India, stronger organization of waste-pickers and materials recycling in Brazilian cities, and vehicle recycling and remanufacture in Ghana's Suame/Kumasi industrial cluster.[67] Linking government and industrial procurement and vehicle repair to this reorganized cluster of enterprises is one example of the government actions that stimulated its growth, and the enterprises rely on associations of materials and vehicle collectors for the continued flow of old vehicles and scrap parts and materials. The business essentially prolongs the life of vehicles and creates a wide range of skilled and unskilled work. Schmitz estimates that more than 12,000 businesses involve 200,000 workers, up from 40,000 employed in the 1980s.[68]

In short, there is now a growing set of policies and strategies to expand poor farmers' and workers' economic opportunities, often while building greater environmental sustainability and profitability into sectors of growing economies. Governments that give priority to improving labor incomes can do so, even with only moderate rates of economic growth. They have a wide range of tools to accomplish this, involving employment, access to land, minimum wages, labor protections (especially for low-income workers in the informal economy), and others. Driven by domestic political movements, and sometimes aided by external donors, governments can impact wages and have significant effects on equity and prosperity. Human rights advocates and proponents of the SDGs are well positioned to be part of an expanded move to adopt such policies.

The SDGs and Access to Productive Assets

The Sustainable Development Goals (SDGs), unlike their predecessors, include multiple targets that focus attention specifically on poor populations' secure access to land, employment at decent wages, financial services, energy, and other productive resources.[69] Whether the SDGs can help encourage sustainable impact on these structural issues will depend on the depth of commitment from governments and donors and the effectiveness of domestic and international political pressure for action and accountability. These factors are the subject of chapter 7. But the presence of goals and verifiable targets and indicators is an essential start. A long list of SDG targets is relevant to labor incomes – from Goals addressing gender equality, education, employment, inequality, and others. The SDGs that address labor issues most directly are summarized in table 5.1.

The targets related to labor rights and the decent work agenda link human rights, labor rights, and the development goals more strongly than ever before in mainstream development policy. Employment-related targets and indicators add new references to working conditions and to policies ensuring that young people gain employment skills, but they create only a general standard related to wages. Instead, they focus on two variables: increasing opportunities for skills and vocational training (4.4), and eliminating gender disparities in the access to such training (4.5).

Table 5.1. Selected SDGs dealing with labor and employment issues

SDG Target	Key Indicators
4.4 By 2030, substantially increase the number of youth and adults who have relevant skills, including **technical and vocational skills,** for employment, decent jobs and entrepreneurship	4.4.1 Proportion of youth and adults with information and communications technology skills, by type of skill
8.3 [Promote] policies that support **productive activities, decent job creation,** entrepreneurship, creativity and innovation, and **encourage the formalization and growth of micro-, small-, and medium-sized enterprises**	8.3.1 Proportion of informal employment in nonagriculture employment, by sex
8.5 By 2030, achieve **full and productive employment and decent work** for all women and men, including for young people and persons with disabilities; equal pay for work of equal value	8.5.1 Average hourly earnings of female and male employees … 8.5.2 Unemployment rate, by sex, age and persons with disabilities
8.6 By 2020, **substantially reduce the proportion of youth not in employment, education, or training**	8.6.1 Secondary completion rates, girls and boys 8.6.3 Youth employment rate, formal and informal sector.
8.8 Protect **labour rights and promote safe and secure working environments** for all workers, including migrant workers, in particular women migrants, and those in precarious employment	8.8.2 Increased national compliance with labor rights, assessed by monitoring ILO reports and national legislation
10.4 Adopt policies, especially **fiscal, wage and social protection policies**, and progressively achieve greater equality	10.4.1 Labor share of GDP, including wages and social protection transfers 10.4.2 Redistributive impact of fiscal policy

Source: United Nations General Assembly (2015).[70] Emphases added.

Two other targets, while not as directly and obviously tied to land and paid labor, offer potential leverage to help advance poor people's access to these productive assets. Target 7.1 calls for "universal access to affordable, reliable and modern energy services" by 2030. It is hard to overestimate the impact that affordable electric energy can have, reshaping education and opening prospects for new livelihoods. Target 5.4 addresses the issue of unpaid domestic work, overwhelmingly by women: "Recognize and value unpaid care and domestic work through the provision of public services, infrastructure and social protection policies and the promotion of shared responsibility within the household and the family as nationally appropriate."

Pandemic and Decent Work

Job losses and setbacks for job security have resulted in the loss of the equivalent of 400 million full-time jobs worldwide, affecting many more workers and households.[71] The impact is particularly harsh for women, who are overrepresented in the sectors most affected, and for workers in the informal economy.[72] Informal workers are affected differently by lockdowns, distancing, and infection depending on their employment – as vendors, recyclers/waste pickers, home workers, domestic workers, construction, or other. But they are uniformly hard hit and have limited access to social protections.[73]

The crisis does demonstrate the value of creating social protection schemes, even when their funding is limited: such schemes have provided a vehicle for governments to make cash grants and vouchers available to workers. Ugo Gentilini of the World Bank maintains a blog updating the social protection response to COVID-19, and the weekly updates through June and July 2020 demonstrate the ability of governments to expand benefits through social protection programs in countries as diverse as Ethiopia, India, the Philippines, Colombia, and Morocco, whose initiatives are featured in a July 2020 update.[74] Measures being taken in many low- and middle-income countries include extending cash transfer programs or food vouchers and related support, and making hand-washing stations, masks, and hand sanitizer more widely available.

Conclusion

Expanding poor people's access to productive assets, in particular to decent work, is a key theme in the SDGs that was largely absent in the MDGs. The shift from goals and targets that prioritize quick-impact interventions to goals and targets intended to motivate and support improved employment opportunities and labor rights means that the SDGs are more aligned with global systems of labor protections and related human rights standards. The labor-related goals, especially in a time of pandemic-induced job losses, have helped to focus support for social-safety-net programs and protections for the most vulnerable, informal sector workers.

Labor rights and the availability of decent work at living wages are one half of the SDGs' effort to make productive assets more broadly and equitably available. Chapter 6 examines a second key priority, secure land tenure.

chapter six

Access to Productive Assets: Land

Like most farmers in dry regions of East Africa, women farmers in most of Malawi struggle to keep their families fed by piecing together livelihoods from diverse sources: growing maize and cassava on their own land or rented plots, working on nearby larger farms when such work is available, migrating to nearby towns for work, and earning any nonfarm income that becomes available. The East African country improved its nutrition standing in the 2000s according to the international data tracked by the MDGs.[1] But these data track only calories consumed, and by other measures low-income households' struggles grew harder, and their diets less secure and less diverse. Families spent an increasing proportion of income on food and reported less diverse diets in the long "hungry season" that precedes each year's maize harvest.[2]

Emergency food aid and cash assistance are essential when droughts cause food prices to soar, as are well-run nutrition programs in schools and effective nutrition monitoring and care at community health clinics. But secure access to land, fertilizer at affordable prices, and support for agro-ecological farming methods to build the soil's productivity will be the keys to long-term sustainable improvement in incomes and nutrition. Poor Malawians will become more food-secure, and will more consistently enjoy the internationally recognized right to adequate food, when they have secure access to land and affordable farm inputs and work available at living wages that allow them to build resilient, sustainable livelihoods and save and invest in their own land and in their families' health and education.

In this chapter I examine the SDGs' potential to support movements for more equitable, secure access to land. In addition to the impact on poor farmers' livelihoods, development agencies' work on land issues offers a window into how they interpret and implement human rights-based strategies, and the ongoing interaction between development and human rights as fields. The cases of land rights advocacy, programs, and policy change examined here suggest that, despite disappointing implementation of broader rights-based approaches at many development agencies, there is great potential for applying human rights principles and practices in some areas of development work, and that the lines between the two sectors are becoming less clear.

I make the case that land is important, and that it is too difficult for rural people to get secure access to land and systematically more difficult for women in many countries. Land reform is difficult, but there are recent national initiatives that show that progress is possible, and many more campaigns and initiatives by social movements and NGOs that point the way. The SDGs address land directly, taking on board human rights principles and creating an opportunity for more rapid progress in the coming years.

Secure Land Tenure and Livelihoods

Secure access to land is fundamental to most rural people's livelihood strategies. In a 2008 review of the research and the agency's strategy, the International Fund for Agricultural Development (IFAD) found that "equitable land distribution" is a key to rapid growth and to reducing rural poverty, and it is a central policy priority for the UN's rural poverty-focused agency.[3] Access to land is a key determinant of incomes, agricultural productivity, and food security, and protecting and expanding land tenure rights and increasing equity and security of land tenure for poor groups and for women are important to poverty reduction.[4]

Land's value for poor households has multiple dimensions. Secure access to land is the basis for producing food for family consumption or for the market, and land is an asset that allows access to credit, a resource to fall back on, and a source of status and respect in many communities. Finally, secure land ownership makes farmers much more likely to invest in long-term improvements: planting trees, adopting new production methods, and acting as stewards of land that is an enduring asset. Deininger, Hoang, and Jin sum up a considerable body of research, concluding that security of tenure is "unambiguously investment-enhancing."[5]

The Seattle-based NGO Landesa's applied research and programming related to land rights has produced some of the most compelling evidence of the transformative impact of secure land ownership rights for the rural poor. Landesa estimates that of people living in poverty on less than the equivalent of $2 a day, 1 billion live in areas where livelihoods are primarily based on land, and are landless or lack secure access to land.[6] Yet there is increasing competition for access to productive land in many places, driven by population growth, demand for biofuel crops, large-scale land purchases, rentals and investments, and declining soil fertility.[7]

To see the positive effects of secure land tenure, consider the impact Landesa has documented of owning even very small plots of land. In a project led by the Indian state government of West Bengal, some 4,300 landless households were given title to a "microplot" of one-tenth of an acre – about the size of a tennis court – along with a well, a hand pump, and a sanitation hookup. Holding secure title to a plot on which to build a house and keep animals and a garden made more diverse and more profitable livelihood strategies possible for previously landless families, encouraged them to invest in farm animals and maintain trees, and increased their independence and status in their communities.[8] This closely studied intervention confirms the importance of secure land tenure in creating opportunities and reducing risk for the rural poor. In Rwanda, these environmental benefits were apparent when a program of land title "regularization" produced "a very large impact on investment and maintenance of soil conservation measures," especially by female-headed households whose land rights were made more secure.[9]

Development theorists and agencies have long recognized the central role of land tenure, but efforts to facilitate broader and more equal access to land and agrarian resources have had limited impact, and have been largely restricted in recent decades to encouraging stronger land markets and access to small-scale plots.

Women and Land

Women's rights to own, control, and inherit land are tenuous in many societies, and because these landholding rights are governed by highly varied formal statutory law and by local customary institutions and law, the causes and solutions are complex. But unequal ownership and inheritance rights in practice lead to stunning inequalities in control and ownership of land, and development, human rights, and women's organizations, along with some governments, are giving high priority to addressing the inequalities. The focus has long been on strengthening the access of poor *households*, but practitioners and several significant scholarly studies have contributed to the understanding that a household's land rights are not enough to assure that women within the households have secure, equal land rights.[10]

Statutory law and policy often limit ownership or inheritance rights. These limitations may include a lack of recognition of joint ownership arrangements and failure to specify that inheritance rights should be equal between men and women. Governments often have limited capacity or will to enforce laws that do guarantee access.[11] These limitations include the absence of comprehensive, accurate, accessible land titling and registration systems; weak or incomplete land records; and limited capacity to implement or enforce these laws.

Pervasive cultural and social biases also restrict women as property-holders. These may constrain women's ownership even in societies with relatively equal legal land rights, such as India or Nigeria, because of widespread discrimination in practice and because of weak enforcement of legal guarantees in the countryside.[12] These limitations are reinforced when women are not fully aware of their rights under the law or able to assert them in legal, family, or community settings. Customary law and authorities are the effective authority in many family matters in rural areas of many societies; especially in sub-Saharan African countries, customary land tenure and adjudicatory systems exist at the local level, side by side with statutory law. Customary tenure rules seldom recognize joint ownership of land and housing: they may disadvantage women in the passing of land after the death of a man, and they are difficult to harmonize or integrate with "modern" land titling practices.[13]

These unequal ownership and inheritance rights in practice lead to stunning inequalities in control and ownership of land, recorded in the FAO's Gender and Land Rights Database.[14] Across the global South, women's representation as landholders – defined as "exercising management control over a landholding" – is highest in Latin America: in Peru, Ecuador, and Chile, for example, women own 30 percent, 25 percent, and 30 percent of landholdings, respectively. But in Central America women are far less represented in landholding. In Guatemala and Belize, women are responsible for only 8 percent of landholdings; in El Salvador, just under 12 percent. Throughout Asia, women's control of landholdings is similarly low, ranging from 10 percent in Bangladesh to 15 percent in Vietnam. Botswana maintains the highest rate of woman landholders in sub-Saharan Africa at almost 35 percent. But the proportion is 18 percent in Uganda, 4 percent in Nigeria, and 15 percent in Ethiopia. (FAO data for land ownership are less complete; where gender-disaggregated ownership figures are available, the percentage of female *ownership* is somewhat larger than female landholding, likely implying that some women who hold legal title do not exercise effective control over decisions.)

These inequalities have profound implications for the women themselves and for their communities. Secure land rights for women foster increased agricultural production and contribute to improved food security.[15] Women increase agricultural yields by 20 to 30 percent on average when given the same access to land as men, and a woman's increased agricultural production supports the household's well-being directly through consumption and indirectly by increasing women's incomes, which they can and do invest in household well-being.[16] Landesa has collected and summarized evidence that shows conclusively that women's access to land and productive assets has a range of positive socioeconomic effects, as well as benefits to agricultural productivity and women's influence in household decision making.[17] Women's land rights can also have important environmental implications.[18]

Agrarian reform was an important component of the vision for transforming poor agrarian economies in the 1950s and 1960s, the early decades of international development practice.[19] National, large-scale redistributive land reforms are widely credited as the basis for broad-based economic growth in Japan, South Korea, India's Kerala State, and other Asian societies.[20] But large-scale redistributive land reform gave way to donor policies emphasizing land markets, and USAID's emphasis on improving land markets, beginning in the 1980s, has had an enduring effect on the agency's land policies.[21]

Effective land administration, including mapping, titling, and the management of land registration can have significant impacts. Titling and registering land accurately and without great expense allows men and women to have more secure tenure and invest in long-term land improvements. A system that includes joint titles between spouses is particularly important. In Nicaragua a joint titling system implemented in 1997 increased the percentage of land titles issued to women from 10 percent in the 1980s to 42 percent by 2000.[22] Administrative systems should create incentives for such titling arrangements, and avoid the disincentive of double fees for joint titles.[23]

Clearly, there is a great deal of room for measures to improve land rights, distribution, and equity. In the next section we turn to a few of the initiatives underway to do so.

Government Policies and Land: Effective Reforms Are Possible

Large-scale redistributive land reforms have been notoriously difficult to enact and implement, and there are few recent examples of redistribution on a large scale. Land rights issues, like labor issues, are politically charged and difficult;[24] one has only to remember the prominence and difficulty of land and agrarian reform for new regimes seeking to solidify their political base in Nicaragua, Zimbabwe, the Philippines, Ethiopia, South Africa, and Colombia.

Many governments have taken more limited, focused initiatives to improve security of tenure and to strengthen ownership rights for women, as well as to increase access to irrigation and fertilizers. A single change in land statutes or regulations, allowing spouses to hold joint titles, can have important effects. The Nicaraguan joint titling system discussed above is one of many: joint titling is now practiced in 115 countries, although the opportunities it creates for women's property rights also encounter cultural and other obstacles. The World Bank reports significant progress in issuing land titles to women in post-tsunami Aceh, Indonesia, and land use certificates to women in Vietnam.[25] Ethiopia adopted joint spousal titles in 2003, and the change "increased women's perception of their tenure security, including in polygamous households; improved agricultural productivity; and increased the participation of female-headed households in the land rental market."[26] But women benefit only if they are aware of their rights, and men's better access to information has hampered implementation, as have polygamous marriage practices in some regions.

Initiatives to expand secure land rights have accelerated with the SDGs. NGOs and UN agencies have created guides and templates for reporting on tenure-related indicators, including indicators of women's rights to land.[27] The FAO's Gender and Land Rights Database, for example, allows users to rate the country's legal framework for gender equality in land tenure, as well as to find the latest statistics on land ownership and use. These global and regional tools will support and encourage continued pressure for policy changes. In Brazil, the women's movement *Espaço Feminista* has embraced land rights issues and launched a sustained effort to leverage the SDG targets for women's land rights in Pernambuco state.[28] *Espaço Feminista's* community-based monitoring method has attracted attention among Brazil's regional neighbors, and steps are being taken to replicate or adapt it in Argentina, Ecuador, and Nicaragua.[29]

In twelve African countries, a Monitoring and Evaluation of Land in Africa (MELA) project, led by Land Policy Initiative (LPI) and International Food Policy Research Institute (IFPRI), is tracking progress in the implementation of the African Union's Declaration on land issues and challenges and of the relevant SDGs. In Tanzania, for example, a national monitoring and reporting framework is bringing new attention to findings from land rights and human rights monitors.[30] Both the Government of Tanzania and civil society organizations have been engaged in initiating reform of marital and inheritance laws – the Customary Law Declaration Order (1963) and the National Land Policy (1995) – some of the most serious legal barriers to women's rights in land.

Colombia's government is giving priority to reforming and regularizing the land registration system, but implementing changes alongside a complex peace process has been challenging.[31] The legal framework provides stronger protections for women's land rights, for example, than exist in practice.[32] But a new law (Law 1900) passed in 2018 further extends land rights, allowing joint registration by couples regardless of legal marital status, and strengthening the status of women heads of household.[33] Colombia has adopted a new information system, LANDex, developed by the Land Policy Initiative, which will help support effective monitoring both internally and by comparison to other countries in the region.

The land policy NGO Landesa and several partners have launched initiatives in Tanzania, India, Liberia, Brazil, and Kenya to close the gender land rights gap during the coming decade. With government cooperation and community-based work by networks of local land rights advocates, the campaign was announced at the 2018 Trust conference (a human rights forum) and features four strategies: mobilize operational partners – both international organizations and local civil society networks – to help close the gap between law and practice; provide pro bono legal support as well as communications and advocacy expertise to strengthen legal implementation policies and practices locally; bring on board media partners to help amplify stories about women's land rights from the ground; and generate financial resources to roll out the campaign.[34]

Dealing effectively with customary land institutions is a persistent challenge.[35] In settings where customary arrangements effectively control land use and land rights, aid donors have supported women's organizations advocating for equitable treatment within the customary system, and have supported women's representation on committees and boards that oversee land distribution, as well as promoting awareness among formal land administration officials of issues where formal and customary systems intersect.[36] The Swedish national aid agency Sida reports that such interventions have subtle but measurable effects: women are more fully represented in land certification processes in Ethiopia; and Tajikistan's District Task Forces on land administration have promoted women's land rights, provided forms of assistance to some 14,000 rural women, and increased the proportion of farms registered to women from 2 percent in 2002 to 14 percent in 2008.[37]

Alongside land itself, access to agricultural inputs, especially water and fertilizer, is also critical. In Africa, Rwanda and Malawi have taken important steps to begin to expand access to productive resources for poor people in rural areas. Their initiatives are exceptions to the general trend under the MDGs, whose "lack of structural transformation and economic diversification has limited poverty reduction efforts in Africa."[38] This means that for many countries the baseline level of poverty remains high, and their vulnerability to "shocks," whether changes in commodity prices or in the weather, remains great. But Rwanda and Malawi show that governments with modest resources can tackle the task of making productive resources available to very poor farmers.

A nationwide rural antipoverty program in Rwanda launched in 2008 began as a targeted effort for the country's 30 poorest *urumenge* or sectors (of a total of 416), and now covers more than half the country's sectors with a multi-strategy program. The strategies include direct income support for the elderly, disabled persons, and other groups; changes in education policy; and two initiatives expanding rural poor people's access to productive assets. The evidence is now clear that the government's rural productivity program has been a success. Rural families that are particularly vulnerable (headed by a child, woman, genocide widow, or disabled person) receive a cow or other livestock; a Crop Intensification Program is more broadly targeted to increase access to seeds, fertilizer, extension services, and crop storage. The program has quadrupled fertilizer use, and yields have doubled for beans and tripled for maize, wheat, and cassava.[39]

Malawi launched a national program to expand irrigation and access to agricultural inputs, especially fertilizer, in 2006. The country's agriculture and rural poverty have been a central preoccupation since the early 2000s, when, after state subsidies for fertilizer were cut off, staple crop production dropped and a famine struck in 2002, devastating the countryside. The Malawian government responded with a sustained effort to make agriculture more productive and resilient, and to expand the livelihood options for the rural poor.

The initiative includes rehabilitating old irrigation schemes and transferring their ownership and maintenance to locally based water users' associations, a proven, successful form of self-management. With a loan from the World Bank, the government created a fund to finance additional small-scale irrigation schemes where farmers previously practiced much less productive dryland farming. The fund also finances technology, seeds, and fertilizer, and provides training in management, irrigation techniques, and accounting.[40] The irrigation program favors small-scale, easily maintained gravity-driven schemes over more complex designs that require powered pumping.

Local impact studies show the powerful effects that modest increases in access to these farming inputs can have: participants report increased harvests, more varied diets that include meat, and food supplies that are enough to take households through the "hungry season," when small farmers' supplies dwindle and the price of maize increases in the market. There are visible signs of improvement, including new corrugated iron roofs, livestock, and bicycles.[41] Agriculture and nutrition in low-income societies are often challenging, but when regional and national policies increase poor farmers' access to land and productive assets, production and well-being are improved.

The SDGs and Land

The SDGs address both the general need for greater security of tenure and the acute discrimination that women face with respect to land ownership. The relevant goals and indicators can be seen in table 6.1.

The goals do not include all that human rights and land rights advocates called for on land (or labor), but they did hit many of the most important variables to track, especially on land tenure. They include indicators not only for agricultural land but for secure tenure to land other than farmland, which was a key recommendation of a set of experts.[42] This is important because owning land, including urban plots of land, is such an effective means of building family assets and rising securely out of poverty.[43] The goals also include a separate, direct sub-goal focused on security of tenure for agricultural land, and indicators that track progress in increasing the share of women with title to agricultural land. Target 2.3 links improvements in land access to other measures that increase the productivity of smallholder farmers.

Finally, land and inheritance rights are tied to women's equal access to economic opportunity and resources in Goal 5 on Gender Equality: "Undertake reforms to give women equal rights to economic resources, as well as access to ownership and control over land and other forms of property, financial services, inheritance and natural resources, in accordance with national laws" (Target 5.a). This explicit focus on women's land rights at the highest levels of development policy and planning creates a new opening and source of leverage for social movements and organizations in human rights and development. It was controversial, and some governments worked to weaken the language. Among the biggest disappointments in the negotiation of land-related goals was the phrase suggesting that improvements in women's land ownership rights be "in accordance with national laws" in target 5.a., and "as nationally appropriate" in target 5.4. Both soften the targets by implying that they are subject to national custom or preferences.

Table 6.1. SDG targets dealing with land issues

Target	Key Indicators
1.4 [Provide] **equal rights to economic resources … ownership and control over land and other forms of property**, inheritance, natural resources, appropriate new technology and financial services …	1.4.2 Proportion of adult population with secure tenure rights to land, with legally recognized documentation, and who perceive their rights to land as secure
2.3 **[D]ouble the agricultural productivity and incomes of small-scale food producers, in particular women**, indigenous peoples, family farmers, pastoralists and fishers, including through secure and **equal access to land, other productive resources and inputs**	2.3.2 Average income of small-scale producers, by sex and indigenous status
5.a Undertake **reforms to give women equal rights to economic resources, as well as access to ownership and control over land** and other forms of property, financial services, inheritance and natural resources, in accordance with national laws	5.a.1 (a) proportion of total agricultural population with ownership or secure rights over agricultural land, by sex; and (b) share of women among owners or rights-bearers of agricultural land …

Source: United Nations General Assembly (2015). Emphases added.

Human Rights-based Approaches and Land: How the SDGs Can Help

Women's rights to own and inherit property are limited in many societies, and because these rights are governed by highly varied statutory law and often by local customary institutions and law, the causes and solutions are complex. But unequal ownership and inheritance rights lead to stunning inequalities in control and ownership of land; and development, human rights, and women's organizations, along with some governments, are giving high priority to addressing the inequalities. The growing global movement to improve land tenure, protect Indigenous peoples' particular rights to land, and secure women's equal land rights is energized by local initiatives in many societies and supported both by development agencies that sponsor projects and programs and by human rights organizations that work mostly through advocacy, mobilization, documentation, and litigation.

Although human rights treaties and covenants themselves say surprisingly little about land rights, extreme and systematic inequalities in access to land have been associated with human rights abuses, and have become the focus of important and creative human rights advocacy and programming.[44] Equitable and secure access to land is essential to the human right to adequate food and housing, and inequalities in law and practice may constitute systematic discrimination, in violation of fundamental human rights principles. So, land – despite human rights documents' relative silence – is an area where the human rights-based approaches have been widely used.

Rights to land and particularly the rights of women to own, use, and inherit land, have been recognized since 2000 internationally in numerous documents and strongly tied to human rights. The FAO Voluntary Guidelines on the Responsible Governance of Tenure of Land, Fisheries and Forests (2012) set out principles for land tenure, including the duty to administer an effective system of land registration; provide access to justice; and maintain a system without discrimination that is transparent, accountable, and open to the participation of affected parties.[45] The standards are "voluntary" in that they do not have the force of law, but "voluntary," as Oxfam's Stéphane Parmentier reminds us, does not mean discretionary or optional.[46] The Voluntary Guidelines emphasize the importance of gender equality, and the UN Conference on Sustainable Development makes women's land tenure rights a central element in working toward equal rights and opportunities in political and economic spheres.[47] Numerous resolutions of the Commission on the Status of Women and the former UN Commission on Human Rights (reconstituted as the Human Rights Council) also recognize equal ownership, access, and control rights as central to meeting governments' obligations not to discriminate.

These rights are spelled out in documents of the Committee on the Elimination of Discrimination against Women, and the UN Committee on Economic, Social, and Cultural Rights. These documents specify, for example, that women should hold equal inheritance rights when a marriage dissolves and that the right to own or inherit property cannot "be restricted on the basis of marital status ..." (General Comment 28). Article 3 of the ICESCR, Articles 2, 3, and 26 of the ICCPR, and the Convention on the Elimination of All Forms of Discrimination against Women (CEDAW) all uphold nondiscrimination and provide strong bases for land and food policies that treat women and men equally. The ICESCR notes women's vulnerability to "forms of discrimination ... in relation to property rights (including homeownership) or rights of access to property or accommodation," and asserts the equal right of women and men to own property and utilize resources, and women's equal rights to marital property and inheritance when a spouse dies or leaves – a life-threatening event for women in some societies.[48]

The FAO Voluntary Guidelines on the Right to Food, adopted by the FAO Council in 2004, include detailed guidance to states on the relation between access to land and food security, linking secure access to land to the human right to food.[49] Making access to land part of a national strategy to realize the right to adequate food, the guidelines note, means putting in place legislation against forced evictions, having clear objectives and time frames attached to goals regarding access to land, and creating and managing public institutions for land tenure administration that perform effectively.[50]

All of this legislating, policymaking, planning, and institution building by governments will only happen with a surge of support. Vocal support comes from community-based organizations, development NGOs, national coalitions, and global human rights groups that employ advocacy, litigation, and community-level organizing and consciousness raising, and that train and deploy paralegals. These strategies are the forte of human rights-based approaches to development, and land tenure is one of the topics where rights-based approaches have been most genuinely and most successfully practiced. Human rights and development NGOs, along with community-based movements in low- and middle-income countries, pursue a variety of strategies to increase secure access to land for women, Indigenous peoples, and impoverished rural communities. Some work at the community level to help women and others understand and assert their rights. Examining the work of a few organizations and networks that are among the leaders of the movement for equitable land access will reveal the range of methods and the influence of human rights approaches.

The Federation of Women Lawyers-Kenya – a women's rights organization of more than 1,000 law practitioners – provides legal aid to women facing gender discrimination, while working to create lasting structural change that improves women's rights throughout Kenya.[51] The Kenya Land Alliance advocates for land laws and policies that protect and promote equitable land ownership. Kenya Land Alliance lobbies and consults for the Kenyan government on topics related to women's land and property rights, while promoting education, dialogue, and research through civic forums.[52]

Likewise, the Uganda Land Alliance (ULA) has trained and deployed "community land rights workers" to strengthen women's property rights. In Luwero District, home to half a million people in central Uganda, twenty community rights workers of the Luwero Land Rights Activists Association (LLRAA) received training in Community-Based Gender and Property Rights, to provide legal counsel to individuals, and raise awareness about women's property rights.[53] They supported clients by convening meetings with local leaders, by educating about the law and land rights, and through mediation services.[54] The results for community-based programs in this and several localities show progress on a local, grassroots scale: ten or a dozen women in each locality were enabled to buy or register land, solely or jointly, directly supported by community land rights workers.[55]

ULA works at the national level as well, combining public protests, sponsored dialogues between groups of rural workers and public officials, and technical work to improve the language of national land law and regulation. But the local level changes wrought by persistent women and supported by trained paralegals are the changes that can transform people's expectations about land ownership, and the power relations that go with them.

The Asia Pacific Forum on Women, Law and Development (APWLD) is a regional coalition that encourages outreach and human rights promotion among its national affiliates in the region, using Participatory Feminist Action Research (PFAR). APWLD supports local and national initiatives by women, using a participatory methodology by which women analyze and develop proposals to solve pressing problems. The region-wide agenda revolves largely around access to productive resources, women's legal equality (including inheritance rights), and wages.[56] Initiatives in 2010 built movements and won initial victories around access to land in Nepal, status of informal workers in the Philippines, wages in Thailand, and related issues in ten regional countries.[57]

Global NGOs on Land Rights

As with human rights NGOs at the national and regional level, global human rights NGOs use a variety of strategies. Some practice the kind of documentation, reporting, and advocacy that have long been associated with advocacy on civil and political human rights. Human Rights Watch, the New York-based global human rights advocate, launched an initiative on women's economic and property rights in 2003. Its report on women's land ownership and property inheritance in Kenya was groundbreaking, meticulously documenting violations of national law by administrators and local authorities. It called international attention to longstanding struggles of women's organizations in Africa, arguing that the violations could "doom development efforts and the fight against HIV/AIDS."[58] A 2017 report on discrimination against widows in Zimbabwe, titled "You Will Get Nothing," continues this work and emphasizes global implications. "More than 250 million widows around the world face multiple abuses, neglect, and social exclusion and too frequently are pushed into extreme poverty … For some, the abuses they face as widows continue a lifetime of gender-based discrimination abuse and deprivation …"[59]

The Global Initiative for Economic, Social and Cultural Rights (GI-ESCR) works to strengthen global and regional norms and understanding of human rights protections for women's land rights. GI-ESCR produced a practitioners' guide to using CEDAW to advance women's land rights.[60] At the regional level, GI-ESCR worked with African colleagues in a successful effort to gain a new resolution from the African Commission on Human and Peoples' Rights that strongly affirms a range of women's rights with respect to land.[61]

The Food Information and Action Network (FIAN) works both on global standard setting and at the national policy level. Using a rapid-response membership network similar to Amnesty International's Urgent Action network, FIAN highlights violations of the right to food, mostly associated with access to agricultural land. Collaborating with the peasant movement *La Via Campesina*, FIAN focuses on agrarian reform and access to land as a key to fulfilling the right to food.[62] Its recent advocacy includes reports and initiatives on land tenure security and the right to food in the Philippines, Brazil, and Mozambique.[63]

In Guatemala, Sierra Leone, and India, ActionAid is implementing projects on women's land rights, funded by the European Commission. The projects' shared goals are to increase organized women's groups' ability to advocate, through training in land rights and (in India) formation of some new groups. The projects aim to increase these groups' engagement with legal and policy processes through advocacy, petitions, and campaigns; by engaging with local officials over specific instances of lost access to land; and by using public events and targeted information and radio to increase mass awareness of women's land issues and of the justice system.[64]

Care works jointly with Landesa in India and Tanzania to develop land-related skills among Care staff while working with communities.[65] Both countries have relatively progressive land laws and pose similar opportunities and challenges to expanding women's ability to advocate, negotiate, and claim their legal rights. The initial collaboration in Tanzania was funded by the Gates Foundation, which asked Landesa to help Care integrate women's land rights into rural development programming.

Three international NGOs or coalitions working on land issues – Namati, Landesa, and International Land Coalition – use approaches that draw on development and human rights methods. By building a "global legal empowerment network" and innovating to increase the impact and accessibility of paralegal and related services, Namati aims to increase poor people's capacity to claim their rights and work for respectful treatment and public services. (Namati's name is a Sanskrit word meaning "to shape something into a curve," a reference to what the Rev. Dr. Martin Luther King called the moral arc of the universe.) Namati's work on land has been innovative, leading to the creation of a methodology and training resources for protecting and strengthening claims to community lands and protecting individual and communal lands from incursions by extractive industries and others.[66] Working on land/environment issues in five countries (Sierra Leone, Kenya, India, Myanmar, and the United States, where the work focuses on environmental justice), the relatively young NGO plans to expand its work to more societies in the coming years.[67]

Landesa, the Seattle-based NGO specializing in land tenure issues, carries out a broad set of research, demonstration projects, and larger-scale projects and programs on land tenure and women's land rights.[68] It implements USAID-funded national policy analysis and assistance programs, working with government ministries and specialized NGOs. A 2016 program, for example, "support[s] the government of Uganda's efforts to lay the groundwork for rural development and stability by strengthening communal and smallholders' rights to land, with a special emphasis on strengthening women's land rights."[69] In Liberia, where land policies are less progressive and less well elaborated, Landesa implements a USAID-funded project to improve national land administration.[70] But Landesa has also coauthored and signed onto statements with human rights NGOs, an unusual step for an NGO working mostly in the development sector.

International Land Coalition brings together some 260 organizations with an interest in land tenure, to promote "people-centered land governance." Members range from the World Bank to small NGOs, and advancing the land-related SDGs is central to the ILC's stated objectives.[71] Arguing that many of the SDGs depend on the success of goals that expand and protect access to land, ILC stresses engagement at the national level and sponsors "National Engagement Strategies" to support members in influencing their own governments, working with more than 300 organizations in twenty countries.[72] In many of those countries ILC reports concrete results: new legislation or administrative procedures, families protected from eviction, households gaining title to land.[73] The ILC's monitoring Dashboard provides data on a set of indicators that track performance on both the SDGs related to land tenure and the Voluntary Guidelines on the Responsible Governance of Tenure.[74]

Advocacy on land rights has a final, vital dimension: it is often complemented by efforts to protect land rights advocates, whose work on a politically volatile subject often puts them at risk. Some development agencies, and almost all the human rights NGOs surveyed, link their work on land rights strongly to protecting the civil and political rights and physical security of land rights advocates. Some give high priority to protecting the rights and safety of land rights and environmental rights activists, and the 2016 killings of land rights activists in Honduras made that country a focus of attention. Human Rights Watch has documented murders and is among the many NGOs pressing for better protections in Honduras and elsewhere.[75] With increased attention to land rights likely under the SDGs, and increased donor-funded advocacy, this protection of human rights defenders will likely be critically important in the coming decade.

The Pandemic and Secure Tenure

It may not be self-evident that the COVID-19 pandemic puts particular pressure on farm households' tenure security, but there are threats to women's land rights, both urban and rural, and to Indigenous peoples' lands. Reports from the World Bank, research groups, and NGOs are documenting threats to loss of urban homesteads and to rural land.[76] Reports from Brazil, Cambodia, Indonesia, Ethiopia, and many other countries show that there is urgent need to protect land rights against landowning firms and investors that are eager to take advantage of the crisis to expand their landholdings.[77]

The Land Rights Now network documents a range of strategies to protect land rights in the pandemic, from direct action by Indigenous peoples' organizations to forbid access to their lands, to urgent action appeals calling for pressure on the Ugandan government to stop "land grabs."[78] The work by human rights NGOs, including Amnesty International and Human Rights Watch, is an important form of support.

Conclusions: Supporting Sustainable, Productive Livelihoods?

The Sustainable Development Goals' focus on improving access to productive assets – especially related to land and labor – is one of several ways that the SDGs embrace a distinctly different development strategy than the MDGs. This strategy of the SDGs is also an indication of the growing, continuing interest – in principle, at least – in human rights-based development approaches.

There is plenty of evidence of goals and targets that call for action on agendas related to the fulfillment of economic and social rights standards, although almost all SDG goals and targets fall short of precisely replicating an existing human rights standard. A range of international and national civil society organizations, including human rights-focused NGOs, are active in local, national, and international settings, often linking their work to the relevant SDGs. They have created some of the kinds of tools – mechanisms, datasets, new networks – that are evidence of determined, concerted effort to link human rights standards to labor and land at the community and national levels.

Is there evidence that this activity is succeeding in prompting governments to improve access to land and decent work for poor people? At the local level and at the national level, a record of programs, initiatives, and legislation has grown in the last decade, particularly on two aspects of the land and labor agenda: women's land ownership rights, and legal protections and recognition for workers in the informal economy. Many of the most visible initiatives began well before the SDGs, and my survey of the experience does not allow any informed speculation as to whether that trend has accelerated.

The content of the SDGs related to land and labor and the high level of involvement by human rights and women's organizations both distinguish these goals from prior global development goals. It would be unduly optimistic, however, to conclude that the SDG experience will encourage stronger integration of human rights and development and lead to dramatic progress on land tenure and inheritance rights. While human rights engagement has the potential to strengthen and clarify standards and their implementation at national levels, weaknesses and limitations in the official SDG indicators and review processes will make parallel, independent monitoring critically important. As the mid-point of the fifteen-year SDG period approaches, the goals have raised multiple questions for the future of human rights-development strategies. By the year 2030, we may have a clearer view of how the two fields intersect, and what the fields can take from this period of human rights-development engagement.

What does the presence of these goals and targets mean for the impact that policy change and external assistance will have on poor people's access to productive assets? Early in the SDG era, the best evidence we have lies in the breadth and level of engagement and the extent to which SDGs focus attention on structural issues. In the final chapter, we trace some of the organizing and mobilization that are taking place around the SDGs, the early implementation of the goals, and the prospects for improved accountability.

chapter seven

Politics and Accountability: Implementing the SDGs

Getting "back to normal" is simply not feasible – because "normal" got us here. The crisis has shown us how deeply connected we are to others and to the planet. COVID-19 is forcing us to revisit our values and design a new area of development that truly balances economic, social and environmental progress as envisioned by the 2030 Agenda and the SDGs.

United Nations Development Programme,
"COVID-19 and the SDGs"[1]

Countries become party to human rights agreements and sign onto goals like the SDGs in part to "bind themselves," to make long-term commitments that will hold despite changes in national politics or in other conditions. Some combination of domestic political pressure and the force of the international commitments, it is hoped, will persuade governments to maintain their commitments to limit atmospheric emissions, not to torture prisoners, and to continue to vaccinate children against deadly diseases. This final chapter assesses the prospects for the SDGs and highlights the role of human rights in reinforcing the many SDG commitments.

The broad, ambitious SDG agenda for global poverty eradication and sustainability was launched at almost exactly the moment that a populist, authoritarian political wave gained influence in many countries, including in some of the world's traditional aid-donor countries. Contrasted with the globalist, cooperative language of the SDGs, the nationalist populist trend is worrisome. It suggests weakened commitments to coordinated action and shared goals, and likely reductions in financial support from some traditional donor countries. It may look like unfortunate timing, but in fact the SDGs' impact in low- and middle-income countries will be driven not mainly by external aid and coordination but by political initiative within societies.

The SDGs articulate specific goals, but they are equally a larger political vision of sustainable and humane paths for global and national development. They define and operationalize a program for sustainable development in light of what was accomplished under the MDGs, of the climate change crisis, of existing human rights commitments, and of countries' varied experiences with the global economy. That political vision must now, in 2020, also provide the principles that guide the difficult global recovery from the pandemic. The diverse conditions and challenges that societies face in that recovery are even more reason to focus on using SDG targets and indicators and the associated human rights standards to reinforce domestic accountability mechanisms.

Although the SDGs were framed and announced before the political events that signaled a rising populist tide in 2016, and of course well before the novel coronavirus emerged, they are well-suited to the current political environment. In this final chapter I want to show why it makes sense to be ambitious and hopeful about global social change and transformation, even in uncertain political times, and I examine some of the dimensions of accountability in global development and human rights. The SDGs became effective in January 2016, and early in their fifteen-year lifespan most of the evidence on implementation is about work in progress rather than about outcomes. The review of implementation in this chapter focuses largely on how the goals and indicators are being monitored, and how human rights agencies bear on the process. How strong and influential is the coalition of actors pushing for their implementation; and how well-prepared are governments to make progress, in terms of data, legislation, policies, and institutions?

SDGs and Human Rights: Political Program and Development Agenda

The SDG goals need to be an effective political program that wins political support in many societies more than a checklist held by donors and aid recipients. If the SDG agenda is seen and promoted in this way, the goals, especially with strong support from human rights, women's, and environmental organizations, can deal with the adverse currents of the global political environment, and even flourish despite them.

This brings us back to an issue discussed in chapter 1: how do global development goals and human rights advocacy work – that is, how do they succeed in motivating positive actions by governments? The MDGs worked largely by focusing governments and donors on a well-defined set of goals and financing programs to advance them. Economic and social rights improvements are achieved by setting standards in law, requiring states to report their performance in meeting them, and encouraging organized groups of rights-holders to act to claim their rights.

The SDGs are, in a sense, a blend of these two dynamics. They are goals, not declarations of rights, and they are supported by external assistance. But they also address issues – land, labor rights, sexual and reproductive health rights, and universal health coverage – that have mobilized substantial support from domestic political coalitions and human rights organizations. Although the SDGs clearly are a list of specific goals and targets, they also represent a political program, a reframing of development that can inspire change at every level. A report from the International Institute for Environment and Development (IIED) captured the spirit of the goals: the SDGs are not so much to be "achieved through a step-wise technical process of analysis and coordination that implements 17 goals and countless targets in every country. Instead it will entail a mix of state-led, market-led, technology-led and citizen-led processes that together aspire to sustainable development, and together achieve wholesale transformation on many fronts."[2]

In this way, as in others, the SDGs echo human rights. Just as human rights are not only a set of international laws and standards but also a set of principles that inspire and help to mobilize citizens, so the SDGs can be much more than a list of goals and targets. To gain momentum in the political environment of the 2020s, they need to be understood not just by planners and aid-agency professionals but by citizen groups, local governments, unions, and social entrepreneurs. Accountability will have to be pursued at all levels. While global reviews of country reports and progress will be important, the political traction for many of the goals will be found in domestic politics.

The key policy changes to promote greater equality, access to productive resources, and better health systems are not mainly driven by external aid. Donor agencies, especially international institutions such as the World Bank, can help support policy changes such as improved land tenure systems, minimum wage increases, and protections for informal sector workers, and they can play a larger role in the costly process of expanding health coverage and services. But fundamentally, changes like these are driven by domestic politics and policy. Policies to reduce inequality, for example, are of necessity mainly financed by domestic taxes or other revenues. Major income support programs in middle-income countries such as Brazil and Mexico have used not only loan financing from the World Bank and the Inter-American Development Bank but also broad tax revenues, including, in Brazil, revenue from a tax on financial transactions.[3]

The significant labor reforms addressing the informal economy and minimum wages in Colombia, Thailand, Bangladesh, Peru, South Africa, the Philippines, and elsewhere, discussed in chapter 5, had support from the ILO and other UN bodies, but the initiatives were driven internally, and while they had some financial costs to governments, the most important changes were legislative or regulatory. The costs of reforms such as Thailand's recognition of informal sector workers, for example, were borne mainly by employers. Those costs are still real, but they don't depend heavily on foreign assistance to bankroll them. Similarly, measures to strengthen land tenure systems and the security of women's land rights involve the administration of new mandates and some out-reach costs, but not major expenditures. This is not to let donor governments off the hook, because there are important roles for international aid in advancing and monitoring the SDGs. Improvements in health systems and expanded primary health care particularly benefit from donor support, and that donor role may be more pronounced in the wake of the COVID-19 pandemic.

Could the SDGs and these national movements also become a response, a counterweight to populist regimes?[4] National proposals to reduce inequality, improve labor rights, or increase minimum wages, for example, could capture support from the same base to which populist rhetoric appeals, and they may benefit from a pandemic-recovery environment in which there is pressure not to return to the *status quo ante pandemic.* At least in some settings, the SDGs can help governments respond to popular demand for a social and economic policy agenda that addresses the grievances that have won populist movements such a following.[5] This would require broad, powerful coalitions supporting the SDG agenda, the subject to which we now turn.

Mobilizing Political Support for Development Goals

Fortunately, the SDGs have attracted a broader base of support than their predecessors achieved. Like the MDGs, the SDGs fall short of human rights principles in many ways. But they offer many more targets and indicators that echo human rights standards and offer leverage for human rights-inspired advocacy, and they have attracted the interest and critical attention of human rights NGOs and the UN human rights apparatus. Development, human rights, and environmental advocates and NGOs are showing a new level of shared commitment to monitoring the SDGs.

Can the SDGs mobilize both humanitarian enthusiasm for quick improvements in people's well-being and concern for addressing inequalities and promoting systemic changes in the challenging context of the COVID-19 pandemic? There is no shortage of criticism of the SDGs, but they also have features that give them much greater potential than the MDGs to tackle the critical problems related to global poverty and inequality. Activists, both outside and within government, can and should win and sustain this support by maximizing the goals' focus and impact on issues neglected by the MDGs: inequalities, health systems, and access to productive resources.

Because the SDGs are broad and ambitious, and because they benefit from the fifteen years' experience of the MDG period, they can be leveraged to engage the human rights community actively against poverty; tackle diseases that are scourges of the poor; build health systems to improve care for all; advance women's sexual and reproductive rights; address the barriers that block poor people from good jobs, secure access to land, and other productive resources; and strengthen mechanisms to hold governments – rich and poor alike – accountable for their commitments.

Engaging the Human Rights Community

Relatively few in the human rights community took an active interest when the MDGs were launched in 2000. But by 2015 all the major international human rights NGOs, the UN Human Rights Office, and human rights scholars had joined the SDG discussion, and human rights advocates are much better positioned to shape and help drive the SDGs' implementation. Economic and social rights advocates are finding ways to link their monitoring of standards in the International Covenant on Economic, Social and Cultural Rights to corresponding goals and targets in the SDGs.[6]

This is good news for advancing the SDG objectives, because human rights advocates can make a contribution that was conspicuously absent in the MDGs by documenting and publicizing government and donor policies that left large populations excluded. MDG monitoring emphasized the positive, identifying and praising rapid progress and encouraging continued effort and replication elsewhere. Human rights monitoring is now strengthening this by also documenting conspicuous failings by governments and donors, and insisting that they be corrected. These include shadow commentaries on countries' voluntary reports, as in the report by South African and international human rights NGOs on that country's report;[7] and reports from a human rights perspective on thematic issues from the goals, such as land tenure rights, women's economic rights, sexual and reproductive health rights, and fiscal and tax policies.[8]

There is already a wide range of human rights advocacy, monitoring, and critique of the SDGs. Some of this work is specifically targeted to the goals; some is supportive without being linked to the SDGs. Other work focuses on coalition building, and on accountability and monitoring, and it began well before 2015.

Beginning in 2013 the Post-2015 Human Rights Caucus brought 350 organizations together in support of a rights-based agenda for the new goals. Dozens of international NGOs sought to influence the detailed discussions of the UN Inter-Agency and Expert Group that was charged with choosing SDG targets.[9] They made appeals in open letters in 2015 and 2016 and won some limited victories in shaping the indicators.[10] The outcome is a set of goals, targets, and indicators that echo human rights standards and principles imperfectly but much more strongly than their predecessor MDGs.[11] The caucus advanced proposals for SDG monitoring mechanisms and other features, and this early engagement by human rights NGOs and UN human rights bodies set the tone for continuing dialogue, showing that human rights activists expect to have a say in the SDG process.

Among human rights organizations, influential publications have signaled active involvement with the SDGs from Human Rights Watch, Amnesty International, and two of the principal focal points for work on economic and social rights: the New York-based Center for Economic and Social Rights (CESR), and the global network ESCR-Net. These latter two voices highlight both the engagement and ambivalence of human rights activists' positions on the SDGs, some engaging actively while acknowledging and critiquing the goals' shortcomings, others taking a more critical view of the goals and the development institutions that monitor them.

While work explicitly focused on the SDGs themselves has been important, much more human rights work focuses on themes that track major SDG objectives. Often this involves coalition building around these themes. The interactions among a set of local and international NGOs working on women's land rights – including GI-ESCR, ActionAid, ULA, FIAN, Landesa, and others – are discussed in chapter 6. In the case of women's land rights, the coalition brings together NGOs, donor agencies, and UN bodies working in rural development, human rights, Indigenous peoples' rights, and the environment.

The networks that have formed around children's welfare issues manifest similar patterns of collaboration. Save the Children (STC), originally founded in 1918 to advocate for children's rights, continues to bridge the human rights/charity divide effectively. STC participates influentially in three overlapping networks. The Education 2030 Framework for Action group, supporting governments' commitments under this 2015 framework, coordinates through UNESCO to press for rapid action on SDG 4. The Global Partnership to End Violence against Children, founded in 2016 coinciding with the SDGs, aims to play a role in monitoring government commitments to action on violence, mainly under Goal 16.2. The Global Partnership maintains a monitoring initiative and progress map, highlighting "pathfinding" countries. An Independent Accountability Panel on Women's, Children's and Adolescents' Health is successor to a similar partnership supporting child and maternal health under the MDGs, and it works alongside a civil society-led Universal Health Care Alliance.[12] At the national level, a global 2018 survey revealed that a national civil society coalition monitors SDG progress in almost every country.[13]

Human rights agencies are active on virtually every social policy and economic theme in the SDGs. Table 7.1 illustrates this, citing some of the principal international human rights NGOs working specifically on these social policy areas and indicating their engagement with the SDGs. Accountability and the institutions, monitoring tools, and reporting needed to increase governments' accountability to development goals are major themes of human rights work on the SDGs, as we will see below.

Table 7.1. Selected international human rights NGOs, social policy agendas, and the SDGs

NGO, Location, Year founded	Agenda
Global Initiative for Economic, Social and Cultural Rights, 2011	Housing and water rights; rights-based approaches to development
International Women's Health Coalition, New York, 1984	Women's sexual and reproductive health rights; a "core partner" in the Equal Measures 2030 Campaign
Food Information and Action Network, Heidelberg, 1986	Right to adequate food, access to land
Center for Economic and Social Rights, New York, 1993	ESC rights; projects on right to water; central role in human rights monitoring of SDG processes
Global Exchange, San Francisco, 1998	"a human rights organization dedicated to promoting social, economic and environmental justice ..."
Mary Robinson Foundation – Climate Justice, Dublin, 2010	Equity and climate justice; food and nutrition security; women's leadership; other
Rights and Resources Washington, DC, 2006	Land and forest resources; uses SDG targets in campaigns for Indigenous land rights
International Initiative on Maternal Mortality and Human Rights, 2007	Maternal health and reproductive rights; active in calling for SDGs to include sexual and reproductive health rights
ESCR-Net, Bangkok, 2002	Broad ESC rights agenda; global network

Sources: Organizations' websites.

Inclusive Health Goals and the Global Women's Movement

The health-related SDG goals and indicators continue to target specific diseases (SDG 3.3) but also embrace full access to reproductive health and reproductive rights (SDG 3.7 and 5.6), and strengthening health systems by working toward universal health coverage (SDG 3.8). SDG 3 takes a pragmatic approach, articulating both the broad goal of universal health coverage and targets that aim to encourage and accelerate progress on the MDG health-related goals.

The SDGs are also positioned to help advance women's reproductive health and family planning goals. These goals and targets dedicated to universal access to reproductive health care and family planning services, together with other goals sought by women's organizations in the SDGs, are important both substantively and politically. Politically they mean that the SDGs can avoid the political failings of the MDGs, which became associated with the US administration's policy on reproductive rights, and lost a powerful potential constituency. To women's and family planning advocates, as Alana Galati writes, "[t]he absence of SRHR from the description of the [MDGs] signaled to donors and countries that they should focus their attention elsewhere."[14]

The SDGs, launched in a different political context, have prompted programmatic and advocacy work by women's health movements worldwide. Many of the principal advocacy NGOs on women's sexual and reproductive health and rights (SRHR) engaged in debating the content of the SDGs and have mobilized to win support from governments and donors to the SDGs' commitments on sexual and reproductive rights. International Planned Parenthood Federation (IPPF) has published two reports on the SDGs and urges its readers to "leverage the SDGs as a way of increasing the political priority of family planning, as well as ensuring the two SDG targets are being fulfilled."[15] Many women's organizations and women's rights activists are also highly critical of the SDGs for stopping short of advancing a full agenda to empower women worldwide, especially economically, and for failing to address sexual rights fully.

In the run-up to 2015, women's organizations formed the Post-2015 Women's Coalition, with more than 300 organizational members working to avoid the failings of the MDGs, and organized and campaigned successfully for SRHR goals. That coalition has now transformed into the Feminist Alliance for Rights. Under the umbrella of the Center for Women's Global Leadership, hosted at Rutgers University, the Feminist Alliance for Rights works to strengthen and collaborate with regional networks of women's organizations, advocate for open participation in SDG and other global processes, and represent feminist perspectives. Its report on the 2017 High-level Political Forum (HLPF) complains that "civil society voices fell on deaf ears," but its most important work may be not at the UN headquarters but in facilitating regional and national events that help women's organizations take a larger role in setting national policy.[16]

Women's advocacy on the SDGs gives a clear view of the multi-level nature of SDG participants. National and regional activist networks work alongside global networks and NGOs. Regional meetings like the June 2017 meeting in Bogotá, Colombia, bring local and national organizations together to develop and coordinate national strategies. Mobilization in Colombia continued through the monitoring and reporting for a national report on gender equality, presented in late 2018 as part of the global Equal Measures 2030 monitoring process.[17]

Implementation, Accountability, and Financing

Five years into the life of the goals, much of what has transpired involves initiatives by governments, including integrating the SDG targets into their own development policy processes, setting up the administrative machinery for implementation, and participating in annual rounds of country reports and reviews before the SDGs' High-level Political Forum. The remainder of this chapter examines some of the approaches governments and NGOs have taken, laying the groundwork for implementation and for demanding accountability.

Implementation poses real management puzzles: how does a government organize a fifteen-year effort to meet a wide-ranging set of goals that cross all of the lines among ministries and departments? The organizational answers are beyond the scope of this discussion, and the answers are varied. The United Nations tries to help by calling attention to varied successful implementation schemes. Finland (and the other Nordic countries) are leaders, devising and funding coordinating agencies that promote and monitor SDG objectives government-wide. (Finland has the advantage of a small population, 5.5 million people, approximately equal to Metro Toronto's.) Colombia, not necessarily among the usual suspects, adopted the SDGs alongside a national plan for peace and reconstruction, after its historic 2016 peace settlement. The country's eagerness for a new path under the slogan "Todo por un Nuevo Pais" (All for a new country) led to a strong launch at both the national and local levels.[18] Colombia, like Mexico, links its national budget and SDG goals through a tool that analyzes text to help policymakers gauge the fit between budget lines and SDG targets. Nepal and at least one Indian state have taken the further step of assigning budget codes linked to SDG targets, so the expenditures related to each SDG target can be tracked.[19]

Local action and the "localization" of SDGs extends involvement in SDG goals to the municipal level. The Cities Alliance estimates that 65 percent of the goals require action by local actors.[20] Goal 11 deals directly with "sustainable urban settlements," but several others address needs such as water and sanitation that are acute in slums and peri-urban settlements, and that are in fact provided by utilities licensed and often owned and managed by local governments. As the agents that execute some of the goals, many cities are deeply involved. Brazil's national league of municipalities is in the forefront of a national effort, led by cities with strong participatory budgeting and other governance innovations, such as Curitiba and Porto Alegre.[21]

But municipalities and even smaller units in other countries are stepping up as well. Clusters of villages in Bangladesh have formed SDG Unions, committed to achieving the SDG targets. The Union is Bangladesh's smallest unit of rural government, and the country's densely organized NGO sector promotes community mobilization and capacity-building strategies through an "SDG Union Strategy." The NGO Hunger Project Bangladesh "has been demonstrating the working of this innovative model in 185 Unions, 61 of which are supported by BRAC, as a low-cost and sustainable means of achieving SDGs."[22] This Union strategy involves citizens, local officials, community-based and national associations and NGOs, and national service delivery agencies in an effort to design and implement local solutions.

Financing

Much of the discussion of implementation of the SDGs focuses on "finance for development," and aid commitments and new finance innovations will be important. Donors have responsibilities, and almost none of the rich countries have lived up to their long-agreed commitment to provide more generous and effective development assistance.[23] Even before the pandemic, there was not much of a taste for bold new initiatives from many donor governments. The United States and many European governments seemed inclined to focus aid on strategic objectives and on stemming the flows of people from immigrant-sending regions. All of this seems to signal a shift away from the global solidarity themes of the SDGs, heightening tensions in North-South relations around immigration and trade agreements.[24] The reluctance in the United States to cooperate through the United Nations and other multilateral bodies further heightens tensions and increases skepticism about the goals. This reluctance and other factors have led to a stagnation of official development assistance from OECD countries in recent years.[25]

The pandemic appears likely to shift some of these dynamics in development finance. Europe is poised to launch a major green recovery initiative, and the United States has marginalized itself politically, especially with its own failed management of the pandemic. The course of the pandemic in the United States is terrible news for my own society, but it may be good news for advancing rights-based approaches to social and economic policies in low- and middle-income countries. The anticipated European Green New Deal's ambitious investment program, aiming to make Europe a carbon-neutral bloc by 2050, has raised expectations of the possibility that an €825 billion investment in sustainability and a sharp shift away from fossil fuel investments and imports will become a model and driving force for some low- and middle-income countries.[26]

The long-term impact on aid funding remains to be seen, but despite the importance of external funding for some social objectives, the most important of the SDGs are not aid-driven. And both realism and a desire for effectiveness and accountability should lead us to focus somewhat less on mobilizing major new aid and more on helping low- and middle-income governments to raise revenue more effectively. The role of realism here may be self-evident. Even before the political swings of 2016 and 2017, Charles Kenny of the Center for Global Development wrote that "[a]id will be a declining factor in achieving the global progress called for in the draft Sustainable Development Goals," though aid might grow as a factor in some low-income countries. But then, as he aptly notes, "development progress has always been primarily about poor people and poor countries achieving things for themselves."[27]

That could be a good thing, because revenues raised domestically have important advantages for the effectiveness and accountability of development initiatives. If low- and middle-income countries could raise 15 percent of their revenues as tax income (fairly standard among the OECD countries), they would raise an additional amount nearly double what is provided through official development assistance.[28] That 15 percent rate may be higher than ideal in some low-income countries, as Long and Miller argue, but the point remains that a great deal of domestic revenue is available, and one recent study argues for special attention to low- and middle-income countries such as Egypt, Nigeria, Pakistan, and Guatemala, where "tax performance" is particularly weak.[29] Why should we wish that poorer countries raise their own taxes? Because experience also shows that when governments rely more on domestic tax revenues, they practice more responsive, accountable decision making and spending, and they build stronger, more capable government institutions.[30]

Like rich countries, low- and middle-income countries lose a great deal of revenue to tax evasion and offshore tax havens, and here the richer countries could help by joining in a concerted effort to restrict illegal financial flows, including tax evasion. NGOs and humanitarian movements, both national and international, have developed impressive, sophisticated analyses of tax policy and their effects on social policy.[31] Even modest progress on improving tax revenues in some low- and middle-income countries could help catalyze many of the social objectives in the SDGs.

Reporting and Accountability

Accountability to international goals, norms, and international law is a perennial weak link in international cooperation. No matter what global issue is at stake – chemical weapons, monetary policy, greenhouse gas emissions, ocean fishing, or the right to food – international organizations have relatively little power to enforce agreements that governments sign. Scott Barrett's 2011 book *Why Cooperate?* highlights important cases where cooperation did occur (think: reducing chlorofluorocarbon emissions to protect the ozone layer), and shows why such cooperation is difficult to achieve.[32]

Since the 1980s, I have been involved as a practitioner and now as a researcher in efforts to build stronger accountability standards for governments and international organizations. During those decades, NGOs have played pivotal roles in shaping some accountability relationships, including, for example, World Bank rules on resettlement of populations for Bank-financed infrastructure projects, and World Bank information-disclosure rules.[33] Accountability for development goals, like accountability for ESC rights, is complex and difficult, as social objectives like improved land rights and expanded sexual and reproductive health services require lengthy, sustained action and funding.

Accountability is described in idealistic terms in some official documents, calling the SDGs the foundation of a system of mutual accountability among countries rich and poor.[34] But during negotiations for the SDGs, it became clear that developing country governments saw it differently. They saw proposals for "robust" accountability as "paternalistic finger-wagging" by the rich countries, and the global SDG accountability processes that emerged were considerably weaker than advocates proposed.[35] So, although accountability to the SDG process and to other international norms and rules remains important, accountability for SDG commitments will depend on stronger accountability of governments to people.

As much as we may wish for a unified, "robust" accountability mechanism that systematically moves governments toward full compliance, what the SDGs have is instead a multi-factor, multi-actor accountability dynamic that varies from country to country and issue to issue. The formal reporting through SDG and human rights processes is important, but just as influential are multiple monitoring, reporting, and advocacy efforts. This is visible in the "Decade of Accountability for the SDGs" initiative, a multi-party campaign launched in 2020. The campaign has begun with a survey to collect effective accountability processes – essentially, an acknowledgment that many political processes will contribute to whatever accountability can be constructed around the SDGs. How is that process playing out, and how does it relate to human rights accountability?[36]

Advocates of human rights approaches to development argue that they offer stronger accountability, but human rights (especially economic and social rights) and global development goals and pledges both suffer acutely from a lack of international enforcement leverage. While high-profile violators of civil and political rights can land in front of tribunals such as the International Criminal Court, there has been no such decisive accountability measure for violators of the health, housing, or food rights of whole populations. This means that effective accountability efforts focus not only at the international level but at enabling domestic political and social movements to push effectively for accountability. Advocates cannot rely only on the oversight mechanisms created for the SDGs themselves because, like most international standards and agreements, the SDGs have no enforcement power. Instead they play an oversight reporting function and create incentives for compliance. Enforcement in almost all matters of economic and social policy has been a matter for domestic politics.

Accountability in human rights terms is more than monitoring or oversight. It has three distinct parts: monitoring, review, and remedial action.[37] It is not enough to track progress toward each goal and target by country; the progress or lack of progress must be reviewed and analyzed, and a remedy proposed and implemented. After a review, it is essential that there be a plan for remedial action, and that the plan be public and transparent enough to be domestically observable and enforceable. This view of the accountability process gives rise to the concern that the annual Voluntary National Reviews of SDG goals are focused too much on "burnishing the image" of the reporting country,[38] and provide too little serious analysis and discussion of corrective action.

Human rights and development view reporting and monitoring differently, and the opportunity to integrate their approaches is one of the SDGs' great challenges and opportunities. The rules for monitoring and accountability specific to the SDGs have provoked discussion, with human rights advocates pressing for a process that is open to input from NGOs and other voices that may dissent from official country reports. The early proposal in 2015 by four human rights and women's rights organizations to shape the formal Global Review Process signaled their engagement in the details of the accountability process. Amnesty International, Center for Reproductive Rights, Center for Economic and Social Rights, and Human Rights Watch joined forces to make a common set of recommendations, and although these were adopted only in part, engagement of human rights advocates in the formal monitoring process and in their own informal reporting is a crucial asset to the SDGs.[39]

At the same time, human rights views of monitoring and accountability for economic and social rights have been shifting. Many human rights advocates have long resisted the kind of quantitative goals and indicators that are the centerpiece of development goals. But there is increasing interest among human rights advocates in using the quantitative indicators as benchmarks and developing quantitative measures of their own. This engagement by human rights advocates can have major benefits, giving advocates multiple strategies and even political venues for action. In chapter 2 we touched on two such indices developed for economic and social rights: the Outcomes, Policy Efforts, Resources, and Assessment (OPERA) and the Social and Economic Rights Fulfillment (SERF) Index. Both are important parts of a wider movement among human rights professionals to develop methods of using data and indicators that are consistent with the spirit of human rights.

Responding to the accountability challenges of economic and social rights themselves, and of the SDGs, the Center for Economic and Social Rights has led an effort to develop and adapt monitoring methods for economic and social rights, and to create resources for domestic human rights advocates. In a monitoring manual and through workshops and training sessions, analysts at CESR and the Asia Pacific Forum promote pragmatic monitoring strategies that are intended to strengthen leverage of ESC Rights and of the SDGs.[40]

The Human Rights Measurement Initiative (HRMI) has developed the methodology and the data further and now makes available country data on countries' social and economic achievements in light of their fiscal constraints, in a single index, promoting the index as a tool for monitoring SDG achievement.[41] The Danish Institute for Human Rights (DIHR) has produced another tool for linking each SDG to the related human rights standards. DIHR publications not only "match" the SDG goals and indicators to related human rights standards, they also highlight the relevance of cross-cutting human rights principles such as nondiscrimination, and analyze gaps in the SDGs and possible strategies for monitoring.[42] DIHR's 2019 report is a guide to using the "Integrated Review and Reporting Tool," replete with examples from Uganda, Brazil, Samoa, Paraguay, and elsewhere.[43]

How Effective Is SDG Reporting?

The SDG process requires governments to report periodically to the High-level Political Forum, which reviews countries' performance. Although the forum lacks enforcement capacity, these Voluntary National Reviews will shape how international donors view aid-recipient countries' performance. Five years into the implementation of the SDGs, there is some experience with governments' reporting, and a coalition of more than a dozen international environment and development NGOs has commissioned annual studies that assess the quality of this reporting and make recommendations for improvement.[44]

The 2018 NGO report is highly critical, although it notes improvements over prior years. Kindornay's 2018 assessment of all of that year's forty-six Voluntary National Review Reports, which were to focus on the theme of "no one left behind," bemoans the fact that, despite specific additional guidance for reporting on this theme, reporting was "limited."[45] The 2018 country reports showed evidence of more civil society involvement but did not create mechanisms to regularize this.[46] The observation that countries were using the reports to "burnish their reputations" is supported by the detailed review, which notes that the reports underemphasize lessons that could be learned from mistakes and failures. The forum's 2018 discussions are praised, on the other hand, for a more productive review of the "leave no one behind" theme that included human rights in some discussions, despite opposition from some governments.[47]

But in 2020, facing the prospect of an SDG process derailed by the pandemic, criticism of the official SDG reporting became more profound. Jensen, who monitors SDG issues for the Danish Institute for Human Rights, summed up the critique of global agencies' work on poverty as a "veil of propaganda" that needs to be pulled back from the realities of global poverty.[48] Alston is similarly frustrated, summing up an extensive critique by complaining that "SDG reporting too often tends to describe the glass as being one-fifth full rather than four-fifths empty."[49]

Separately, detailed independent reviews of performance by the governments of Kenya and Nepal, focused on inclusion and inequality issues in health, also found a mixed picture.[50] Geographically remote and marginalized groups' health needs are not well-served, nor are they accurately reported, but improvements in health services are promising. In Kenya, for example, increased health spending, decentralized services, the waiving of health-care fees, and a much-improved data system are all positive steps.[51]

Governments' reports on their own progress are important, but they are never going to provide the basis for a candid, factual evaluation. Other NGOs and researchers issue independent assessments of progress in particular countries or on issues of interest. The July 2018 national report by South Africa, for example, was critiqued in a shadow report and information sheet produced by the Center for Economic and Social Rights, Institute for Economic Justice, and Section 27.[52] The SDG Knowledge Hub maintained by the International Institute for Sustainable Development (IISD) assembles a multitude of independent and "shadow" reports that are an important resource for monitoring and accountability. Independent reports provide a corrective to the diplomatic and unduly positive reporting in the official UN documents.[53]

But while the SDGs' written procedures explicitly make room for reports from firms or NGOs that offer an independent perspective on governments' performance, NGOs have been disappointed by the limited space and exposure that has been provided for independent reporting. At the July 2017 High-level Political Forum, for example, where reports from forty-four countries were reviewed and discussed, the schedule allowed little time for more than a formal discussion. Donald and Annunziato, writing for CESR, cite "obstruction and resistance that greeted civil society's eagerness to participate," and worry that the pro-forma discussions of important themes and country reports suggest that "on the current trajectory the prognosis for achievement of the 2030 Agenda is woeful."[54]

Independent Reporting Contributes to Accountability

Multiple efforts to monitor progress on specific SDGs have sprouted since the targets and indicators were finalized. Some are explicitly linked to human rights standards, many are focused on a single target or topic, and all contribute to the collective effort to develop effective monitoring that will motivate rapid progress and document shortfalls. Alongside the SDG review process, UN human rights bodies receive regular reports from all governments that are parties to the various human rights agreements, and these also permit input from domestic or international NGOs or other knowledgeable private citizens. Save the Children UK proposes a series of measures by which the UN Human Rights Council's periodic review of countries and other regular human rights processes should begin to refer specifically to the relevant SDG standards when they write country reviews.[55]

This kind of linkage between UN human rights reviews and the SDGs is becoming more frequent as economic and social rights advocates develop ways to link their monitoring of ESC rights standards to corresponding goals and targets in the SDGs. Using a database created by the Danish Institute for Human Rights, Jensen shows that a high percentage of several hundred recommendations made in 2016 and 2017 by UN human rights mechanisms make explicit reference to one or more SDG goals or targets, showing "relatively widespread engagement by UN human rights mechanisms with the SDGs ..."[56]

Global NGOs and research groups have also contributed to the monitoring process. The Overseas Development Institute's 2017 "Leave No One Behind Index" illustrates the contribution that such unofficial monitoring can make.[57] The index tracks three indicators of readiness: availability of data through recent household surveys, enactment of core policies and legislation, and whether the government meets relevant spending targets. Trends in low- and middle-income countries' readiness – with data, policies, and finance in place – have been mixed in the first years, but the 2019 briefing shows a worrying trend, with countries' data readiness improving but a slight increase in the number of countries that do *not* have appropriate policies in place.[58] Eighty-one countries are ready by all three standards, and forty-one of those are low- or middle-income countries. But only one low-income country, Rwanda, is fully "ready," and only nine lower-middle-income countries (annual incomes below between $1,095 and $3,995) are entirely "ready." The ODI index of readiness is important, and although it is not based on readiness for the goals that are the main focus of this book, it makes it clear that many low-income countries are not on track to make the kind of progress envisioned by the SDGs.

Nine NGOs and foundations have united to create Equal Measures 2030, a data hub and periodic report on SDG Gender Equality. The Gender Equality Index includes data on fifty-one indicators that relate to fourteen of the SDGs, and data from 129 countries.[59] The index is intended to strengthen advocacy and policy initiatives to advance gender equality related to all of the SDGs, and Equal Measures 2030 has also produced guides to using the data. The 2019 report is not encouraging, as this summary statement shows: "nearly 40 percent of the world's girls and women – 1.4 billion – live in countries failing on gender equality."[60] The NGO Arrow also maintains a database on sexual and reproductive health rights indicators.[61]

Finally, informal interactions among government officials and the UN agencies and NGOs on a particular goal may be more influential than formal reviews. UNICEF, for example, would be likely to have strong relationships and frequent interaction with ministries responsible for health, education, women, and children. Its 2017 report showing that targeted investment in the health and well-being of the poorest and most marginalized populations would have the greatest impact on saving and improving lives is an important tool in its dialogue with governments.[62] In the case of water and sanitation (SDG 6) in West Africa, the NGO International Rescue Committee has acted informally in this consultative role with several governments and is forming an Africa Joint Learning Initiative, with UNICEF and UNDP support, to facilitate regional interaction and progress.[63]

But despite the many international venues open for advocacy, the most important political setting in almost every case will be domestic. At national as well as municipal levels, concrete plans, programs, and legislation will have the greatest effect on the human outcomes of the SDGs.

SDG Indicators, Reporting, and Domestic Politics

The growing role of data in political decision making has given new currency to the conventional wisdom that "if you don't count it, it doesn't count." But how useful are all the data-collection exercises funded by international development donors and national governments, in the context of the SDGs? Global monitoring is only effective if someone is keeping count, and if the scorekeepers' data are credible. The substantial investments being made in data collection must not only inform UN progress reports but also serve the information needs of citizens and organizations in civil society, the voices that may be able to motivate sustainable change.

The SDGs have designated 230 official indicators for the goals. Discussion of these often seems to assume that indicators exist so that a global authority can track and compare countries' progress and publish regional trends in its annual reports. Casey Dunning of the Center for Global Development, for example, worries (correctly) that many of the indicators require data that aren't available reliably, or regularly, from many countries.[64] In September 2019, 104 of the indicators had been categorized as "Tier 1," meaning that they have a clear methodology, and that data are available in at least 50 percent of countries.[65]

But countries are free to adopt indicators for each target that suit their situations. Expert groups responsible for the indicators have created a flexible system that can be driven by national priorities.[66] The European Union, for example, has selected 100 indicators covering the seventeen goals and established the datasets to track them.[67] Laos has designated 238 indicators to track its five-year development plan, roughly half of them identical to the global SDG indicators, and the remainder adapted or additional, including indicators related to safety from unexploded landmines that remain a distinct threat.[68] Colombia configured the goals and targets differently, and tracks eighty-two goals, using 156 indicators.[69]

The indicators are also being deployed in subnational initiatives such as the coalition of organizations around women's land rights in Brazil's Pernambuco State. Meetings in February 2017 involved local land rights movements and women's organizations with state and local governments to link land rights issues in the region to a set of SDG indicators and agree to a set of initiatives and further discussions.[70] Adopting indicators is only a first step, but the Pernambuco initiative has treated data and indicators as tools available to all, and in August 2019 negotiations with Bonito municipality in Pernambuco led to the announcement of a land regularization program slated to give secure title to 35,000 households.[71]

In Colombia, a sixteen-city network is using indicators to measure and encourage comparisons of progress on a set of city-relevant indicators.[72] Their strategy is based on the premise that "if Colombia has a centralized information platform run by a legitimate institution ... then Colombian cities will be better positioned to successfully localize and align development plans with the SDGs and the 2030 Agenda."[73]

This is something like what Rosga and Satterthwaite called for in an earlier debate over human rights and development indicators, suggesting that they should be designed with national political needs in mind. They urged that we "find ... ways to utilize human rights indicators as a tool of global governance that allows the *governed* to form strategic political alliances with global bodies in the task of holding their governors to account."[74] This is an important reason why a "one-size fits all" approach to standards and accountability won't work; data are useful for making international comparisons and charting regional trends, but their more important function is as a basis for local political action and decision making.

This approach sees accountability primarily as a function of domestic politics, reinforced by international agreements and donors. It is an approach that makes sense, in most countries and for many issues, for the decade of work ahead on the SDGs. Changes in national policy and practice that begin to address extreme inequalities, take steps to put productive resources in the hands of poor and excluded populations, and build stronger health systems that are inclusive and protect patients financially will all be driven largely by domestic politics when they come. International norms, in the form of development goals and human rights standards, can help to speed them along and strengthen them. Those should be our objectives for the SDGs.

Conclusions

How can we assess the SDGs' capacity to support constructive change and accountability? The SDGs suffer from some serious weaknesses, and they are not a recipe for universal, uniform progress on the full range of economic, social, governance, and environmental issues they address. They are, as critics observe, extremely broad, and there is little prospect of most societies meeting all of them. They lack "teeth," having no strong accountability mechanism for countries that do little to meet their agreed commitments. These are serious flaws, and they require careful consideration of the assets and tools available. I have argued that there are assets and strengths of three kinds: (1) the contents of the goals and targets; (2) the timing of the SDGs, which allows them to build on momentum and awareness created under the MDGs; and (3) the strength of the constituencies they have garnered.

The SDGs' goals themselves build and improve on the MDGs in important ways. They address inequalities directly, and they aim in several ways to increase poor and marginalized peoples' access to productive assets rather than only to social benefits. Land, labor, and access to energy, issues at the core of any vision of economic development, are now also important aspects of our global development *goals*. The SDGs also tackle systemic health-care issues, while continuing to push forward progress on specific diseases and conditions, by encouraging health system improvements that move toward universal health coverage.

The SDGs benefit from following on the heels of the MDGs. Fifteen years of MDG promotion means that, at the birth of the SDGs, there was already broad familiarity with the idea of global and national goals, the beginnings (at least) of data collection and monitoring systems, and consciousness of how citizen involvement might contribute to the effort.

These assets are closely related to the third of the assets/strengths mentioned above: the SDGs are winning attention and support from a broader and potentially effective constituency that includes human rights advocates and global networks of women's organizations. This support is visible at both the international and national levels, but it may be most critical in national and subnational arenas, where critical decisions related to land rights, health coverage, protections for informal sector workers, wages, and social guarantees are made. Much of this book has traced the actions of local and national work that collectively will advance the goals.

But despite these strengths, analysts of the SDGs bemoan the weak accountability mechanisms. Country reporting before the High-level Political Forum subjects governments to the scrutiny of their peers, but with no sanctions available for falling short of SDG targets. "Accountability," critics argue, is a taboo word at the United Nations, so much so that the SDG offices use the term "reporting back" in its place when describing required reports. Human rights advocates are particularly critical of the SDGs on this score, but human rights critics should acknowledge that there are also no strong accountability mechanisms for economic and social human rights in the United Nations. The standards and covenants create binding obligations under international law, but very few such obligations under international law can subject governments to real accountability.

So, rather than imagining a strong form of effective international accountability that many may wish for, the tasks at hand are to support measures that strengthen domestic voices and political accountability and to promote international models that make equity and broad-based economic strategies attractive to governments with limited resources. That is the opportunity that the SDGs offer, an opportunity strengthened by their ties to human rights and made urgent by the challenges that face humanity.

Conclusions

Through global agreements that span a thirty-year period, from the beginning of the MDGs in 2000 to the conclusion of the SDG period in 2030, the world's governments have made commitments to dramatically improve the physical quality of life for many of the world's people. Governments pursue these goals with varied motives and political postures, and proponents in the United Nations and a range of humanitarian, human rights, and environmental organizations work to exploit whatever leverage the goals provide.

The generation-long effort will surely be remembered for progress during the MDG period in reducing the incidence of dread diseases and lowering the number of people who suffer extreme poverty and malnutrition. The SDGs, taking in the second half of the thirty-year effort, aim to continue this success and raise the stakes in several ways. They are linked to the Paris Climate Accords, they engage a broader set of social and development policy issues, and they apply to both wealthier and poorer societies. And, as I have argued, they bring elements of human rights standards and principles to bear on vital challenges that the MDGs avoided: inequality, health systems and universal health coverage, and poor people's access to land and decent work.

Despite the MDGs' important impacts on child and maternal health, school enrollments, and other important measures of well-being, they ignored challenges that are key to enduring change: income inequality, poor people's land and labor rights, and the quality of health systems and health coverage. In this book I have assessed three propositions about their successors, the SDGs, propositions that together make up a guardedly hopeful view of what might be accomplished between now and 2030. In these final pages I will review those propositions: that the SDGs do address the three key priorities; that low- and middle-income country societies have made progress on all three, providing models showing that progress is not driven primarily by external aid and that gains are possible with modest resources; and that human rights advocates, women's organizations, and other movements are engaged in a new way with the SDGs, helping to create mechanisms that make real progress and accountability possible.

First, unlike the MDGs, the SDGs do address inequality, land and labor, and health systems; the fact that they do so, although imperfectly, is important. These issues, neglected in the MDGs, are among the foundations of a sustainable and equitable development path, and they are among the most difficult challenges governments face in development policy. The SDGs address them directly in Goals 2 and 5 (land), 8 (labor), 10 and 5 (inequality), and 3 (universal health coverage).

The goals are far from perfect. They were negotiated by governments, some of which effectively resisted stronger ties to human rights and worked to avoid creating difficult obligations. This resistance can be seen in the softening of the target for income inequality, which measures the proportion of national income reaching the bottom 40 percent of the income distribution, with no explicit attention to the concentration of income at the top. It is also evident in the language of Goal 5, on gender equality, which weakens the target by adding the phrase "in accordance with national laws." Similarly, the targets related to universal health coverage do not spell out the obligations of governments to give priority to health investments that serve marginalized groups, and governments will inevitably feel great pressure to invest in services demanded by urban middle-class citizens.

But even with these limitations, the goals that emerged in 2016 do align more strongly with human rights than did the MDGs. In the case of land and labor, the fact that the SDGs include goals or targets explicitly calling for reforms is an important step, and they have made the SDGs a source of leverage for advocates. Income distribution – and the target calling for increasing the proportion of national income to reach the lowest 40 percent – is also a source of leverage for pro-poor redistributive policies, including tax policy, income support programs, streamlined remittance transactions, and others. The SDGs clearly refocus attention in public health to the issues of health systems and universal health coverage, and they have helped to inspire national and global initiatives promoting expanded coverage and financial protection. The fact that 11 million people in African countries are driven into extreme poverty in a single year simply by paying for health care should be motivation enough to grapple with the challenges of creating and adapting systems that expand coverage and provide financial protection.

Human rights principles have clear and important implications for how that coverage should be expanded. Spending should give priority to expanding basic essential services to populations with least access, and that means resisting the potent political pressure to prioritize higher-level health care for urban middle-class populations. That is a challenge that few governments can meet consistently, and in the cases examined in chapter 4 – Thailand, Ghana, Rwanda, and Brazil – it is a tension and a struggle. One essential strategy in the interim for meeting the health-care needs of poor and remote populations is used on a large scale in Brazil and elsewhere: train and deploy community health workers to play a lead role in teams offering care in underserved areas.

Similarly, formalizing the system of land rights requires vigilance to ensure that rights are secured by all citizens and not primarily by those with the best access to political influence and legal representation. The work of national organizations pressing for women's land rights is an important corrective to this, as experience in Uganda, Kenya, Mozambique, Sierra Leone, Burma, Laos, India, and other societies has shown.

So, the fact that the content of the SDGs does address inequality, access to land and labor rights, and health systems and coverage means that development and human rights priorities are more closely aligned, consistent, and (potentially) mutually supportive than they were with the MDGs. Their impact will depend largely on initiatives from low- and middle-income country governments and on pressure and support from various constituencies, both domestic and international.

With respect to this second proposition, low- and middle-income societies have already been tackling the challenges of inequality, land, labor, and health coverage, using strategies and policies that can be advanced further under the SDGs. The experience here is positive but uneven, and there is a stronger record of initiatives on land, labor, and health coverage than on income inequality. Clarifying land rights and removing or weakening the most serious obstacles to women's ownership and inheritance of land have now inspired a broad and influential movement across the low- and middle-income countries, with organizations adapting and promoting legal strategies (Namati) and administrative and policy expertise (Landesa), building women's movements for land and economic rights in Asia, and training networks of paralegals and other support to counter the influence of traditional authorities and norms. Their human rights education, litigation, and community-based strategies are among the diverse means by which human rights advocacy and development practice are becoming more integrated in their efforts to increase security and equity of land tenure.

Progress in improving the pay and conditions of low-income workers has been greatest where it is arguably needed most, among workers in the informal economy. A number of strategies have been used successfully. Informal networks of recyclers have won contracts and formal recognition in several South American cities. Bangkok's 440,000 home workers have won recognition, social security benefits, and other protections, and informal workers in many settings have benefited indirectly from the effects of minimum wage laws. Domestic workers, among the most vulnerable in the informal sector, have organized and won contract protections in the Philippines, Bolivia, and elsewhere. It bears repeating that what North Americans call the "gig economy" is the norm for workers in most of the world: informal sector workers are 61 percent of the world's workforce, and focusing on their well-being is a potent strategy for addressing poverty and income inequality, and promoting greater gender equality.

Third, human rights advocates and the global women's movement are actively promoting, critiquing, and monitoring the SDGs. That engagement, which was largely absent during the MDGs, creates a stronger, more diverse coalition of advocates that can bring to bear the data, principles, and political energy to motivate action. Several years into the SDG period, the engagement of human rights and women's movements is clear, but the results in terms of accountability and of outcomes remain to be demonstrated.

Finance and Accountability

Much of the discussion about implementation and accountability for the broad goals set in the SDGs has focused on two themes: will wealthy governments provide adequate financing, and will the UN reporting and review processes create meaningful accountability for the rapid progress the goals require?

Finance for the SDGs is important, but unlike the MDGs they are not essentially driven by external aid commitments. For this reason, I have argued that the primary focus should be not on aid commitments to finance SDG-related initiatives but on domestic political mobilization and, at least in many countries, domestic mobilization of finance through improved tax systems. Many of the high-priority measures needed to implement land and labor reforms and some of the most important steps to address income inequality do not require massive public expenditures. Expanded health coverage and building stronger health systems clearly will require major new spending, however, and external assistance will be important.

Accountability and closing the gaps between policy commitments and actual services delivered are critical challenges for every government and advocate in implementing the SDGs. Success will depend on the functioning of a diffuse, networked set of monitoring efforts at national, regional, and global levels. These efforts feature databases, innovative indicators that measure governments' readiness to implement policies, "shadow reports" to supplement government reporting to the United Nations, ongoing monitoring and critique of formal UN processes, and expert groups organized around the themes. These networks, as described beginning in chapter 3, have no formal power to hold governments accountable, and have been disappointed at the limited roles they have been granted in the annual UN SDG fora to date.

These networks deploy a range of strategies that feature carrots and sticks, data and images, and cooperation and confrontation. Holding up successful initiatives for praise and replication, on the one hand, and taking governments to court to force implementation of land rights or to extend health coverage, on the other, have both advanced land and health rights in cases reviewed here. Linking innovative measures of governments' effort to human rights standards and SDG targets has been promoted and practiced by human rights advocates. Working with national and subnational governments to demonstrate, for example, the impact of a secure deed to even a tiny plot of land has proven effective in India, as has publicly shaming state or national governments for failing to protect citizens' legal rights.

Accountability of more than a hundred governments to multiple goals overseen by separate networks of UN, NGO, and other actors may not be the ideal scenario one would draw up to maximize accountability for development initiatives. However, the formal, centralized reporting structure, through the UN annual High-level Political Forum (HLPF), has not as yet demonstrated that it can be an open, candid process, and, whatever improvements may be made in the HLPF, this combination of carrots and sticks – data-based, cooperative, and confrontational strategies – will be an important facet of reporting and accountability under the SDGs.

Human Rights and Development

The analysis and progress report on the SDGs presented here is important in its own right because of the SDGs' potential impact on the lives of hundreds of millions of people. It is also of interest because the SDGs offer new insight into the ongoing interaction between human rights and development as fields of practice. For some respected human rights scholars, the articulation of global social, economic, and environmental goals that do not explicitly and directly link to existing human rights standards is problematic.[1] By failing to cite and link goals to human rights standards explicitly, they argue, the goals undercut the existing, agreed set of global standards found in human rights covenants, creating confusion and compromise at best.

My observation is that among many human rights practitioners, and particularly the UN bodies and NGOs that lead the human rights field in practice, the SDGs appear as opportunities to advance their practice. These advocates also recognize the gaps between human rights standards and SDG targets or indicators; they vigorously criticize the weaknesses of the global goals but nonetheless see them as opportunities to advance agendas related to gender equality, land rights, decent work, inequality, and health coverage. They have taken action to highlight the importance of income disparities and the options for tax, fiscal, and other policies to address them. They make this case in the context of debates over the SDGs because the SDGs provide a broad forum and platform and an important chance to influence national policies.

Human rights advocates have expanded their work to strengthen the measurement and assessment of economic and social rights performance, promoted them effectively through the Human Rights Measurement Initiative, and begun using them as a tool to monitor SDG performance. And they have expanded their work both on universal health coverage and on land rights, focusing on land rights of the groups most vulnerable to losing their main economic asset, including women and Indigenous peoples.

Viewed from the perspective of the development field, the potential impact of the human rights-development interaction is even more positive. Although most development agencies that embrace rights-based approaches rhetorically have not implemented them rigorously, the number of development organizations that straddle the two fields is growing. Save the Children, Namati, Landesa, and ActionAid are among the prominent international NGOs matching this description, and work that integrates the two fields has been the norm among organizations in the global South for some time.

The First Five Years and After

I have laid out a hopeful view of what can be accomplished under the SDGs. Building on the gains of the MDGs is a priority to continue reductions of targeted diseases and increase access to education in countries where enrollments are low. The experience of pursuing global goals under the MDGs is helping, as governments and organizations in civil society are already familiar with the idea of ambitious global targets. And external aid can continue to support initiatives that benefit most from external funding, particularly the costly process of expanding health coverage. The SDGs also correct some of the MDGs' failings, refocusing on the long-term foundations of sustainable development for individuals and communities, and taking on the challenges of universal health coverage and building health systems.

Still, the record of implementation in the first five years has been a mixed bag. That voluntary country reports at annual UN global fora have lacked candor and rigor should not be surprising, as governments generally do what they can to present the best possible view of their records. What is disappointing is the relatively weak and pro-forma discussion of those reports at the annual HLPF, and – critically important – the very limited space provided for discussion of independent perspectives on country reports and thematic reports.

Measures of national governments' readiness to implement the SDGs, in terms of data, policies, and finance, are worrisome, too. One would hope that governments with a strong commitment to the goals would have the data and supportive policies in order after the first few years. Many do, and have arranged financing as well, and half of the eighty-one countries rated "ready" on all three categories are low- and middle-income countries. But progress is slowest among lower-income countries, and with only one low-income country represented in the fully "ready" category, preparatory work urgently needs to be done.

Even a hopeful observer like myself does not imagine that most of the world's governments can accomplish even most of these ambitious goals. Globally, the SDGs will not succeed in literally "leaving no one behind" in the push for universal freedom from poverty and hunger, or for access to decent work. But advocates can aspire to motivating a growing number of countries and development financing agencies to promote and implement policies that reach toward the groups most often left behind during the MDGs – rural dwellers, people who live with a disability, women, members of Indigenous or other ethnic minorities, and other people who have been excluded from economic and social gains in many societies. That shift would signal a major change in the approach that governments and most international development agencies take to "poverty alleviation." Failure to accomplish this would reinforce the skepticism and anger of these populations and of critics of the international development enterprise. But success would be a genuine move toward the spirit of human rights and could produce accomplishments worthy of the generation-long global goal-setting effort.

Notes

Introduction

1 Carmen, Raff, & Miguel Sabrado. (2000). "Setting the Scene: 'Those Who Don't Eat and Those Who Don't Sleep.'" Ch. 1 in Raff Carmen & Miguel Sobrado (Eds.), *A Future for the Excluded: Job Creation and Income Generation by the Poor: Clodomir Santos de Morais and the Organization Workshop*. London: Zed Books.
2 Fanzo, Jessica. (2018). "Does Global Goal Setting Matter for Nutrition and Health?" *AMA Journal of Ethics, 20*(10), E979–86. doi: 10.1001/amajethics.2018.979.
3 Center for Economic and Social Rights. (2020). "Resourcing a Just Recovery from COVID-19." https://www.cesr.org/covid19.
4 Alston, Philip. (2020). "The Parlous State of Poverty Eradication. Report of the Special Rapporteur on Extreme Poverty and Human Rights." Human Rights Council Forty-fourth session, 15 June–3 July 2020. https://chrgj.org/wp-content/uploads/2020/07/Alston-Poverty-Report-FINAL.pdf.
5 Ibid., 19.
6 Lieberman, Amy. (2020, 29 April). "A Look at How UN Development Funds Are Recalibrating SDG Funding." Joint SDG Fund. https://jointsdgfund.org/index.php/article/look-how-un-development-funds-are-recalibrating-sdg-funding.
7 IISD (International Institute for Sustainable Development). (2020, 21 July). "As Decade of Action Has Become a Decade of Recovery, HLPF Focuses on Pandemic Response." SDG Knowledge Hub. https://sdg.iisd.org/news/as-decade-of-action-has-become-a-decade-of-recovery-hlpf-focuses-on-pandemic-response/.
8 Ibid.

1. Human Rights and Global Development Goals

1 Easterly, William. (2015, 28 September). "The SDGs Should Stand for Senseless, Dreamy, Garbled." *Foreign Policy*. http://foreignpolicy.com/2015/09/28/the-sdgs-are-utopian-and-worthless-mdgs-development-rise-of-the-rest/. Accessed 16 August 2016.
2 Naidoo, Robin, & Brendan Fisher. (2020). "Sustainable Development Goals: Pandemic Reset." *Nature*. https://media.nature.com/original/magazine-assets/d41586-020-01999-x/d41586-020-01999-x.pdf.

3 United Nations. (2014). *The Millennium Development Goals Report 2014.* http://www.un.org/millenniumgoals/2014%20MDG%20report/MDG%202014%20 English%20web.pdf. Accessed 26 June 2017.

4 Ibid.

5 Devereux, Stephen, Bapu Vaitla, & Samuel Hauenstein Swan. (2008). *Seasons of Hunger.* London: Pluto Press

6 Narayan, Deepak, Robert Chambers, Meera K. Shah, & Patti Petesch. (2000). *Voices of the Poor: Crying Out for Change.* New York: Oxford University Press for the World Bank.

7 Low-income countries are those with average per capita income in 2021 below $1,035; middle-income countries have per capita income in 2021 between $1,036 and $12,535. Middle income is divided into lower and upper categories, at the per capita income level of $4,075. World Bank. (2020). "World Bank Country and Lending Groups." https://datahelpdesk.worldbank.org/knowledgebase /articles/906519-world-bank-country-and-lending-groups.

8 Sumner, Andy. (2010). "Global Poverty and the New Bottom Billion: What if Three-quarters of the World's Poor Live in Middle-income Countries?" IDS (Institute of Development Studies) Working Paper, No. 349, 2.

9 Collier, Paul. (2007). *The Bottom Billion: Why the Poorest Countries Are Failing and What Can Be Done about It.* Oxford: Oxford University Press.

10 Sumner, Andy. (2010). "Global Poverty and the New Bottom Billion: What if Three-quarters of the World's Poor Live in Middle-income Countries?" IDS Working Paper, No. 349, 2.

11 United Nations. (2014). *The Millennium Development Goals Report 2014.* http://www.un.org/millenniumgoals/2014%20MDG%20report/MDG%202014%20 English%20web.pdf. Accessed 26 June 2017.

12 Díaz-Martinez, Elisa, & Elizabeth Gibbons. (2013). "The Questionable Power of the Millennium Development Goal to Reduce Child Mortality," 25. Working paper: The Power of Numbers Working Paper Series, School of Public Health, François-Xavier Bagnoud Center for Health and Human Rights, Harvard University, Cambridge, MA.

13 Pogge, Thomas. (2004). "The First United Nations Millennium Development Goal: A Cause for Celebration?" *Journal of Human Development*, 5(3), 377–97.

14 United Nations. (2015). *The Millennium Development Goals Report 2015.* https://www.un.org/millenniumgoals/2015_MDG_Report/pdf/MDG%202015%20 rev%20(July%201).pdf.

15 Roser, Max, Hannah Ritchie, & Bernadeta Dadonaite. (2019, November). "Child Mortality." Our World in Data. https://ourworldindata.org/child-mortality.

16 Nelson, Paul, & Ellen Dorsey. (2008). *New Rights Advocacy.* Washington, DC: Georgetown University Press.

17 United Nations General Assembly. (2000, 18 September). *United Nations Millennium Declaration, Resolution Adopted by the General Assembly.* A/RES/55/2. Available at: https://www.refworld.org/docid/3b00f4ea3.html. Accessed 15 July 2020.

18 United Nations Secretary-General. (2001, 6 September). *Road Map towards the Implementation of the United Nations Millennium Declaration, Report of the Secretary-General.* U.N. GAOR, 56th Sess. Follow-up to the outcome of the Millennium Summit, U.N. Doc. A/56/326.

19 Lennox, Corinne. (2005). "The Millennium Development Goals and Minority Rights, April 2005." Presentation at the side-event "Millenium+5, the MDGs and Human Rights," organized by the Conference of NGOs in Consultative Relationship with the United Nations (CONGO).

20 United Nations. (2009). *Millennium Development Goals Report 2009*. New York: United Nations.

21 Yamin, Alicia, Jessica Cole, Tiffany R. Moore Simas, & Marion Brown. (2007, November). *Deadly Delays: Maternal Mortality in Peru: A Rights-based Approach to Safe Motherhood*. Physicians for Human Rights. http://physiciansforhumanrights .org/library/report-2007-11-28.html.

22 Harman, Sophie. (2014, October). "Ebola and the Politics of a Global Health Crisis." *E-International Relations*.

23 United Nations Millennium Project. (2005). "Investing in Development: A Practical Plan to Achieve the Millennium Development Goals. Overview," 27. http://www .omdg.org/en/images/investing_dev.pdf. Accessed 16 November 2020.

24 Nowak, Manfred. (2005). "A Human Rights Approach to Poverty." *Human Rights in Development Yearbook 2002. Empowerment, Participation, Accountability and Non-Discrimination: Operationalising a Human Rights-based Approach to Development*, 15–36; see especially 28–9. Leiden: Martinus Nijhoff Publishers.

25 Fukuda-Parr, Sakiko. (2016). "From the Millennium Development Goals to the Sustainable Development Goals: Shifts in Purpose, Concept, and Politics of Global Goal Setting for Development." *Gender & Development, 24*(1), 43–52. DOI: 10.1080/13552074.2016.1145895.

26 Michel, James. (2005, September–October). "The Birth of the MDGs." *DACNews*, 3 pp., on file with author.

27 Bissio, Roberto. (2003, April). "Civil Society and the MDGs." *UNDP Development Policy Journal, 3*, 151–60; Tomlinson, Brian. (2005, May). *The Politics of the Millennium Development Goals: Contributions to Strategies for Ending Poverty?* A Background Paper, Canadian Council for International Cooperation. On file with the author.

28 Honniball, Arron, & Otto Spijkers. (2014). "MDGs and SDGs: Lessons Learnt from Global Public Participation in the Drafting of the UN Development Goals." *Vereinte Nationen – German Review on the United Nations, 63*, 251–6.

29 United Nations. (2016). "High-level Political Forum on Sustainable Development," 3. https://sustainabledevelopment.un.org/majorgroups/hlpf. Accessed 29 August 2016.

30 Ibid.

31 Ibid., 10.

32 Post-2015 Human Rights Caucus. (2014, June). "Human Rights for All Post-2015: A Litmus Test." https://www.cesr.org/human-rights-all-post-2015-litmus-test-0.

33 Campaign for People's Goals for Sustainable Development. (2012, 31 October). "Campaign for People's Goals for Sustainable Development." https:// sustainabledevelopment.un.org/content/documents/778campaign.pdf.

34 Post-2015 Human Rights Caucus. (2014, June). "Human Rights for All Post-2015: A Litmus Test." https://www.cesr.org/human-rights-all-post-2015-litmus -test-0; Amnesty International, Center for Economic and Social Rights, Center for Reproductive Rights, & Human Rights Watch. (2015, July). "Post-2015 Outcome

Document: Redlines and Proposals on Follow-up and Review." https://www.hrw
.org/news/2015/07/22/post-2015-outcome-document-redlines-and-proposals
-follow-and-review. Accessed 25 August 2016.

35 United Nations SDG Knowledge Platform. (2016). "High-level Political Forum on
Sustainable Development 2016 – Ensuring That No One Is Left Behind." https://
sustainabledevelopment.un.org/hlpf/2016.

36 Marks, Stephen P. (2014). "Prospects for Human Rights in the Post-2015
Development Agenda." In Julia Kozma, Anna Müller-Funk, & Manfred Nowak
(Eds.), *Vienna +20: Advancing the Protection of Human Rights Achievements,
Challenges and Perspectives 20 Years after the World Conference*, 291–306. Ludwig
Boltzmann Institute of Human Rights, Studies Series, vol. 31. Vienna: Neuer
Wissenschaftlicher Verlag.

37 Brolan, C.E., P.S. Hill, & G. Ooms. (2015, 21 August). "'Everywhere but Not
Specifically Somewhere': A Qualitative Study on Why the Right to Health Is Not
Explicit in the Post-2015 Negotiations." *BMC International Health and Human Rights,*
15(22). doi:10.1186/s12914-015-0061-z.

38 MacNaughton, Gillian. (2019). "The Mysterious Disappearance of Human Rights
in the 2030 Development Agenda." In Rajini Srikanth & Elora Halim Chowdhury
(Eds.), *Interdisciplinary Approaches to Human Rights: History, Politics, Practice*, 131–47.
New York: Routledge.

39 Fredman, Sandra. (2018). *Working Together: Human Rights, the Sustainable
Development Goals and Gender Equality*. London: The British Academy.

40 Post-2015 Women's Coalition. (2012). "The Post 2015 Development Agenda: What's
at Stake for the World's Women?" http://wedo.org/the-post-2015-development
-agenda-perspectives-from-the-post-2015-womens-coalition/. Accessed 16 August
2016.

41 Quintos, Paul. (2015, 23 April). "Intervention for the Session on Follow-up
and Review of FFD and Post-2015 MOI." Campaign for People's Goals for
Sustainable Development. https://sustainabledevelopment.un.org/content
/documents/14124IBON%20International.pdf.

42 Esquivel, Valeria. (2016). "Power and the Sustainable Development Goals: A
Feminist Analysis." *Gender & Development, 24*(1), 9–23; Sen, Gita. (2019). "Gender
Equality and Women's Empowerment: Feminist Mobilization for the SDGs." *Global
Policy, 10*(1), 28–38.

43 Danish Institute for Human Rights. (2015). *Human Rights Guide to the Sustainable
Development Goals*. http://sdg.humanrights.dk/. Accessed 29 August 2016.

44 Kuruvilla, Shyama, Flavia Bustreo, Paul Hunt, Amarjit Singh, Eric Friedman,
Thiago Luchesi, et al. (2012). "The Millennium Development Goals and Human
Rights: Realizing Shared Commitments." *Human Rights Quarterly, 34*(1), 141–77.

45 See, for example, Winkler, Inga T., & Carmel Williams. (2018). *The Sustainable
Development Goals and Human Rights: A Critical Early Review*. New York: Routledge.

46 Jensen, Steven L.B. (2019, 4 July). "UN Human Rights Mechanisms Proving
Effective SDGs Monitor." Open Global Rights. https://www.openglobalrights.
org/un-human-rights-mechanisms-proving-effective-sdgs-monitor/.

47 Center for Economic and Social Rights. (2015). "Strong Commitments in Final
SDG Text, Despite Sordid Final Compromises." http://www.cesr.org/strong
-commitments-final-sdg-text-despite-sordid-final-compromises. Accessed 26 June
2017.

48 Ibid.
49 Donald, Kate. (2015, September). "Winning a Place for Human Rights in the New Sustainable Development Agenda." *Open Global Rights*. https://www .openglobalrights.org/Winning-a-place-for-human-rights-in-the-new-sustainable -development-agenda/.
50 Hege, Elisabeth, & Damien Demailly. (n.d.). "How Do NGOs Mobilize around the SDGs and What Are the Ways Forward? A French-German Comparison." IDDRI Working Paper. https://www.iddri.org/sites/default/files/import/publications/ working-paper-sdgs-and-ngos_eh-dd.pdf.
51 International Organizations Clinic, NYU University School of Law, & UNDP. (2016). "Accountability through Civic Participation in the Post-2015 Development Agenda."
52 Hege, E., & D. Demailly. (2018). "NGO Mobilisation around the SDGs." Studies No. 01/18. Paris: IDDRI, 14.
53 Jolly, R. (2004). "Global Development Goals: UN Experience." *Journal of Human Development*, 5(1), 70.
54 Ibid., 72.
55 Motta, Sara C., & Alf Gunwald Nilsen (Eds.). (2011). *Social Movements in the Global South: Dispossession, Development and Resistance*. New York: Palgrave-Macmillan.
56 Friedman, Steven, & Shauna Mottiar. (2005, December). "A Rewarding Engagement? The Treatment Action Campaign and the Politics of HIV/AIDS." *Politics and Society*, 33(4), 511–65
57 Carter, Miguel. (2015). *Challenging Inequality: The Landless Rural Workers' Movement and Agrarian Reform in Brazil*. Durham, NC: Duke University Press.
58 Mander, Harsh, & Abha Joshi. (n.d.). "The Movement for Right to Information in India: People's Power for the Control of Corruption." https://www. humanrightsinitiative.org/programs/ai/rti/india/articles/The%20Movement%20 for%20RTI%20in%20India.pdf.
59 Villarino, Eliza. (2013, 16 October). "The Plight of the Girl Child." https://www .devex.com/news/the-plight-of-the-girl-child-82106.
60 In each case, five were selected from NGOs involved in poverty, employment, and health; five from NGOs working in health-related fields; ten were chosen at random from the Global Call to Action against Poverty list of supporting civil-society organizations. The southern NGOs and social movements include large NGOs such as Bangladesh Rural Action Committee (BRAC), the South African Treatment Action Campaign, and the Self-Employed Women's Association in India, as well as smaller NGOs working in health, agriculture, gender, and income generation.

2. Principles and Practice, Human Rights and Development

1 Levine, Iain. (2016). "Building a Better World by Righting Development." https:// www.hrw.org/blog-feed/righting-development#blog-281197. Accessed 4 March 2017.
2 Oxfam International. (2017). "Our Commitment to Human Rights." https://www .oxfam.org/en/our-commitment-human-rights.
3 Friedman, Steven, & Shauna Mottiar. (2005, December). "A Rewarding Engagement? The Treatment Action Campaign and the Politics of HIV/AIDS." *Politics and Society*, 33(4), 511–65.

4 Geffen, Nathan. (2010). *Debunking Delusions: The Inside Story of the Treatment Action Campaign.* Johannesburg: Jacana Media.
5 Cornwall, Andrea. (2008). "Unpacking 'Participation': Meanings, Models and Practices." *Community Development Journal,* 269–83.
6 Raftopoulos, Malayna, & Damien Short. (2019). "Implementing Free Prior and Informed Consent: The United Nations Declaration on the Rights of Indigenous Peoples (2007), the Challenges of REDD+ and the Case for the Precautionary Principle." *The International Journal of Human Rights,* 23(1–2), 87–103. DOI: 10.1080/13642987.2019.1579990.
7 Business and Human Rights Resource Centre. (2015). "Oil Palm Uganda Lawsuit." https://business-humanrights.org/en/oil-palm-uganda-lawsuit-re-land-grabs-in-uganda. Accessed 12 February 2017; Yeargan, Stephanie Carey. (2016). "Meet the Teams: Core to Care: Get the Land Right." http://sxdaccelerator.care.org/meet-the-teams-core-to-care-get-the-land-right/. Accessed 27 June 2017; Pearce, F. (2016). *Common Ground: Securing Land Rights and Safeguarding the Earth.* International Land Coalition. https://www.oxfam.org/sites/www.oxfam.org/files/file_attachments/bp-common-ground-land-rights-020316-en_0.pdf; Oxfam International. (n.d.). "Our Commitment to Human Rights." https://www.oxfam.org/en/our-commitment-human-rights. Accessed 4 March 2017.
8 Wickeri, Elisabeth, & Anil Kalhan. (2010). "Land Rights Issues in International Human Rights Law." Institute for Human Rights and Business. https://www.ihrb.org/pdf/Land_Rights_Issues_in_International_HRL.pdf. Accessed 25 February 2017.
9 Kent, George. (2005). *Freedom from Want: The Human Right to Adequate Food.* Washington, DC: Georgetown University Press.
10 Office of the High Commissioner for Human Rights. (n.d.). "The Right to Adequate Food." Fact Sheet 34. https://www.ohchr.org/Documents/Publications/Fact Sheet34en.pdf. Accessed 10 October 2019.
11 De Beco, Gauthier. (2013). "Human Rights Indicators: From Theoretical Debate to Practical Application." *Journal of Human Rights Practice,* 5(2), 380–97. DOI:10.1093/jhuman/hut003.
12 Blyberg, Ann, & Helena Hofbauer. (2014). "Progressive Realization: Article 2 and Governments' Budgets." International Budget Partnership. http://www.internationalbudget.org/wp-content/uploads/Progressive-Realization-booklet.pdf. Accessed 25 February 2017.
13 Office of the High Commissioner for Human Rights. (2012). *Human Rights Indicators: A Guide to Measurement and Implementation.* https://www.ohchr.org/Documents/Publications/Human_rights_indicators_en.pdf.
14 Office of the High Commissioner for Human Rights. (2012). "Guiding Principles on Extreme Poverty and Human Rights," iv. https://www.ohchr.org/Documents/Publications/OHCHR_ExtremePovertyandHumanRights_EN.pdf. Accessed 2 January 2020;
15 CESR. (n.d.). "The OPERA Framework." https://www.cesr.org/opera-framework.
16 Fukuda-Parr, Sakiko, Terra Lawson-Remer, & Susan Randolph. (2008). "Measuring the Progressive Realization of Human Rights Obligations: An Index of Economic and Social Rights Fulfillment." *Economics Working Papers.* 200822. https://opencommons.uconn.edu/econ_wpapers/200822; Fukuda-Parr, Sakiko, Terra Lawson-Remer, & Susan Randolph. (2015). *Fulfilling Social and Economic Rights.* Oxford: Oxford University Press.

17 UN Committee on ESCR. (2009). "General Comment No. 20: Non-discrimination in Economic, Social and Cultural Rights." Article 2, para. 2, of the International Covenant on Economic, Social and Cultural Rights. https://digitallibrary.un.org /record/659980?ln=en.

18 Ibid., para 13.

19 Silva, Jose Adan. (2016, 5 December). "Nicaraguan Women Push for Access to Land, Not Just on Paper." *Global Issues.* http://www.globalissues.org/news/2016 /12/05/22710. Accessed 2 February 2017.

20 Office of the High Commissioner for Human Rights. (n.d.). *International Covenant on Economic, Social, and Cultural Rights,* Article 12. https://www.ohchr.org/en /professionalinterest/pages/cescr.aspx.

21 McBroom, Kerry. (2016, June). "Litigation as TB Rights Advocacy: A New Delhi Case Study." *Health and Human Rights Journal, 18*(1), 69–83.

22 On drug policy, see Csete, Joanne, Adeeba Kamarulzaman, Michel Kazatchkine, Frederick Altice, Marek Balicki, Julia Buxton, et al. (2016, 2 April). "Public Health and International Drug Policy." *Lancet, 387*(10026), 1427–80.

23 Office of the High Commissioner for Human Rights. (n.d.). "Issues in Focus." http://www.ohchr.org/EN/Issues/Health/Pages/IssuesFocus.aspx. Accessed 9 January 2017.

24 UN Committee on ESCR. (2000). "General Comment No. 14: The Right to the Highest Attainable Standard of Health." Article 12 of the International Covenant on Economic, Social and Cultural Rights. https://digitallibrary.un.org/record /425041?ln=en.

25 United Nations General Assembly. (2010). "The Human Right to Water and Sanitation." Resolution adopted by the General Assembly on 28 July 2010, 64/292. https://undocs.org/en/A/RES/64/292. Accessed 13 November 2020.

26 Office of the High Commissioner for Human Rights. (2010). "The Right to Water." Fact Sheet No. 35. http://www.ohchr.org/Documents/Publications /FactSheet35en.pdf.

27 Ibid.; and Smets, Henri. (2009). "Access to Drinking Water at an Affordable Price in Developing Countries." In M. El Moujabber, L. Mandi, G. Trisorio Liuzzi, I. Martin, A. Rabi, & R. Rodriguez (Eds.), *Technological Perspectives for Rational Use of Water Resources in the Mediterranean Region,* 57–68. Bari: CIHEAM, 2009. Options Méditerranéennes: Série A. Séminaires Méditerranéens, n. 88, United Nations.

28 Nelson, Paul J. (2017). "Citizens, Consumers, Workers, Activists: Civil Society during and after Water Privatization Struggles." *Journal of Civil Society, 13*(2), 202–21.

29 Watkins, Kevin. (2006, 9 November). *Human Development Report 2006 – Beyond Scarcity: Power, Poverty and the Global Water Crisis.* UNDP Human Development Reports. Available at SSRN: https://ssrn.com/abstract=2294691. Accessed 15 November 2020; Szabo, Andrea. (2015). "The Value of Free Water: Analyzing South Africa's Free Basic Water Policy." *Econometrica, 83*(5), 1913–61.

30 Pruce, Joel. (2015). *The Social Practice of Human Rights.* London: Palgrave /Macmillan.

31 Theis, J. (2003). *Brief Introduction to Rights-based Programming.* Save the Children–Sweden. http://www.crin.org/docs/resources/publications/hrbap/brief_intro _RBA.doc. Accessed 20 November 2014.

32 Nelson, Paul J., & Ellen Dorsey. (2003, December). "At the Nexus of Human Rights and Development: New Methods and Strategies of Global NGOs." *World*

Development, 31(12), 2013–26; UNDP. (2000). *Human Development Report 2000*. New York: Oxford University Press.

33 Kindornay, Shannon, James Ron, & Charli Carpenter. (2012, May). "Rights-based Approaches to Development: Implications for NGOs." *Human Rights Quarterly, 34*(2), 473.

34 Schmitz, Hans Peter. (2012). "A Human Rights-based Approach (HRBA) in Practice: Evaluating NGO Development Efforts." *Polity, 44*(4), 534; Grugel, Jean, & Nicola Piper. (2009). "Do Rights Promote Development?" *Global Social Policy, 9*(1), 79.

35 Nelson, Paul, & Ellen Dorsey. (2018). "Who Practices Rights-based Development? A Progress Report on Work at the Nexus of Human Rights and Development." *World Development, 104*, 97–107.

36 Eyben, R. (2003). "The Rise of Rights: Rights-based Approaches to International Development." IDS Policy Briefing 17. Brighton: IDS. https://opendocs.ids.ac.uk/opendocs/handle/123456789/768.

37 Cornwall, Andrea, & Celestine Nyamu-Musembi. (2004). "Putting the 'Rights-based Approach' to Development into Perspective." *Third World Quarterly, 25*(8), 1415–37.

38 Destrooper, T. (2016). "Linking Discourse and Practice: The Human Rights-based Approach to Development in the Village Assaini Program in the Kongo Central." *Human Rights Quarterly, 38*(3), 787–813.

39 Nelson, Paul, & Ellen Dorsey. (2018). "Who Practices Rights-based Development? A Progress Report on Work at the Nexus of Human Rights and Development." *World Development, 104*, 97–107.

40 Fukuda-Parr, Sakiko. (2010, January). "Reducing Inequality – the Missing MDG." *IDS Bulletin, 41*(1), Special Issue: The MDGs and Beyond, 26–35; Fukuda-Parr, Sakiko, & Alicia Ely Yamin (Eds.). (2015). *The MDGs, Capabilities and Human Rights: The Power of Numbers to Shape Agendas*. New York: Routledge.

41 Travis, P., S. Bennet, A. Haines, T. Pang, Z. Bhutta, A.A. Hyder, et al. (2004). "Overcoming Health-systems Constraints to Achieve the Millennium Development Goals." *Lancet, 364*, 900–6.

42 Nelson, Paul J. (2007). "Human Rights, the Millennium Development Goals, and the Future of Development Cooperation." *World Development, 35*(12), 2041–55; Nelson, Paul, & Ellen Dorsey. (2008). *New Rights Advocacy: Changing Strategies of Development and Human Rights NGOs*. Washington, DC: Georgetown University Press.

43 Gauri, Varun, & Siri Gloppen. (2012). "Human Rights-based Approaches to Development: Concepts, Evidence, and Policy." *Polity, 44*(4), 485–503.

44 International Women's Rights Action Watch Asia-Pacific. (2010). "Participation in ICESCR and CEDAW Reporting Processes." https://docs.escr-net.org/usr_doc/CEDAW_CESCR_reporting_guidelines_FINAL_Oct_6_2010.pdf. Accessed 14 December 2016.

45 Burchfield, Lauren, & Jessica Corsi. (2010). "Between Starvation and Globalization: Realizing the Right to Food in India." *Michigan Journal of International Law, 31*(4), 691. https://repository.law.umich.edu/mjil/vol31/iss4/1. Accessed 19 December 2019; Friedman, Stephen, & Shauna Mottiar. (2005). "A Rewarding Engagement? The Treatment Action Campaign and the Politics of HIV/AIDS." *Politics and Society, 33*(4), 511–65.

46 Nelson, Paul, & Ellen Dorsey. (2018). "Who Practices Rights-based Development? A Progress Report on Work at the Nexus of Human Rights and Development." *World Development, 104*, 97–107.

47 Namati. (2019). *Annual Report 2018*. https://namati.org/news-stories/namatis
-2018-annual-report-now-available/.

48 Deva, Surya. (2017). "Access to Justice for Socio-economic Rights: Lessons from the
Indian Experience." https://voelkerrechtsblog.org/access-to-justice-for-socio
-economic-rights-lessons-from-the-indian-experience/. Accessed 19 December 2019.

49 McBroom, Kerry. (2016, June). "Litigation as TB Rights Advocacy: A New Delhi
Case Study." *Health and Human Rights Journal, 18*(1), 69–83.

50 Open Society Foundations. (2016). "Advancing Public Health through Strategic
Litigation: Lessons from Five Countries." https://www.opensocietyfoundations.
org/sites/default/files/advancing-public-health-through-strategic-litigation
-20160622.pdf. Accessed 8 June 2017.

51 McBroom, Kerry. (2016, June). "Litigation as TB Rights Advocacy: A New Delhi
Case Study." *Health and Human Rights Journal, 18*(1), 75.

52 Patel, Akshay, Sudha Sharma, Audrey Prost, Genevieve Sander, & Paul Hunt.
(2013). "Maternal and Child Health in Nepal." In Flavia Bustreo & Paul Hunt
(Eds.), *Women's and Children's Health: Evidence of Impact of Human Rights*, 26–33.
Geneva: World Health Organization.

53 Feinglass, Ellie, Nadja Gomes, & Vivek Maru. (2016). "Transforming Policy into
Justice: The Role of Health Advocates in Mozambique." *Health and Human Rights
Journal, 18*(2), 233–46.

54 Ibid.

55 Ibid.

56 Barros De Luca, G., S. Valongueiro, E. Leocádio, J. Martines, I.A. de Carvalho, &
P. Hunt. (2013). "Sexual, Reproductive and Maternal Health in Brazil." In Flavia
Bustreo & Paul Hunt (Eds.), *Women's and Children's Health: Evidence of Impact of
Human Rights*, 34–41. Geneva: World Health Organization.

57 Ibid., 40.

58 Helfer, Laurence R. (2015). "Pharmaceutical Patents and the Human Right to
Health: The Contested Evolution of the Transnational Legal Order on Access to
Medicines." In Terence C. Halliday & Gregory Shaffer (Eds.), *Transnational Legal
Orders*, 311–39. Cambridge: Cambridge University Press.

59 Yamin, A.E., & O. Parra-Vera. (2009). "How Do Courts Set Health Policy? The Case
of the Colombian Constitutional Court." *PLoS Med, 6*(2): e1000032, 49. https://doi
.org/10.1371/journal.pmed.1000032.

60 Nelson, Paul. (2017). "Citizens, Consumers, Workers, Activists: Civil Society
during and after Water Privatization Struggles." *Journal of Civil Society, 13*(2),
202–21; Sultana, Farhana, & Alex Loftus (Eds.). (2012). *The Right to Water*. New
York: Earthscan.

61 Bakker, Karen. (2010). *Privatizing Water: Governance Failure and the World Urban
Water Crisis*. Ithaca, NY: Cornell University Press; Punjabi, Bharat, Roger Keil,
Vinay Gadwani, Farhana Sultana, Alana Boland, & Karen Bakker. (2015).
"Debate on Karen Bakker's Privatizing Water: Governance Failure and the
World's Urban Water Crisis." *International Journal of Urban and Regional Research*.
DOI:10.1111/1468-2427.12281.

62 Santos, C., & A. Villarreal. (2005). "Uruguay: Victorious Social Struggle for Water."
In B. Balanyá, B. Brennan, O. Hoedeman, S. Kishimoto, & P. Terhorst (Eds.),
Reclaiming Public Water – Achievements, Struggles and Visions from around the World,
173–89. Transnational Institute and Corporate Europe Observatory.

63 Takacs, David. (2016). "South Africa and the Human Right to Water: Equity, Ecology and the Public Trust Doctrine," 34. *Berkeley Journal of International Law, 55*. UC Hastings Research Paper No. 226.

64 Nelson, Paul. (2017). "Citizens, Consumers, Workers, Activists: Civil Society during and after Water Privatization Struggles." *Journal of Civil Society, 13*(2), 202–21.

65 Christman, Jordan. (2017, 19 June). "Paraguay's Strategic Success in Water Accessibility." The Center for Water Security and Cooperation. https://www .ourwatersecurity.org/single-post/2017/06/19/Paraguay%E2%80%99s-Strategic -Success-in-Water-Accessibility; Slawson, Nicola. (2017, 26 May). "Rural Water Access: Why Should Countries Follow Paraguay's Lead?" *Guardian*. https://www .theguardian.com/global-development-professionals-network/2017/may/26 /rural-water-access-paraguay-success-lessons. Accessed 22 January 2020.

66 De Albuquerque, Catarina. (2012). *On the Right Track: Good Practices in Realising the Rights to Water and Sanitation,* 65. Geneva: UNESCO WWAP.

67 GI-ESCR. (2015). "A Human Rights-based Approach to Water in Informal Settlements." http://globalinitiative-escr.org/wp-content/uploads/2015/08 /GI-ESCR-Practitioners-Guilde-on-Right-to-Water.pdf.

68 Ibid.; Rana, M., & A. Piracha. (2018). "Supplying Water to the Urban Poor." *Management of Environmental Quality, 29*(4), 608–22. https://doi.org/10.1108 /MEQ-11-2017-0127.

69 Hanchett, S., S. Akhter, M.H. Khan, S. Mezulianik, & V. Blagbrough. (2003). "Water, Sanitation and Hygiene in Bangladeshi Slums: An Evaluation of the WaterAid– Bangladesh Urban Programme." *Environment and Urbanization, 15*(2), 43–56. https://doi.org/10.1177/095624780301500219.

70 Sharma, Manoj, & Melissa Alipalo. (2017). *The Dhaka Water Services Turnaround. How Dhaka Is Connecting Slums, Saving Water, Raising Revenues, and Becoming One of South Asia's Best Public Water Utilities.* Manila: Asian Development Bank; Yeasmin, F., F. Sultana, L. Unicomb, F.A. Nizame, M. Rahman, H. Kabir, et al. (2019). "Piloting a Shared Source Water Treatment Intervention among Elementary Schools in Bangladesh." *American Journal of Tropical Medicine and Hygiene, 101*(5), 984–93. doi:10.4269/ajtmh.18–09.

3. Challenging Inequalities

1 Quinn, Sandra Crouse, & Supriya Kumar. (2014, September). "Health Inequalities and Infectious Disease Epidemics: A Challenge for Global Health Security." *Biosecurity and Bioterrorism: Biodefense Strategy, Practice, and Science, 12*(5), 263–73.

2 Stewart, Frances. (2016). *Horizontal Inequalities and Violence: Understanding Group Violence in Multiethnic Societies.* London: Palgrave; Wilkinson, Richard, & Kate Pickett. (2010). *The Spirit Level: Why Greater Equality Makes Societies Stronger.* London: Bloomsbury; Wilkinson, Richard, & Kate Pickett. (2019). *The Inner Level.* London: Penguin.

3 Hasell, Joe. (2018, 19 November). "Is Income Inequality Rising around the World?" Our World in Data. https://ourworldindata.org/income-inequality-since-1990.

4 World Bank. (2020). "Gini Index: World Bank Estimate." https://data.worldbank .org/indicator/SI.POV.GINI. Gini coefficient scores are also sometimes converted to percentages, making the scale zero to 100.

5 UNDP. (2013, November). *Humanity Divided: Confronting Inequality in Developing Countries.* New York: UNDP Bureau for Development Policy, 64–5. https://www .undp.org/content/undp/en/home/librarypage/poverty-reduction/humanity -divided--confronting-inequality-in-developing-countries.html. Accessed 15 November 2020.

6 Inequality.org. (n.d.). "Facts – Global Inequality." https://inequality.org/facts /global-inequality/.

7 Hasell, Joe. (2018, 19 November). "Is Income Inequality Rising around the World?" Our World in Data. https://ourworldindata.org/income-inequality-since-1990.

8 Moser, Carolyn (Ed.). (2007). *Reducing Global Poverty: The Case for Asset Accumulation.* Washington, DC: Brookings Institution.

9 World Inequality Lab. (2018). *World Inequality Report 2018.* https://wir2018.wid .world/. Accessed 4 December 2019.

10 Nagarajam, M. (2013, 24 August). "Urban Rural Health Indicators during Eleventh Plan." *Govpreneur.*

11 Pan-American Health Organization & World Health Organization. (2018). "Core Indicators, Health Situation in the Americas." https://iris.paho.org/bitstream /handle/10665.2/49511/CoreIndicators2018_eng.pdf?sequence=1&isAllowed =y. Accessed 15 November, 2020.

12 Centers for Disease Control. (2011, January). "CDC Health Disparities and Inequalities Report – United States, 2011." Atlanta, GA: Centers for Disease Control, 50.

13 Rights and Resources Initiative. (2017). "From Risk and Conflict to Peace and Prosperity: The Urgency of Securing Community Land Rights in a Turbulent World." http://rightsandresources.org/wp-content/uploads/2017/01/From -Risk-and-Conflict-to-Peace-and-Prosperity_RRI-Annual-Review-2016-2017 _English.pdf. Accessed 28 June 2017.

14 Mason, Nathaniel, & Beatrice Mosello. (2017). "How to Reduce Inequalities in Access to WASH: Synthesis Report." London: ODI and WaterAid.

15 UNFPA. (2016). "Universal Access to Reproductive Health." http://www.unfpa .org/sites/default/files/pub-pdf/UNFPA_Reproductive_Paper_20160120_online .pdf. Accessed 28 June 2017.

16 Watson, William. (2015). *The Inequality Trap: Fighting Capitalism instead of Poverty.* Toronto: University of Toronto Press.

17 Ibid.; *Economist.* (2004, 11 March). "Poverty and Inequality: A Question of Justice? The Toll of Global Poverty Is a Scandal. But Deploring Economic 'Injustice' Is No Answer." https://www.economist.com/leaders/2004/03/11/a-question-of -justice.

18 Milanovich, Branko. (2015). *Global Inequality: A New Approach for the Age of Globalization.* Cambridge, MA: Harvard University Press; Piketty, Thomas. (2014). *Capitalism in the Twenty-first Century.* Cambridge, MA: Harvard University Press; Bourguignon, François. (2015). *The Globalization of Inequality.* Princeton, NJ: Princeton University Press.

19 Berg, Andres G., & Jonathan D. Ostry. (2011). "Inequality and Unsustainable Growth: Two Sides of the Same Coin?" IMF Staff discussion note SDN 11/08. https://www.imf.org/external/pubs/ft/sdn/2011/sdn1108.pdf; Easterly, W. (2002). "Inequality Does Cause Underdevelopment." Washington, DC: Center for Global Development Working Paper 1, summarized in: UNDP. (2013, November).

Humanity Divided: Confronting Inequality in Developing Countries. New York: UNDP Bureau for Development Policy, 43.

20 Ravallion, M. (2005). "Inequality Is Bad for the Poor." World Bank Policy Research, Working Paper 3677. Washington, DC: The World Bank; Wade, R. (2005). "Does Inequality Matter?" *Challenge, 48*(5), 12–38.

21 Cornia, Giovanni (Ed.). (2004). *Inequality Growth and Poverty in an Era of Liberalization and Globalization.* Oxford: Oxford University Press. Retrieved 15 November 2020, from https://oxford.universitypressscholarship.com/view/10.1 093/0199271410.001.0001/acprof-9780199271412; Birdsall, Nancy. (2007). "Income Distribution: Effects on Growth and Development." Washington, DC: Center for Global Development, Working Paper 118.

22 Sabates-Wheeler, Rachel. (2005). "Asset Inequality and Agricultural Growth: How Are Patterns of Asset Inequality Established and Reproduced?" Washington, DC: World Bank. https://openknowledge.worldbank.org/handle/10986/9049 License: CC BY 3.0 IGO. Accessed 15 November 2020.

23 Wilkinson, Richard, & Kate Pickett. (2010). *The Spirit Level: Why Greater Equality Makes Societies Stronger.* London: Bloomsbury; Wilkinson, Richard, & Kate Pickett. (2019). *The Inner Level.* London: Penguin.

24 Paes de Barros, R., F.H.G. Ferreira, J.R. Molinas Vega, & J. Saavedra Chanduvi. (2008). *Measuring Inequality of Opportunities in Latin America and the Caribbean.* Washington, DC: World Bank.

25 International Labour Organization. (2011). *World of Work Report 2011: Income Inequalities in the Age of Financial Globalization.* Geneva: ILO.

26 Langer, Armin, & Frances Stewart. (2015). "Regional Imbalances, Horizontal Inequalities, and Violent Conflicts." World Bank Other Operational Studies. Washington, DC: The World Bank.

27 Fleurbaey, M. (2007). "Poverty as a Form of Oppression." In Thomas Pogge (Ed.), *Freedom from Poverty as a Human Right: Who Owes What to the Very Poor?* Oxford: UNESCO/Oxford University Press, 145.

28 Gaventa, John. (2016). "Can Participation 'Fix' Inequality? Unpacking the Relationship between the Economic and Political Citizenship." Coady International Institute, Innovation Series No. 5.

29 Birdsall, Nancy. (2007). "Income Distribution: Effects on Growth and Development." Washington, DC: Center for Global Development, Working Paper 118.

30 Kaya, A., & A. Keba. (2011). "Why Global Inequality Matters: Derivative Global Egalitarianism." *Journal of International Political Theory, 7*(2), 140–64.

31 Reeves, Richard. (2017). *Dream Hoarders: How the American Upper Middle Class Is Leaving Everyone Else in the Dust, Why That Is a Problem, and What to Do about It.* Washington, DC: Brookings Institution Press.

32 Bourguignon, F., F.H.G. Ferreira, & M. Walton. (2007). "Equity, Efficiency and Inequality Traps: A Research Agenda." *Journal of Economic Inequality, 5*(2), 235–56.

33 UNDP. (2013, November). *Humanity Divided: Confronting Inequality in Developing Countries.* New York: UNDP Bureau for Development Policy, 49.

34 Broberg, Morten, & Hans-Otto Sano. (2018). "Strengths and Weaknesses in a Human Rights-based Approach to International Development – An Analysis of a Rights-based Approach to Development Assistance Based on

Practical Experiences." *The International Journal of Human Rights,* 22(5), 664–80. DOI: 10.1080/13642987.2017.1408591.

35 Alston, Philip. (2015). "Extreme Inequality as the Antithesis of Human Rights." https://www.openglobalrights.org/extreme-inequality-as-the-antithesis-of -human-rights/; Alston, Philip, & Nicki Reisch. (2019). *Tax, Inequality, and Human Rights.* Oxford: Oxford University Press; MacNaughton, Gillian. (2017). "Vertical Inequalities: Are the SDGs and Human Rights up to the Challenges?" *International Journal of Human Rights, 21*(8), 1050–72.

36 Balakrishnan, Radhika, & James Heintz. (2015, 29 October). "How Inequality Threatens All Human Rights." openDemocracy.

37 Heintz, James, Diane Elson, & Radhika Balakrishnan. (2015, 4 August). "What Does Inequality Have to Do with Human Rights?" Working Paper 392, Political Economy Research Institute, University of Massachusetts Amherst. https://www .peri.umass.edu/publication/item/687-what-does-inequality-have-to-do-with -human-rights. Accessed 15 November 2020.

38 Saíz, Ignacio, & Gaby Oré Aguilar. (2016). "Tackling Inequality as Injustice: Four Challenges for the Human Rights Agenda." openGlobalRights. https://www .opendemocracy.net/openglobalrights/gaby-or-aguilar-ignacio-saiz/tackling -inequality-as-injustice-four-challenges-for-h. Accessed 28 August 2016; United Nations Human Rights Council. (2016, 12 January). "Report of the Independent Expert on the Effects of Foreign Debt and Other Related International Financial Obligations on the Full Enjoyment of Human Rights, Particularly Economic, Social and Cultural Rights." https://documents-dds-ny.un.org/doc/UNDOC/GEN /G16/004/23/PDF/G1600423.pdf?OpenElement. Accessed 10 May 2017.

39 Heintz, James, Diane Elson, & Radhika Balakrishnan. (2015, 4 August). "What Does Inequality Have to Do with Human Rights?," 1. Working Paper 392, Political Economy Research Institute, University of Massachusetts Amherst. https://www .peri.umass.edu/publication/item/687-what-does-inequality-have-to-do-with -human-rights. Accessed 15 November 2020.

40 Physicians for Human Rights. (2007). *Deadly Delays: Maternal Mortality in Peru: A Rights-based Approach to Safe Motherhood.* http://physiciansforhumanrights.org /library/report-2007-11-28.html.

41 Tax Justice Network. (n.d.). https://www.taxjustice.net/.

42 May, Alex. (2017). "Why Tax Dodging Is a Human Rights Issue." Oxfam. https:// views-voices.oxfam.org.uk/2017/11/tax-dodging-human-rights-issue/. Accessed 22 November 2020; CESR. (n.d.). "Advancing Tax Justice through Human Rights." http://archive.cesr.org/article.php@id=1694.html. Accessed 15 November 2020.

43 UNICEF. (2010, September). "Progress for Children: Achieving the MDGs with Equity." No. 9. https://www.unicef.org/publications/files/Progress_for_Children -No.9_EN_081710.pdf.

44 Lennox, Corinne. (2013). "Addressing Health Inequalities in the Post-2015 Development Framework." *State of the World's Minorities and Indigenous Peoples 2013.* https://minorityrights.org/wp-content/uploads/old-site-downloads /download-1273-Addressing-health-inequalities-in-the-post-2015-development -framework.pdf.

45 Pan American Health Organization. (2012). "Health Determinants and Inequalities." Ch. 2 in *Health in the Americas, 2012 Edition, Regional Volume.* https://www.paho.org/salud-en-las-americas-2012/index.

php?option=com_docman&view=download&category_slug=hia-2012
-regional-volume-19&alias=156-chapter-2-health-determinants-inequalities
-156&Itemid=231&lang=en. Accessed 15 November 2020; USAID. (2013). "The
Issue of Inequalities: A Look at the Underlying Causes of Maternal and Child
Death in Latin America and the Caribbean." Impact Blog. http://blog.usaid
.gov/2013/09/the-issue-of-inequalities-a-look-at-the-underlying-causes-of
-maternal-and-child-death-in-latin-america-and-the-caribbean/.

46 Lintelo, Dolf te. (2011). "Summary: Inequality and Social Justice Roundtable
Consultation." Institute of Development Studies and MDG Achievement Fund,
2011. http://www.ids.ac.uk/publication/inequality-and-social-justice
-roundtable-consultation; Lamba, Payal, & Anuj Sabharwal. (2014). "Public Health
in India: Challenges Ahead." http://papers.ssrn.com/sol3/papers.cfm?abstract
_id=2424919. Accessed 18 August 2016.

47 UNICEF. (2010, September). "Progress for Children: Achieving the MDGs with
Equity." No. 9, 23. https://www.unicef.org/publications/files/Progress_for
_Children-No.9_EN_081710.pdf.

48 Ibid.

49 Mendes, Helen. (2007, 30 April). "Millennium Development Goals 'beyond Brazil's
Reach.'" The Science and Development Network; Beghin, Nathalie. (2008). "Notes
on Inequality and Poverty in Brazil: Current Situation and Challenges." Oxfam
International Background Paper.

50 Dorsey, Ellen, Mayra Gomez, Bert Thiele, & Paul Nelson. (2010). "Falling Short
of Our Goals: Transforming the Millennium Development Goals into Millennium
Development Rights." *Netherlands Quarterly of Human Rights*, 28(4), 516–22.

51 USAID. (2013). "The Issue of Inequalities: A Look at the Underlying Causes of
Maternal and Child Death in Latin America and the Caribbean." Impact Blog.
http://blog.usaid.gov/2013/09/the-issue-of-inequalities-a-look-at-the
-underlying-causes-of-maternal-and-child-death-in-latin-america-and-the
-caribbean/.

52 Macan-Markar, Marwaan. (2010). "Inequality Gap Strains Thailand's MDG
Achievements." Inter-Press Service. http://www.ipsnews.net/2010/05/thailand
-inequality-gap-stains-thailandrsquos-mdg-achievements/. Accessed 15 November 2020.

53 United Nations Development Programme. (2010, 8 September). "Achieving
MDGs in India: Elimination of Inequalities and Harnessing New Opportunities for
Implementation of Policies and Programmes." On file with author; 4 pages, pp. 2 and 4.

54 United Nations Children's Fund – India. (2006). "Child Budgeting in India:
Analysis of Recent Allocations in the Union Budget," 2. https://vdocuments.
site/child-budgeting-in-india-unicef-child-budgeting-in-india-with-successi.html.
Accessed 15 November 2020.

55 UN High Commissioner on Human Rights & Center for Economic and Social
Rights. (2013). "Who Will Be Accountable? Human Rights and the Post-2015
Development Agenda." New York and Geneva: United Nations, 7–8.

56 United Nations. (2015). *The Millennium Development Goals Report 2015*. https://
www.un.org/millenniumgoals/2015_MDG_Report/pdf/MDG%202015%20
rev%20(July%201).pdf.

57 Overseas Development Institute. (2010). "Millennium Development Goals Report
Card: Measuring Progress Across Countries." https://www.odi.org/sites/odi.org
.uk/files/odi-assets/publications-opinion-files/6172.pdf. Accessed 22 August 2016.

58 Ministry of Foreign Affairs, People's Republic of China. (2016).
59 UNDP. (2013). *Humanity Divided: Confronting Inequality in Developing Countries.* http://www.undp.org/content/undp/en/home/librarypage/poverty-reduction /humanity-divided-confronting-inequality-in-developing-countries.html. Accessed 10 August 2016.
60 Ivins, Courtney. (2014). "Inequality Matters: BRICS Inequalities Fact Sheet." Oxfam/BRIC Policy Center.
61 Morley, Samuel. (2007). "Public Policies for Reducing Inequality and Poverty," 5. Paper prepared for a workshop on problems of inequality in the developing world, Project on Democracy and Development, Princeton University.
62 Bastagli, Francesca. (2010). "Poverty, Inequality and Public Cash Transfers: Lessons from Latin America." Working Paper, LSE. http://eprints.lse.ac.uk/36840/1 /Poverty%20inequality%20and%20public%20cash%20transfers%20%28lsero%29 .pdf. Accessed 15 November, 2020.
63 Lustig, Nora, Luis F. Lopez-Calva, & Eduardo Ortiz-Jaurez. (2013). "Declining Inequality in Latin America in the 2000s: The Cases of Argentina, Brazil, and Mexico." *World Development, 44*, 129–41.
64 Ivins, Courtney. (2014). "Inequality Matters: BRICS Inequalities Fact Sheet." Oxfam/BRIC Policy Center.
65 Anderson, E. (2016). "Equality as a Global Goal." *Ethics & International Affairs, 30*(2), 189–200; Donald, Kate. (2016). "Will Inequality Get Left Behind in the 2030 Agenda?" CESR, *Spotlights on the SDGs*, 80–6. https://www.2030spotlight. org/sites/default/files/contentpix/spotlight/pdfs/spotlight_ch2_10.pdf.
66 Doyle, Michael W., & Joseph E. Stiglitz. (2014). "Eliminating Extreme Inequality: A Sustainable Development Goal, 2015–2030." *Ethics and International Affairs, 28*(1), 5–13.
67 World Bank. (2019, 29 October). "Data, Low & Middle Income." https://data .worldbank.org/income-level/low-and-middle-income.
68 New Economics Foundation. (n.d.). "Reducing Economic Inequality as a Sustainable Development Goal. Measuring up the Options for beyond 2015." http://b.3cdn.net/nefoundation/226c9ea56ee0c9e510_gqm6b9zpz.pdf. Accessed 10 August 2016.
69 Donald, Kate. (2016, 31 March). "Tackling Inequality as Injustice: Four Challenges for the Human Rights Agenda." CESR. https://www.cesr.org /tackling-inequality-injustice-four-challenges-human-rights-agenda; Donald, Kate. (2016). "Will Inequality Get Left behind in the 2030 Agenda?" CESR, *Spotlights on the SDGs*, 80–6. https://www.2030spotlight.org/sites/default /files/contentpix/spotlight/pdfs/spotlight_ch2_10.pdf; Fukuda-Parr, Sakiko. (2010). "Reducing Inequality – The Missing MDG: A Content Review of PRSPs and Bilateral Donor Policy Statements." IDS Bulletin *41*(1), 26–35; MacNaughton, Gillian. (2017). "Vertical Inequalities: Are the SDGs and Human Rights up to the Challenges?" *International Journal of Human Rights, 21*(8), 1050–72; Shaheen, Faiza. (2016). "Inequality within and among Countries." In Noha Shawki (Ed.), *International Norms, Normative Change, and the UN Sustainable Development Goals*, 99–113. Lanham, MD: Lexington.
70 MacNaughton, Gillian. (2017). "Vertical Inequalities: Are the SDGs and Human Rights up to the Challenges?" *International Journal of Human Rights, 21*(8), 1050–72.
71 Fukuda-Parr, Sakiko. (2019). "Keeping Out Extreme Inequality from the SDG Agenda – The Politics of Indicators." *Global Policy Review, 10*, Supplement 1, 61–9.

72 Donald, Kate. (2016). "Will Inequality Get Left behind in the 2030 Agenda?" CESR, *Spotlights on the SDGs*, 81. https://www.2030spotlight.org/sites/default/files /contentpix/spotlight/pdfs/spotlight_ch2_10.pdf.

73 Pathfinders. (2019). "Inequality and Exclusion." https://cic.nyu.edu/sites/default /files/pathfinders-inequality-challenge-paper-updated-october.pdf. Accessed 20 January 2020.

74 United Nations. (2017, 17 July). *The Sustainable Development Goals Report 2017*. https://www.un.org/development/desa/publications/sdg-report-2017.html. For a critique, see Donald, Kate. (2017, 19 June). "The Politics of 'Progress': UN Report Paints a Highly Partial Picture of SDG Implementation." https://www.cesr.org /politics-%E2%80%98progress%E2%80%99-un-report-paints-highly-partial-picture -sdg-implementation. Accessed 23 November 2020.

75 United Nations. (2018, 20 June). *The Sustainable Development Goals Report 2018*. https://www.un.org/development/desa/publications/the-sustainable- development-goals-report-2018.html.

76 ActionAid. (2016, September). "Inequality SDGs: Countries Still Not Ready." https://actionaid.org/sites/default/files/us_not_ready_still_waiting_4_pager _final.pdf. Accessed 23 November 2020; ActionAid. (2016, 22 September). "Not Ready, Still Waiting: Governments Have a Long Way to Go in Preparing to Address Gender Inequality and the SDGs." https://actionaid.org/publications/2016/not -ready-still-waiting.

77 Lawson, Max, & Matthew Martin. (2018). "The Commitment to Reducing Inequality Index." Oxfam International & Development Finance International. https://www.oxfam.org/en/research/commitment-reducing-inequality -index-2018.

78 CESR. (2019, 6 July). "South Africa: Is Resource Mobilization Reducing Inequality?" https://www.cesr.org/south-africa-resource-mobilization-reducing -inequality. Accessed 23 November 2020.

79 Save the Children. (2014). "Leaving No One Behind: Embedding Equity in the Post-2015 Framework through Stepping Stone Targets." London: Save the Children. http://www.savethechildren.org.uk/sites/default/files/images /Leaving_No_One_Behind.pdf. Accessed 20 June 2017.

80 Global Partnership for Education. (2019). "Unlock Education for Everyone." https://www.globalpartnership.org/blog/unlock-education-everyone. Accessed 3 December 2019.

81 UN Sustainable Development Goals Knowledge Platform. (n.d.). "SDG-Education 2030 Steering Committee." https://sustainabledevelopment.un.org/index/php? page=view&type=30022&nr=100&menu=3170. Accessed 3 December 2019.

82 Donald, Kate. (2016). "Will Inequality Get Left Behind in the 2030 Agenda?" CESR, *Spotlights on the SDGs*, 81. https://www.2030spotlight.org/sites/default/files /contentpix/spotlight/pdfs/spotlight_ch2_10.pdf.

83 Max Lawson, Anam Parvaz Butt, Rowan Harvey, Diana Sarosi, Clare Coffey, Kim Piaget, & Julie Thekkudan. (2020, 20 January). "Time to Care: Unpaid and Underpaid Care Work and the Global Inequality Crisis." https://www.oxfam.org /en/research/time-care.

84 Oxfam. (2017, February). "Fiscal Accountability for Inequality Reduction." Concept Note. https://oxfamilibrary.openrepository.com/bitstream

/handle/10546/620087/pg-fair-concept-note-010217-en.pdf; Oxfam & Development Finance International. (2018). "The Commitment to Reducing Inequality Index, 2018." https://oxfamlibrary.openrepository.com/bitstream /handle/10546/620553/rr-commitment-reducing-inequality-index-2018-091018 -en.pdf. Accessed 17 July 2019.

85 Fight Inequality Alliance. (n.d.). "What Is the Fight Inequality Alliance?" https:// www.fightinequality.org/about.

86 Pathfinders. (2019). "Inequality and Exclusion." https://cic.nyu.edu/sites /default/files/pathfinders-inequality-challenge-paper-updated-october.pdf. Accessed 20 January 2020.

87 International Organization for Migration. (2020). "COVID-19 Analytical Snapshot #16: International Remittances: Understanding the Migration & Mobility Implications of COVID-19." https://www.iom.int/sites/default/files /documents/covid-19_analytical_snapshot_16_-_international_remittances.pdf.

88 World Bank. (2019, September). "Remittance Prices World Wide." *RPW Report*, Issue 31. https://remittanceprices.worldbank.org/sites/default/files/rpw _report_sept_2019.pdf.

89 Cecchetti, Stephen, & Kim Schoenholtz. (2018, 27 March). "The Stubbornly High Cost of Remittances." VoxEU. https://voxeu.org/article/stubbornly-high-cost -remittances.

90 Besley, Timothy, & Torsten Persson. (2014). "Why Do Developing Countries Tax So Little?" *Journal of Economic Perspectives*, 28(4), 99–120.

91 Cobham, Alex, & Petr Janský. (2018). "Global Distribution of Revenue Loss from Corporate Tax Avoidance: Re-estimation and Country Results." *Journal of International Development*, 30, 206–32.

92 Prichard, Wilson, Paola Salardi, & Paul Segal. (2014, 1 September) "Taxation, Non-tax Revenue and Democracy: New Evidence Using New Cross-country Data." ICTD (International Centre for Tax and Development) Working Paper 23. Available at https://ssrn.com/abstract=2496872 or http://dx.doi.org/10.2139 /ssrn.2496872.

93 Owens, Jeffrey, & Richard Parry. (2009, June). "Why Tax Matters for Development." In OECD *Observer*, No 273. Available at www.oecdobserver.org/tax.

94 CESR & Christian Aid. (2014). "A Post-2015 Fiscal Revolution, Human Rights Policy Brief." https://developmenteducation.ie/resource/a-post-2015-fiscal -revolution-human-rights-policy-brief/. Accessed 15 November 2020.

95 Ibid.

96 Ibid.

97 See CESR. (n.d.). "Advancing Tax Justice through Human Rights." http://archive .cesr.org/article.php@id=1694.html. Accessed 15 November 2020.

98 ITC & OECD. (2015). "Examples of Successful DRM Reforms and the Role of International Co-operation Discussion Paper." https://www.oecd.org/ctp/tax -global/examples-of-successful-DRM-reforms-and-the-role-of-international-co -operation.pdf. Accessed 3 December 2019.

99 Jalipa, Caroline. (2019). "Investments in Children: Evidence from Tanzania, Uganda, and Zambia." Tax Justice Network–Africa & Save the Children. https:// resourcecentre.savethechildren.net/library/investments-children-evidence-tanzania -uganda-and-zambia.

100 Sempere, Kas. (2018). "Tax Justice – How to Integrate Local Experiences into an International Campaign?" https://www.ictd.ac/blog/tax-justice-how -to-integrate-local-experiences-into-an-international-campaign/. Accessed 3 December 2019; Oxfam. (2018). "Influencing Tax Policy Reform in Vietnam: The Case of Decree 20." https://oxfamilibrary.openrepository.com/bitstream /handle/10546/620531/cs-influencing-tax-policy-vietnam-070818-en .pdf?sequence=1. Accessed 3 December 2019.

101 Green, Duncan, & Maria Faciolince. (2018, 10 August). "What Kind of Tax Campaigning Works Best in Developing Countries – Top-down or Bottom-up?" The From Poverty to Power Blog.

102 UN Women & COVID-19 Working Group. (2020). "Spotlight on Gender, Covid-19 and the SDGs: Will the Pandemic Derail Hard-won Progress on Gender Equality?" https://data.unwomen.org/sites/default/files/documents /Publications/Spotlight-Gender-COVID-19-SDGs.pdf.

103 Robinson, Mary. (2020). "COVID-19 Grassroots Justice Fund." http://www .covidjusticefund.org.

104 Piketty, Thomas. (2014). *Capital in the Twenty-first Century*. Cambridge, MA, and London: The Belknap Press of Harvard University Press.

105 Scheidel, Walter. (2017). *The Great Leveler: Violence and the History of Inequality from the Stone Age to the Twenty-first Century*. Princeton Economic History of the Western World. Princeton, NJ: Princeton University Press.

106 *Economist*. (2020, 16 May). "Why the Pandemic Could Eventually Lower Inequality. History Suggests It Could Precipitate Shifts towards a More Equal Income Distribution." Finance & economics.

107 Mason, Nathaniel, & Beatrice Mosello. (2017). "How to Reduce Inequalities in Access to WASH: Synthesis Report." London: ODI and WaterAid; Save the Children. (2014). "Leaving No One Behind: Embedding Equity in the Post-2015 Framework through Stepping Stone Targets." London: Save the Children. http:// www.savethechildren.org.uk/sites/default/files/images/Leaving_No_One _Behind.pdf. Accessed 20 June 2017.

4. Health Systems

  1 Summers, Aimee, Tolbert G. Nyenswah, Joel M. Montgomery, John Neatherlin, & Jordan W. Tappero. (2014). "Challenges in Responding to the Ebola Epidemic – Four Rural Counties, Liberia, August–November 2014." *Morbidity and Mortality Weekly Report*, 63(50), 1202–4; Sood, N., & Z. Wagner. (2017). "Social Health Insurance for the Poor: Lessons from a Health Insurance Programme in Karnataka, India." *BMJ Glob Health*, 2018;3:e000582. doi:10.1136 /bmjgh-2017-000582.

  2 UNICEF. (2010). "Brief: Moving towards Universal Health Coverage to Realize the Right to Healthcare for Every Child."

  3 World Bank. (2016). "UHC in Africa: A Framework for Action." 4. http:// documents.worldbank.org/curated/en/735071472096342073/pdf/108008-v1 -REVISED-PUBLIC-Main-report-TICAD-UHC-Framework-FINAL.pdf. Accessed 17 March 2017.

  4 World Bank. (2018). "Out of Pocket Expenditure (% of current health expenditure)." https://data.worldbank.org/indicator/SH.XPD.OOPC.CH.ZS.

5 Wagstaff, Adam, Gabriela Flores, Justine Hsu, Marc-François Smitz, Kateryna Chepynoga, Leander R. Buisman, et al. (2018). "Progress on Catastrophic Health Spending in 133 Countries: A Retrospective Observational Study." *Lancet*, 6:e169–79.

6 Krishna, A. (2011). *One Illness Away: Why People Become Poor and How They Escape Poverty*. New York: Oxford University Press.

7 Averill, Ceri. (2013, 9 October). "Universal Health Coverage: Why Health Insurance Schemes Are Leaving the Poor Behind." Briefing Paper 176, Oxfam International. https://www.oxfam.org/sites/www.oxfam.org/files/file _attachments/bp176-universal-health-coverage-091013-en__3.pdf. Accessed 29 January 2017.

8 Ibid.

9 Limwattananon, S., V. Tangcharoensathien, & P. Prakonsai. (2006). "Catastrophic and Poverty Impacts of Health Payments: Results from National Household Surveys in Thailand." *Bulletin of the World Health Organization, 85*. https://apps .who.int/iris/handle/10665/269988. Accessed 15 November 2020.

10 USAID. (2014, April–May). "Lifting Cambodia's Poorest People out of Poverty with Health Insurance." Frontlines. https://2012-2017.usaid.gov/news -information/frontlines/extreme-poverty/lifting-some-cambodias-poorest -out-of-poverty-health-insurance. Accessed 15 November 2020.

11 World Bank. (2019). Data. Population, total. https://data.worldbank.org /indicator/SP.POP.TOTL?view=chart. Accessed 23 November 2020.

12 Sood, N., & Z. Wagner. (2017). "Social Health Insurance for the Poor: Lessons from a Health Insurance Programme in Karnataka, India." *BMJ Glob Health,* 2018;3:e000582. doi:10.1136/bmjgh-2017-000582.

13 Van Doorslaer, Eddy, Owen O'Donnell, Ravi P. Rannan-Eliya, Aparnaa Somanathan, Shiva Raj Adhikari, Baktygul Akkazieva, et al. (2005, May). "Paying Out-of-pocket for Health Care in Asia: Catastrophic and Poverty Impact." EQUITAP Project Working Paper #2. http://www.equitap.org/publications/docs /EquitapWP2.pdf. Accessed 12 May 2017.

14 Rodin, Judith, & David DeFerranti. (2012). "Universal Health Coverage: The Third Global Health Transition?" *Lancet, 380*(9845), 861–2. DOI: 10.1016/S0140 -6736(12)61340-3.

15 Chapman, Audrey R. (2016). *Global Health, Human Rights and the Challenge of Neoliberal Policies*. Cambridge: Cambridge University Press.

16 Yamin, Alicia Ely. (2017). "Taking the Right to Health Seriously: Implications for Health Systems, Courts, and Achieving Universal Health Coverage." *Human Rights Quarterly, 39*(2), 341–68. doi:10.1353/hrq.2017.0021. Quotation at 351.

17 Ibid., 353.

18 Ibid.

19 WHO. (2019, 21 March). "Ten Threats to Global Health in 2019." https://www .who.int/vietnam/news/feature-stories/detail/ten-threats-to-global-health -in-2019; WHO. (2019). *Primary Health Care on the Road to Universal Health Coverage: 2019 Monitoring Report: Executive Summary*. Geneva: World Health Organization. License: CC BY-NC-SA 3.0 IGO. https://www.who.int/docs/default-source/ documents/2019-uhc-report-executive-summary.

20 Salama, Peter, & Ala Alwan. (2016, June). "Building Health Systems in Fragile States: The Instructive Example of Afghanistan." *Lancet, 4*, 351–2.

21 Travis, Phyllida, Sara Bennett, Andy Haines, Tikki Pang, Zulfiqar Bhutta, Adnan
   Ali Hyder, et al. (2004). "Overcoming Health-systems Constraints to Achieve the
   Millennium Development Goals." *Lancet, 364*, 900–6; Sandro Galea quoted in
   Bristol, Nellie. (2015, 7 April). "SDGs Require both Systems and Disease-specific
   Funding." Blog Post, "Smart Global Health." https://www.csis.org/blogs/smart
   -global-health/sdgs-require-both-systems-and-disease-specific-funding. Accessed
   18 March 2017.
22 Garrett, Laurie. (2013, August). "Existential Challenges to Global Health." New
   York: New York University Center on Global Cooperation.
23 Yamin, Alicia Ely, & Vanessa M. Boulanger. (2013). "From Transforming Power
   to Counting Numbers: The Evolution of Sexual and Reproductive Health and
   Rights in Development; and Where We Want to Go from Here." Working paper,
   The Power of Numbers Working Paper Series, School of Public Health, François-
   Xavier Bagnoud Center for Health and Human Rights, Harvard University,
   Cambridge, MA. https://fxb.harvard.edu/working-papers/. Accessed 23
   January 2020.
24 Alkema, Leontine, Vladimira Kantorova, Clare Menozzi, & Ann Biddlecom. (2013).
   "National, Regional, and Global Rates and Trends in Contraceptive Prevalence
   and Unmet Need for Family Planning between 1990 and 2015: A Systematic and
   Comprehensive Analysis." *Lancet, 381*, 1642–52.
25 Harman, Sophie. (2014, October). "Ebola and the Politics of a Global Health
   Crisis." *E-International Relations*, paragraph 4.
26 Ibid.
27 UNFPA. (2002). "Maternal Mortality Update 2002. Focus on Emergency Obstetric
   Care." https://www.unfpa.org/sites/default/files/pub-pdf/mmupdate-2002
   _eng.pdf; WHO. (2015, February). "Strategies toward Ending Preventable Maternal
   Mortality (EPMM)." https://www.who.int/reproductivehealth/topics/maternal
   _perinatal/epmm/en/.
28 Yamin, Alicia Ely, & Vanessa M. Boulanger. (2013). "From Transforming Power to
   Counting Numbers: The Evolution of Sexual and Reproductive Health and Rights
   in Development; and Where We Want to Go from Here." Working paper, The
   Power of Numbers Working Paper Series, School of Public Health, François-Xavier
   Bagnoud Center for Health and Human Rights, Harvard University, Cambridge,
   MA, 19. https://fxb.harvard.edu/working-papers/.
29 Physicians for Human Rights. (2007). *Deadly Delays: Maternal Mortality in Peru: A
   Rights-based Approach to Safe Motherhood.* http://physiciansforhumanrights.org
   /library/report-2007-11-28.html.
30 Wagstaff, Adam, Gabriela Flores, Justine Hsu, Marc-François Smitz, Kateryna
   Chepynoga, Leander R. Buisman, et al. (2018). "Progress on Catastrophic Health
   Spending in 133 Countries: A Retrospective Observational Study." *Lancet, 6*:e169–79.
   http://dx.doi.org/10.1016/S2214-109X(17)30429-1.
31 UNICEF. (n.d.). "SDG Briefing Note #6: Universal Health Coverage." file:///C:/
   Users/pjnelson/Downloads/SDG-briefing-note-6_universal-health-coverage.pdf.
   Accessed 21 October 2019.
32 Wagstaff, Adam, Gabriela Flores, Justine Hsu, Marc-François Smitz, Kateryna
   Chepynoga, Leander R. Buisman, et al. (2018). "Progress on Catastrophic Health
   Spending in 133 Countries: A Retrospective Observational Study." *Lancet, 6*:e169–79.
   http://dx.doi.org/10.1016/S2214-109X(17)30429-1.

33 USAID. (2015). "USAID's Vision for Health System Strengthening 2015–2019."
    https://www.usaid.gov/sites/default/files/documents/1864/HSS-Vision.pdf.
    Accessed 18 March 2017.

34 Wright, Simon, Ariana Childs Graham, & Bruno Rivalan. (2017). "We Should
    Spend at Least Three-quarters of Our Time on Domestic Resource Mobilisation
    if We Are Serious about Universal Health Coverage and Primary Health Care."
    https://medium.com/health-for-all/we-should-spend-at-least-three-quarters-of
    -our-time-on-domestic-resource-mobilisation-if-we-8ef849cba7ec. Accessed 30 June
    2017.

35 Sakolsatayadorn, Piyasakol. (2017). "Thailand: At the Forefront of Universal
    Health Coverage." https://medium.com/health-for-all/thailand-at-the-forefront
    -of-universal-health-coverage-d1bb9c0c3e79. Accessed 30 June 2017.

36 UHC2030. (2018). "Accelerating Political Momentum for Universal Health Coverage:
    UHC2030 Framework for Advocates." https://www.uhc2030.org/fileadmin
    /uploads/uhc2030/Documents/About_UHC2030/mgt_arrangemts___docs
    /UHC2030_Official_documents/UHC2030_Advocacy_Strategy_final_March
    _2018.pdf.

37 Shaw, R. Paul, Hong Wang, Daniel Kress, & Dana Hovig. (2015). "Donor and
    Domestic Financing of Primary Health Care in Low Income Countries." *Health
    Systems and Reform, 1*(1), 72–88, 74.

38 Mukherjee, J.S., J.K. Joseph, M.L. Rich, & S.S. Shin. (2003). "Clinical and
    Programmatic Considerations in the Treatment of MDR-TB in Children: A Series of
    16 Patients from Lima, Peru." *International Journal of Tuberculosis and Lung Disease,
    7*(7), 637–44.

39 Partners in Health. (2016). "We Build Health Systems: Caring for People in
    Chiapas, Mexico." http://www.pih.org/blog/we-build-health-systems-caring
    -for-people-in-chiapas. Accessed 15 May 2017.

40 Muchiri, Stephen. (2017). "How Kenya Can Achieve the SDGs and Universal
    Health Coverage." https://medium.com/health-for-all/how-kenya-can-achieve
    -the-sdgs-and-universal-health-coverage-21433e744e05. Accessed 30 June 2017.

41 Leal, Maria do Carmo, Ana Paula Esteves-Pereira, Elaine Fernandes Viellas,
    Rosa Maria Soares Madeira Domingues, & Silvana Granado Nogueira da
    Gama. (2020, 20 January). "Prenatal Care in the Brazilian Public Health
    Services." *Revista de Saúde Pública, 54*, 08. Epub. https://dx.doi.org/10.11606
    /s1518-8787.2020054001458; Assefa, Yibeltal, Degu Jerene, Sileshi Lulseged, Gorik
    Ooms, & Wim Van Damme. (2009). "Rapid Scale-up of Antiretroviral Treatment
    in Ethiopia: Successes and System-Wide Effects." PLOSMedicine. *Health in Action,
    6*(4). https://journals.plos.org/plosmedicine/article/file?id=10.1371/journal.
    pmed.1000056&type=printable; Manandhar, Dharma S., David Osrin, Bhim
    Prasad Shrestha, Natasha Mesko, Joanna Morrison, Kirti Man Tumbahangphe,
    et al. (2004). "Effect of a Participatory Intervention with Women's Groups on
    Birth Outcomes in Nepal: Cluster-randomised Controlled Trial." *Lancet, 364,*
    970–9; Mosquera, Paola, Jinneth Hernández, Román Vega, Jorge Martinez,
    Ronald Labont, David Sanders, & Miguel San Sebastian. (2012). "The Impact of
    Primary Healthcare in Reducing Inequalities in Child Health Outcomes, Bogotá –
    Colombia: An Ecological Analysis." *International Journal for Equity in Health, 11*(66).
    http://www.equityhealthj.com/content/11/1/66. Accessed 22 June
    2017; Christopher, Jason B., Alex Le May, Simon Lewin, & David A. Ross. (2011).

"Thirty Years after Alma-Ata: A Systematic Review of the Impact of Community Health Workers Delivering Curative Interventions against Malaria, Pneumonia and Diarrhoea on Child Mortality and Morbidity in sub-Saharan Africa." *Human Resources for Health, 9*(27). https://human-resources-health.biomedcentral.com/articles/10.1186/1478-4491-9-27. Accessed 22 June 2017.

42 Emery, Neal. (2013, 20 February). "Rwanda's Historic Health Recovery: What the U.S. Might Learn," 1. *The Atlantic.* http://www.theatlantic.com/health/archive/2013/02/rwandas-historic-health-recovery-what-the-us-might-learn/273226/.

43 Ministry of Health Rwanda, PMNCH, WHO, World Bank, AHPSR, & participants in the Rwanda multistakeholder policy review. (2014). *Success Factors for Women's and Children's Health: Rwanda.* http://www.who.int/pmnch/knowledge/publications/rwanda_country_report.pdf. Accessed 13 May 2017.

44 Worley, Heidi. (2015). "Rwanda's Success in Improving Maternal Health." Population Reference Bureau. http://www.prb.org/Publications/Articles/2015/rwanda-maternal-health.aspx.

45 Farmer, Paul, Cameron T. Nutt, Claire M. Wagner, Claude Sekabaraga, Tej Nuthulaganti, Jonathan L. Weigel, et al. (2013). "Reduced Premature Mortality in Rwanda: Lessons from Success." *British Medical Journal, 346*(65). www.bmj.com/content/346/bmj.f65.full.pdf+html. Accessed 22 January 2017.

46 Ministry of Health, Rwanda, P. Basinga, P.J. Gertler, A. Binagwaho, A.L. Soucat, J. Sturdy, & C.M. Vermeersch. (2011). "Effect on Maternal and Child Health Services in Rwanda of Payment to Primary Health-care Providers for Performance: An Impact Evaluation." *Lancet, 377*(9775), 1421–8. doi:10.1016/S0140-6736(11)60177-3. http://www.thelancet.com/journals/lancet/article/PIIS0140-6736(11)60177-3/fulltext. Accessed 13 May 2017.

47 Rosenberg, Tina. (2012, 3 July). "In Rwanda, Health Care Coverage That Eludes the U.S." *The New York Times.* http://opinionator.blogs.nytimes.com/2012/07/03/rwandas-health-care-miracle/.

48 Naik, Reshma, Lindsay Morgan, & Jenna Wright. (2014). "The Role of Health Insurance in Family Planning." Population Reference Bureau Policy Brief. http://www.prb.org/pdf15/health-insurance-family-planning.pdf. Accessed 23 January 2017.

49 Chemouni, Benjamin. (2018). "The Political Path to Universal Health Coverage: Power, Ideas and Community-based Health Insurance in Rwanda." *World Development, 106,* 87–98.

50 Averill, Ceri. (2013, 9 October). "Universal Health Coverage: Why Health Insurance Schemes Are Leaving the Poor Behind." Briefing Paper 176, Oxfam International. https://www.oxfam.org/sites/www.oxfam.org/files/file_attachments/bp176-universal-health-coverage-091013-en__3.pdf. Accessed 29 January 2017.

51 Witter, S., & B. Garshong. (2009). "Something Old or Something New? Social Health Insurance in Ghana." *BMC International Health and Human Rights, 9*(20).

52 Alhassan R.K., E. Nketiah-Amponsah, & D.K. Arhinful. (2016). "A Review of the National Health Insurance Scheme in Ghana: What Are the Sustainability Threats and Prospects?" *PLoS ONE, 11*(11), e0165151. doi:10.1371/journal. pone.0165151. Accessed 23 May 2017.

53 Kotoh, A.M., & S. Van der Geest. (2016). "Why Are the Poor Less Covered in Ghana's National Health Insurance? A Critical Analysis of Policy and Practice."

International Journal for Equity in Health. doi: 10.1186/s12939-016-0320-1. https://www.ncbi.nlm.nih.gov/pubmed/26911139. Accessed 23 May 2017.

54 Chapman, Audrey R. (2016). *Global Health, Human Rights and the Challenge of Neoliberal Policies.* Cambridge: Cambridge University Press.

55 Averill, Ceri. (2013, 9 October). "Universal Health Coverage: Why Health Insurance Schemes Are Leaving the Poor Behind." Briefing Paper 176, Oxfam International. https://www.oxfam.org/sites/www.oxfam.org/files/file_attachments/bp176-universal-health-coverage-091013-en__3.pdf. Accessed 29 January 2017.

56 Limwattananon, Supon, Viroj Tangcharoensathien, & Phusit Prakongsai. (2007). "Catastrophic and Poverty Impacts of Health Payments: Results from National Household Surveys in Thailand." *Bulletin of the World Health Organization, 85*(8), 600–6. World Health Organization. http://dx.doi.org/10.2471/BLT.06.033720. Accessed 15 November 2020.

57 Averill, Ceri. (2013, 9 October). "Universal Health Coverage: Why Health Insurance Schemes Are Leaving the Poor Behind." Briefing Paper 176, Oxfam International. https://www.oxfam.org/sites/www.oxfam.org/files/file_attachments/bp176-universal-health-coverage-091013-en__3.pdf. Accessed 29 January 2017.

58 Chapman, Audrey R. (2016). *Global Health, Human Rights and the Challenge of Neoliberal Policies.* Cambridge: Cambridge University Press, 303; Chapman, Audrey R. (2017). "Evaluating the Health-related Targets in the Sustainable Development Goals from a Human Rights Perspective." *The International Journal of Human Rights, 21*(8), 1098–1113. DOI: 10.1080/13642987.2017.1348704.

59 Schmidt, Harald, Lawrence O. Gastin, & Ezekiel J. Emanuel. (2015, 29 June). "Public Health, Universal Health Coverage, and Sustainable Development Goals: Can They Coexist?" *Lancet, 386*(9996), 928–30. DOI: https://doi.org/10.1016/S0140-6736(15)60244-6.

60 Ibid.

61 Averill, Ceri. (2013, 9 October). "Universal Health Coverage: Why Health Insurance Schemes Are Leaving the Poor Behind." Briefing Paper 176, Oxfam International. https://www.oxfam.org/sites/www.oxfam.org/files/file_attachments/bp176-universal-health-coverage-091013-en__3.pdf. Accessed 29 January 2017.

62 World Health Organization. (2010). *Health Systems Financing: The Path to Universal Coverage.* https://www.who.int/whr/2010/10_summary_en.pdf?ua=1. Accessed 31 December 2019.

63 Lagomarsino, G., A. Garabrant, A. Adyas, R. Muga, & N. Otoo. (2012). "Moving towards Universal Health Coverage: Health Insurance Reforms in Nine Developing Countries in Africa and Asia." *Lancet, 380*, 933–44; Leal, M.C., C.L. Szwarcwald, P.V.B. Almeida, E.M.L. Aquino, L. Barreto, F. Barros, & C. Victora. (2018). "Reproductive, Maternal, Neonatal and Child Health in the 30 Years since the Creation of the Unified Health System (SUS)." *Ciênc. saúde coletiva, 23*(6). http://dx.doi.org/10.1590/1413-81232018236.03942018.

64 Jowett, M., M.P. Brunal, G. Flores, & J. Cylus. (2016). "Spending Targets for Health: No Magic Number." Geneva: World Health Organization; (WHO/HIS/HGF/HF WorkingPaper/16.1; Health Financing Working Paper No. 1); http://apps.who.int/iris/bitstream/10665/250048/1/WHO-HIS-HGFHFWorkingPaper-16.1-eng.pdf. Accessed 14 May 2017.

65 Kim, Yong Jim, Paul Farmer, & E. Porter. (2013). "Redefining Global Health-care Delivery." *Lancet, 382,* 1060–9.
66 Gwatkin, Davidson R., Abbas Bhuiya, & Cesar J. Victora. (2004). "Making Health Systems More Equitable." *Lancet, 364,* 1273–80.
67 Balabanova, Dina, Anne Mills, Lesong Conteh, Baktygul Akkazieva, Hailom Bantayerga, Umakant Dash, et al. (2013). "Good Health at Low Cost 25 Years On: Lessons for the Future of Health Systems Strengthening." *Lancet, 381,* 2118–33.
68 Ibid.
69 Chen, Lincoln. (2010). "Striking the Right Balance: Health Workforce Retention in Remote and Rural Areas." *Bulletin of the World Health Organization, 88*(1-1). doi:10.2471/BLT.10.078477. Accessed 15 November 2020.
70 Wadge, Hester, Yasser Bhatti, Alexander Carter, Matthew Harris, Greg Parston, & Ara Darzi. (2016). "Brazil's Family Health Strategy: Using Community Health Workers to Provide Primary Care." The Commonwealth Fund. http://www
.commonwealthfund.org/publications/case-studies/2016/dec/~/media/files
/publications/case-study/2016/dec/1914_wadge_brazil_family_hlt_strategy
_frugal_case_study_v2.pdf.
71 Ibid.
72 UN Secretary General's High-level Panel on Access to Medicines. (2016). *Report of the SG's High-level Panel on Access to Medicines: Promoting Innovation and Access to Health Technologies.* https://static1.squarespace.com
/static/562094dee4b0d00c1a3ef761/t/57d9c6ebf5e231b2f02cd3d4/1473890031320
/UNSG+HLP+Report+FINAL+12+Sept+2016.pdf. Accessed 22 April 2017.
73 Ibid.
74 Alvarez-Uria, Gerardo, Dixon Thomas, Seeba Zachariah, Rajarajeshwari Byram, & Shanmugamari Kannan. (2014). "Cost-analysis of the WHO Essential Medicines List in a Resource-limited Setting: Experience from a District Hospital in India." *Journal of Clinical and Diagnostic Research, 8*(5): HM01–HM03. doi: 10.7860
/JCDR/2014/7976.4352.
75 MSF. (2019). "Access to Medicines: Medicines Shouldn't Be a Luxury." https://
www.msf.org/access-medicines-depth-access-campaign.
76 Baker, Brook. (2009, July). "Patents, Pricing, and Access to Essential Medicines in Developing Countries." *American Medical Association Journal of Ethics, 11*(7), 527–32.
77 MSF. (2019). "Access to Medicines: Medicines Shouldn't Be a Luxury." https://
www.msf.org/access-medicines-depth-access-campaign; Kishore, Sandeep, Kavitha Kalappa, Jordan D. Jarvis, Paul H. Park, Rachel Belt, Thirukumaran Balasubramaniam, & Rachel Kiddell-Monroe. (2015). "Overcoming Obstacles to Enable Access to Medicines for Noncommunicable Diseases in Poor Countries." *Health Affairs, 34*(9), 1569–77. doi: 10.1377/hlthaff.2015.0375.
78 Røttingen, J.A., S. Regmi, M. Eide, A.J. Young, R.F. Viergever, C. Årdal, et al. (2013). "Mapping of Available Health Research and Development Data: What's There, What's Missing, What Role Is There for a Global Observatory?" *Lancet, 382*(9900), 1286–1307.
79 Shadmi, E., Y. Chen, I. Dourado, I. Fran-Perach, J. Furler, P. Hangoma, et al. (2020, 26 June). "Health Equity and COVID-19: Global Perspectives." *International Journal for Equity in Health, 19*(1), 104. doi:10.1186/s12939-020-01218-z; Pollack, T., G. Thwaites, M. Rabaa, M. Choisy, R. van Doorn, D.H. Luong, et al. (2020). "Emerging

COVID-19 Success Story: Vietnam's Commitment to Containment." Blog post, "Our World in Data." https://ourworldindata.org/covid-exemplar-vietnam.

80 Kadakia, Kushal, & Andrea Thoumi. (2020). "The Coronavirus Is a Siren for the Health-related Sustainable Development Goals." Future Development, Brookings Institution. https://www.brookings.edu/blog/future-development/2020/05/13 /the-coronavirus-is-a-siren-for-the-health-related-sustainable-development-goals/.

81 Perry, H.B., R.S. Dhillon, A. Liu, K. Chitnis, R. Panjabi, D. Palazuelos, et al. (2016). "Community Health Worker Programmes after the 2013–2016 Ebola Outbreak." *Bulletin of the World Health Organization, 94*(7), 551–3. https://doi.org/10.2471 /BLT.15.164020; Partners in Health. (2016). "We Build Health Systems: Caring for People in Chiapas, Mexico." http://www.pih.org/blog/we-build-health-systems -caring-for-people-in-chiapas. Accessed 15 May 2017; Pollack, T., G. Thwaites, M. Rabaa, M. Choisy, R. van Doorn, D.H. Luong, et al. (2020). "Emerging COVID-19 Success Story: Vietnam's Commitment to Containment." Blog post, "Our World in Data." https://ourworldindata.org/covid-exemplar-vietnam.

82 McDonnell, Anthony, Ana F. Urrutia, & Emma Samman. (2019, December). "Reaching Universal Health Coverage: A Political Economy Review of Trends across 49 Countries." ODI Working Paper 570. https://www.odi.org/sites/odi .org.uk/files/resource-documents/200623_uhc_paper_final.pdf.

5. Access to Productive Assets: Labor

1 Edwards, M. (2011). *Thick Problems and Thin Solutions: How NGOs Can Bridge the Gap.* The Hague: Hivos.

2 Scoones, Ian. (2015). *Sustainable Livelihoods and Rural Development: Agrarian Change and Peasant Studies.* Rugby: Practical Action Publishing.

3 World Bank. (2018). "Poverty and Shared Prosperity 2018: Piecing Together the Poverty Puzzle." https://www.worldbank.org/en/publication/poverty-and -shared-prosperity.

4 ILO. (2018). *World Employment and Social Outlook: Trends 2018.* https://www.ilo .org/global/research/global-reports/weso/2018/WCMS_615594/lang-en/index .htm.

5 Ibid.

6 Fields, Gary S. (2014). "Self-employment and Poverty in Developing Countries." IZA World of Labor 2014, 6. doi: 10.15185/izawol.60.

7 UN Women. (2019). "Facts and Figures: Economic Empowerment." https://www .unwomen.org/en/what-we-do/economic-empowerment/facts-and-figures. Accessed 9 January 2020.

8 Fields, Gary S. (2013). "Self-employment in the Developing World." Background paper submitted to the High-level Panel on the Post-2015 Development Agenda, May 2013, 1. http://www.post2015hlp.org/wp-content/uploads/2013/05/Fields _Self-Employment-in-the-Developing-World.pdf. Accessed 17 September 2016.

9 Nowak, M. (2005). "A Human Rights Approach to Poverty." In *Human Rights in Development Yearbook 2002. Empowerment, Participation, Accountability and Non-discrimination: Operationalising a Human Rights-based Approach to Development*, 15–36. Leiden: Martinus Nijhoff Publishers.

10 Maxwell, S. (2001). "Heaven or Hubris: Reflections on the New 'New Poverty Agenda.'" *Development Policy Review, 21*(1), 5–25.

11 UN Millennium Project. (2005). *A Practical Plan to Achieve the Millennium Development Goals*. http://www.unmillenniumproject.org/reports/fullreport.htm. Accessed 25 April 2015.

12 Brooks, S., M. Leach, H. Lucas, & E. Millstone. (2009). "Silver Bullets, Grand Challenges and the New Philanthropy." STEPS Working Paper 24. Brighton: STEPS Centre. http://www.ids.ac.uk/files/dmfile/STEPSWorkingPaper24.pdf. Accessed 7 June 2017.

13 UN. (2016). *The Millennium Development Goals Report 2015*. https://www.un.org/millenniumgoals/2015_MDG_Report/pdf/MDG%202015%20rev%20(July%201).pdf.

14 Kenny, Charles, with Sarah Dykstra. (2013). "The Global Partnership for Development: A Review of MDG 8 and Proposals for the Post-2015 Development Agenda." Washington, DC: Center for Global Development. http://www.cgdev.org/sites/default/files/global-partnership-development_0.pdf. Accessed 30 December 2016.

15 OECD. (n.d.). "Trends in Aid to Agriculture and Rural Development (ARD)." http://www.oecd.org/dac/stats/Trends%20in%20aid%20to%20Agriculture%20and%20Rural%20Development.pdf.

16 Food and Agriculture Organization of the United Nations. (2009, September). "Rapid Assessment of Aid Flows for Agricultural Development in Sub-Saharan Africa." Investment Centre Division Discussion Paper. http://www.fao.org/fileadmin/templates/tci/pdf/SSAAid09.pdf. Accessed 30 December 2016.

17 Swindale, Anne, & Paula Belinsky. (2006, 2 September). "Household Dietary Diversity Score (HDDS) for Measurement of Household Food Access: Indicator Guide VERSION 2." http://www.fantaproject.org/sites/default/files/resources/HDDS_v2_Sep06_0.pdf. Accessed 12 February 2017.

18 Fukuda-Parr, Sakiko, & Amy Orr. (2013). "The MDG Hunger Target and the Contested Visions of Food Security." Harvard School of Public Health, Harvard University FXB Center for Health and Human Rights, and The New School, Working Paper Series, *The Power of Numbers: A Critical Review of MDG Targets for Human Development and Human Rights*, 38–9.

19 UN Economic Commission for Africa. (2015). *MDG Report 2015: Lessons Learned in Implementing the MDGs*. http://www.undp.org/content/undp/en/home/librarypage/mdg/mdg-reports/africa-collection.html. Accessed 7 September 2016; United Nations Department of Economic and Social Affairs, Youth. (2018). *World Youth Report: Youth and the 2030 Agenda for Sustainable Development*. https://www.un.org/development/desa/youth/world-youth-report/wyr2018.html.

20 UN Economic Commission for Africa. (2015). *MDG Report 2015: Lessons Learned in Implementing the MDGs*, 66. http://www.undp.org/content/undp/en/home/librarypage/mdg/mdg-reports/africa-collection.html.

21 Ministry of Rural Development (India). (2019). "The Mahatma Gandhi National Rural Employment Guarantee Act 2005." https://nrega.nic.in/netnrega/home.aspx. Accessed 13 December 2019.

22 Zepeda, Eduardo, Scott McDonald, Manoj Panda, & Ganesh Kumar. (2013). *Employing India, Guaranteeing Jobs for the Rural Poor*. Carnegie Endowment and UNDP. http://carnegieendowment.org/2013/02/11/employing-india-guaranteeing-jobs-for-rural-poor-pub-50856. Accessed 17 September 2016.

23 Anderson, Stephen, & Elisabeth Farmer. (2015). *USAID Office of Food for Peace Food Security Country Framework for Ethiopia FY 2016 – FY 2020*. Washington, DC: Food Economy Group. https://www.usaid.gov/sites/default/files/documents/1866 /Ethiopia%20Food%20Security%20Country%20Framework_Final%20Oct%202015 .pdf. Accessed 13 December 2019.

24 Admassie A., & D. Abebaw. (2014). "Rural Poverty and Marginalization in Ethiopia: A Review of Development Interventions." In J. von Braun & F. Gatzweiler (Eds.), *Marginality*. Dordrecht: Springer.

25 Gebre, Samuel. (2019, July). "Ethiopian PM Says Reforms Will Deliver 3 Million Jobs in 2019–20." Bloomburg. https://www.bloomberg.com/news /articles/2019-07-02/ethiopian-pm-says-reforms-will-deliver-3-million-jobs -in-2019-20.

26 Nguyen, Khiem. (2020, 7 July). "Policy Seminar: Social Safety Nets as a COVID-19 Response to Protect Food Security and Nutrition." International Food Policy Research Institute. https://www.ifpri.org/blog/policy-seminar-social-safety-nets -covid-19-response-protect-food-security-and-nutrition.

27 Gentilini, Ugo. (2020). "Weekly Social Protection Links." https://www .ugogentilini.net/.

28 World Bank. (2015, June). "Working to End Poverty in Latin America and the Caribbean – Workers, Jobs, and Wages," 34. LAC Poverty and Labor Brief. Washington, DC: World Bank. Doi: 10.1596/978-1-4648-0685-8. http://documents. worldbank.org/curated/en/612441468196449946/pdf/97209-REVISED-WP -PUBLIC-Box394816B.pdf. Accessed 7 September 2016.

29 ILO. (2014, 5 December). "Wages in Asia and the Pacific: Dynamic but Uneven Progress." Supplement to the Global Wage Report 2014/15. http://www.ilo .org/wcmsp5/groups/public/-asia/-ro-bangkok/-sro-bangkok/documents /publication/wcms_325219.pdf. Accessed 4 February 2017.

30 World Bank. (2015, June). "Working to End Poverty in Latin America and the Caribbean – Workers, Jobs, and Wages," 38–9. LAC Poverty and Labor Brief. Washington, DC: World Bank. Doi: 10.1596/978-1-4648-0685-8.

31 Soares, Sergei, & Joana Silva. (2018). "The Effects of Minimum Wage Policy on Wage Inequality – Evidence from Latin America." *Policy in Focus, 15*(2), 12–17.

32 ILO. (2018). *Minimum Wage Policy Guide*. https://www.ilo.org/global/topics /wages/minimum-wages/lang--en/index.htm. Accessed 15 November 2020.

33 Singapore Business Review. (2019, 7 May). "SEA May Lose Business Appeal as Minimum Wage Skyrockets 82% in 2019." https://sbr.com.sg/economy/asia/sea -may-lose-business-appeal-minimum-wage-skyrockets-82-in-2019.

34 Asia Floor Wage Alliance. (n.d.). "Living Wage Now." https://asia.floorwage.org/.

35 ILO. (2014, 5 December). "Wages in Asia and the Pacific: Dynamic but Uneven Progress." Supplement to the Global Wage Report 2014/15. http://www.ilo .org/wcmsp5/groups/public/-asia/-ro-bangkok/-sro-bangkok/documents /publication/wcms_325219.pdf. Accessed 4 February 2017.

36 Ibid.

37 Botos, K. (2013, 1 October). "Economic Growth without Jobs?" *Public Finance Quarterly* online. http://www.penzugyiszemle.hu/fokuszban/gazdasagi-novekedes -munkahelyek-nelkul.

38 Ibid.

39 World Bank. (2017). "Growing the Rural Nonfarm Economy to Alleviate Poverty: An Evaluation of the Contribution of the World Bank Group." http://ieg .worldbankgroup.org/sites/default/files/Data/Evaluation/files/RuralNonFarm .pdf. Accessed 23 November 2020.

40 Wiggins, Steve, & Peter Hazell. (2011). "Access to Rural Non-farm Employment and Enterprise Development." Background paper for the IFAD Rural Poverty Report 2011. http://citeseerx.ist.psu.edu/viewdoc/download?doi=10.1.1.639.971& rep=rep1&type=pdf. Accessed 5 February 2017.

41 Ibid.

42 Villalobos Barría, Carlos, & Stephan Klasen. (2016). "The Impact of SENAI's Vocational Training Programme on Employment, Wages, and Mobility in Brazil: What Lessons for Sub Saharan Africa?" *The Quarterly Review of Economics and Finance, 62*, 74–96.

43 Wiggins, Steve, & Peter Hazell. (2011). "Access to Rural Non-farm Employment and Enterprise Development." Background paper for the IFAD Rural Poverty Report 2011. http://citeseerx.ist.psu.edu/viewdoc/download?doi=10.1.1.639.971& rep=rep1&type=pdf. Accessed 5 February 2017.

44 Trade Union Development Cooperation Network. (2018). "A Trade Union Take on the SDGs." https://www.ituc-csi.org/IMG/pdf/tudcn_sdgs_global_report_2018 _en.pdf.

45 ILO. (2018). "Building Social Protection Floors with the ILO Together, to Change Millions of Lives in Senegal." https://www.social-protection.org/gimi /RessourcePDF.action?ressource.ressourceId=52900.

46 Fields, Gary. (2012). "Challenges and Policy Lessons for the Growth-Employment-Poverty Nexus in Developing Countries." *Journal of Labor Policy, 1*(6). http://www .izajolp.com/content/1/1/6.

47 UN Habitat. (2006). "Innovative Policies for the Urban Informal Economy," 17. http://unhabitat.org/books/innovative-policies-for-the-urban-informal -economy/. Accessed 18 September 2016.

48 Fields, Gary. (2012). "Challenges and Policy Lessons for the Growth-Employment-Poverty Nexus in Developing Countries" *Journal of Labor Policy, 1*(6). http://www .izajolp.com/content/1/1/6.

49 WIEGO (Women in Informal Employment: Globalizing and Organizing). (2016). "Impact: Colombia's Triumphant *Recicladores.*" http://wiego.org/sites/wiego .org/files/resources/files/Impact_Colombias_Triumphant_Recicladores.pdf. Accessed 15 November 2020.

50 WIEGO. (n.d.). "Links with Poverty." http://wiego.org/informal-economy /links-poverty. Accessed 18 September 2016; WIEGO. (n.d.). "Winning Legal Rights for Thailand's Homeworkers." https://www.wiego.org/sites/default /files/resources/files/WIEGO-Winning-legal-rights-Thailands-homeworkers.pdf. Accessed 15 November 2020.

51 WIEGO. (n.d.). "Links with Poverty." http://wiego.org/informal-economy/links -poverty.

52 Frankson, Liest. (2017, 6 September). "Waste Project Expected to Create Jobs." *Infrastructure News.* https://infrastructurenews.co.za/2017/09/06/waste-project -expected-to-create-jobs/; Stuart, Elizabeth, Emma Samman, & Abigail Hunt. (2018, January). "Informal Is the New Normal: Improving the Lives of Workers at Risk of Being Left Behind." Working and discussion papers, Overseas Development

Institute. https://www.odi.org/publications/11025-informal-new-normal
-improving-lives-workers-risk-being-left-behind; WIEGO. (2018). "Your Toolkit on
ILO Convention 189 – The Domestic Workers' Convention." http://www.wiego
.org/sites/default/files/resources/files/Domestic_Worker_Toolkit_WIEGO
_IDWF_Web.pdf. Accessed 16 September 2019.

53 Aying, Maricel. (n.d.). "Salient Features of Kasambahay Law IRR." https://www
.scribd.com/document/186009525/Salient-Features-of-Kasambahay-Law-IRR.

54 WIEGO. (2018). "Your Toolkit on ILO Convention 189 – The Domestic Workers'
Convention." http://www.wiego.org/sites/default/files/resources/files
/Domestic_Worker_Toolkit_WIEGO_IDWF_Web.pdf. Accessed 16 September 2019.

55 Castaño, Pablo. (2018, January). "Laws, Legitimacy and Ongoing Struggle: Lessons
from Bolivian Policies on Domestic Workers' Rights." WIEGO Policy No. 17.

56 Ibid.

57 UN Women. (n.d.). "Domestic Workers Count Too: Implementing Protections for
Domestic Workers." https://www.ituc-csi.org/IMG/pdf/unwomen_iutc
_factsheets.pdf. Accessed 20 September 2019.

58 ILO. (2017). "Towards Safer Working Conditions in the Bangladesh Ready-made
Garment Sector." https://www.ilo.org/wcmsp5/groups/public/-asia/-ro
-bangkok/-ilo-dhaka/documents/publication/wcms_614088.pdf. Accessed
17 September 2019; US Department of Labor. (2018). "CLIMB: Child Labor
Improvements in Bangladesh." https://www.dol.gov/agencies/ilab/climb.
Accessed 17 September 2019.

59 Díaz, Juan Jóse, Juan Chacaltuna, Jamele Rigolini, & Claudia Ruiz. (2018, 12
September). "Pathways to Formalization: Going Beyond the Formality Dichotomy:
The Case of Peru." Washington, DC: World Bank. https://elibrary.worldbank.org
/doi/abs/10.1596/1813-9450-8551. Accessed 15 November 2020.

60 Latitud R. (2020). "Latitud R: Que Hacemos? (What Do we Do?)." https://latitudr
.org/que-hacemos/. Accessed 15 November 2020.

61 World Bank Open Data. (2019). https://data.worldbank.org/indicator/ny.gdp
.mktp.kd.zg.

62 Alston, Philip. (2020). "The Parlous State of Poverty Eradication. Report of the
Special Rapporteur on Extreme Poverty and Human Rights." Human Rights
Council Forty-fourth session, 15 June–3 July 2020. https://chrgj.org/wp-content
/uploads/2020/07/Alston-Poverty-Report-FINAL.pdf.

63 UN Department of Economic and Social Affairs. (2018). *World Youth Report: Youth
and the 2030 Agenda for Sustainable Development.* New York: United Nations; Steiner,
Roberto, Norberto Rojas, & Natalia Millán. (2010). "Evaluación de impacto del
programa jóvenes rurales emprendedores del Servicio Nacional de Aprendizaje
– SENA: Informe final." Calle, Colombia: Cen-tro de Investigación Económica y
Social (Fedesarrollo). Available from http://www.repository.fedesarrollo.org.co
/handle/11445/350. Accessed 15 November 2020.

64 UNESCO-UNEVOC. (2017, 23–27 October). "UNEVOC TVET Leadership
Programme for Southern and Eastern Africa Capacity Building for
Transformational TVET Leaders: Vision, Knowledge and Skills." Harare,
Zimbabwe HARHAR/ED/2017/TVET/1. https://unesdoc.unesco.org
/ark:/48223/pf0000261548.locale=en. Accessed 23 November 2020; UN Department
of Economic and Social Affairs. (2018). *World Youth Report: Youth and the 2030
Agenda for Sustainable Development.* New York: United Nations.

65 Ismail, Zenobia. (2018). "Lessons Learned from Youth Employment Programmes in Developing Countries." https://gsdrc.org/wp-content/uploads/2018/03/Lessons_Learned_from_Youth_Employment_Programmes.pdf.

66 Gower, Richard, & Patrick Schröder. (2016). "Virtuous Circle: How the Circular Economy Can Create Jobs and Save Lives in Low and Middle-income Countries." Tearfund and Institute for Development Studies. http://www.ids.ac.uk/files/dmfile/TearfundVirtuousCircle-2.pdf. Accessed 15 June 2017.

67 Sundaravadivel, M., S. Vigneswaran, & C. Visvanathan. (2006). *Waste Minimization in Metal Finishing Industries.* www.eolss.net/sample-chapters/c07/e2-14-02-05.pdf. Accessed 24 April 2016; Pochman, M. (2015). *Policies for the Formalization of Micro and Small Enterprises in Brazil.* ILO; Schmitz, H. (2015). "Africa's Biggest Recycling Hub?" IDS blog. www.ids.ac.uk/opinion/africa-s-biggest-recycling-hub; Simonds, Matt. (n.d.). "Decent Work for All by 2030: Taking on the Private Sector." SDG 8, *Spotlights on the SDGs,* 68–72. Accessed 5 February 2017.

68 Schmitz, H. (2015). "Africa's Biggest Recycling Hub?" IDS blog. www.ids.ac.uk/opinion/africa-s-biggest-recycling-hub.

69 MacNaughton, Gillian, & Diane F. Frey. (2016). "Decent Work, Human Rights and the Sustainable Development Goals." *Georgetown Journal of International Law, 47,* 609–63.

70 United Nations General Assembly. (2015). "Transforming Our World: The 2030 Agenda for Sustainable Development." Resolution adopted by the General Assembly on 25 September 2015. Resolution 70/1. http://www.un.org/ga/search/view_doc.asp?symbol=A/RES/70/1&Lang=E. Accessed 4 September 2016.

71 ILO. (2020). "ILO Monitor: COVID-19 and the World of Work. Fifth edition: Updated estimates and analysis." https://www.ilo.org/wcmsp5/groups/public/@dgreports/@dcomm/documents/briefingnote/wcms_749399.pdf.

72 Dias, Sonia. (2020). "How Cooperatives Can Help Brazil's Waste Pickers Build Back from COVID-19." ILO Blog. http://iloblog.org/2020/07/03/how-cooperatives-can-help-waste-pickers-build-back-from-covid-19/.

73 WIEGO. (2020). "Impact of Public Health Measures on Informal Workers Livelihoods and Health." https://www.wiego.org/sites/default/files/resources/file/Impact_on_livelihoods_COVID-19_final_EN_1.pdf.

74 Gentilini, Ugo. (2020). "Weekly Social Protection Links." https://www.ugogentilini.net/.

6. Access to Productive Assets: Land

1 Malawi National Statistical Office. (2017). *Malawi Demographic and Health Survey 2016–2016.* https://dhsprogram.com/pubs/pdf/FR319/FR319.pdf. Accessed 16 December 2019.

2 Devereux, Stephen, Bapu Vaitla, & Samuel Hauenstein Swan. (2008). *Seasons of Hunger.* London: Pluto Press.

3 IFAD. (2008). "Improving Access to Land and Tenure Security." http://www.cpahq.org/cpahq/cpadocs/Land%20Access%20Rural%20Communities.pdf. Accessed 30 September 2016.

4 Boto, Isolina, Estherine Fotabong, Felicity Proctor, Isaura Lopes, & Hawa Kebe. (2012). "Major Drivers for Rural Transformation in Africa: Resources on Rural Transformation in Africa." Brussels Rural Development Briefings, Briefing No. 24,

Resources on Rural Transformation in Africa, at https://brusselsbriefings.files
.wordpress.com/2012/10/br-24-rural-transformation-in-africa-eng.pdf. Accessed
16 November 2020; Landesa (Center for Women's Land Rights). (2012). "Women's
Secure Rights to Land: Benefits, Barriers and Best Practices." Issue Brief. http://
www.landesa.org/wp-content/uploads/Landesa-Women-and-Land-Issue-Brief
.pdf. Accessed 17 September 2016; IFAD. (n.d.). "Land Tenure Security and Poverty
Reduction." https://www.ifad.org/documents/10180/0f715abf-3f59-41f6-ac08
-28403ebd271f. Accessed 14 September 2016.

5 Deininger, Klaus, Tram Hoang, & Songqing Jin. (2016). "Does Tenure Security
Allow More Efficiency-enhancing Land Transactions? Evidence from Vietnam over
a Ten-year Period." Agricultural and Applied Economics Association, 2016 Annual
Meeting, 31 July–2 August 2016, Boston, MA 236565.

6 Prosterman, Roy, Robert Mitchell, & Tim Hanstad. (2009). *One Billion Rising: Law,
Land, and the Alleviation of Global Poverty.* Leiden: University of Leiden, 2009.

7 Stehfest, Elke, Willem Jan van Zeist, Hugo Valin, Petr Havlik, Alexander Popp,
Page Kyle, et al. (2019). "Key Determinants of Global Land-use Projections."
Nature, 10(2166), 1–10. https://doi.org/10.1038/s41467-019-09945-w.

8 Santos, F., D. Fletschner, V. Savath, & A. Peterman. (2014). "Can Government-
allocated Land Contribute to Food Security? Intrahousehold Analysis of West
Bengal's Microplot Allocation Program." *World Development, 64*, 860–72. https://
doi.org/10.1016/j.worlddev.2014.07.017.

9 Ali, D.A., K. Deininger, & M. Goldstein. (2014). "Environmental and Gender
Impacts of Land Tenure Regularization in Africa: Pilot Evidence from Rwanda."
Journal of Development Economics, 110, 262–75; Asia-Pacific Forum on Law and
Development. (2017). "Changing Development from the Inside-Out." http://
apwld.org/wp-content/uploads/2018/10/2017-BOOM-RIW-FPAR-Regional
-Report.pdf; Robinson, Brian E., Yuta J. Masuda, Allison Kelly, Maggie Holland,
Charles Bedford, Malcolm Childress, et al. (2018, March/April). "Incorporating
Land Tenure Security into Conservation." *Conservation Letters, 11*(2), 1–12.

10 Agarwal, B. (1994). *A Field of One's Own: Gender and Land Rights in South Asia.*
Cambridge: Cambridge University Press; Deere, Carmen Diana, & Magdalena
León. (2001). *Empowering Women: Land and Property Rights in Latin America.*
Pittsburgh: University of Pittsburgh Press; Lastarria-Cornhiel, S. (1997). "Impact of
Privatization on Gender and Property Rights in Africa." *World Development, 25*(8),
1317–33; Quisumbing, A.R., & J. Maluccio. (2003, 4 June). "Resources at Marriage
and Intrahousehold Allocation: Evidence from Bangladesh, Ethiopia, Indonesia,
and South Africa." *Oxford Bulletin of Economic Statistics, 65*(3), 283–327; Lastarria-
Cornhiel, Susana, Julia A. Behrman, Ruth Meinzen-Dick, & Agnes R. Quisumbing.
(2014). "Gender Equity and Land: Toward Secure and Effective Access for Rural
Women." In Agnes R. Quisumbing, Ruth Meinzen-Dick, Terri L. Raney, André
Croppenstedt, Julia A. Behrman, & Amber Peterman (Eds.), *Gender in Agriculture:
Closing the Knowledge Gap,* 117–44. Washington, DC: IFPRI, Springer and FAO.

11 Asiimwe, J. (2014). "Making Women's Land Rights a Reality in Uganda: Advocacy for
Co-ownership by Spouses." *Yale Human Rights and Development Journal, 4*(1). http://
digitalcommons.law.yale.edu/cgi/viewcontent.cgi?article=1026&context=yhrdlj.

12 Gómez, Mayra, & D. Hien Tran. (2012, October). "Women's Land and Property
Rights and the Post-2015 Development Agenda." Global Thematic Consultation on
Addressing Inequalities.

13 Benbih, K., & J. Katz. (2014). "Land Tenure Rights for Women under Customary Law." https://landwise.resourceequity.org/records/2738; Scalise, E. (2009). "Women's Inheritance Rights to Land and Property in South Asia: A Study of Afghanistan, Bangladesh, India, Nepal, Pakistan, and Sri Lanka." *Rural Institute Development Report*. https://www.landesa.org/wp-content/uploads/WJF -Womens-Inheritance-Six-South-Asian-Countries.FINAL_12-15-09.pdf.
14 Food and Agriculture Organization of the United Nations. (n.d.). "Gender and Land Rights Database." http://www.fao.org/gender-landrights-database/data -map/statistics/en/. Accessed 23 December 2019.
15 Open Societies Foundation. (2014). "Securing Women's Land and Property Rights." https://www.opensocietyfoundations.org/publications/securing-womens-land -and-property-rights.
16 Ibid.
17 Landesa. (n.d.). "Gender and Land: Good Practices and Lessons Learned from Four Millennium Challenge Corporation Compact-funded Land Projects." https:// www.yumpu.com/en/document/read/31428981/landesa-gender-land-report -mcc-2014.
18 Duncan, Jennifer, & Fiona Noonan. (2016). "Women's Land Rights Key to Enacting Gender-responsive International Climate Change Action." http://voices .nationalgeographic.com/2016/09/07/womens-land-rights-key-to-enacting -gender-responsive-international-climate-change-action/. Retrieved 29 December 2016.
19 El-Ghonemi, M.R. (2003). "Land Reform Development Challenges of 1963–2003 Continue into the 21st Century." *Land Reform (FAO), 2,* 32–43.
20 Grabowski, Richard. (2002). "East Asia, Land Reform and Economic Development." *Canadian Journal of Development Studies, 23*(1), 105–26; Kay, Cristobál. (2002). "Why East Asia Overtook Latin America: Agrarian Reform, Industrialisation and Development." *Third World Quarterly, 23*(6), 1073–1102.
21 El-Ghomenei, M.R. (2003). "Land Reform Development Challenges of 1963–2003 Continue into the 21st Century." *Land Reform (FAO), 2,* 32–43.
22 Sida. (n.d.) "Quick Guide to What and How: Increasing Women's Access to Land." Women's Economic Empowerment Series. http://www.oecd.org/dac/gender -development/47566053.pdf. Accessed 9 March 2016.
23 Ibid., 5.
24 Albertus, Michael. (2015). *Autocracy and Redistribution: The Politics of Land Reform.* Cambridge: Cambridge University Press.
25 Bell, Keith C. (n.d.). "Study on Gender Impacts of Land Titling in Post-Tsunami Aceh, Indonesia." http://documents1.worldbank.org/curated /pt/126381468285613599/pdf/635270WP0P075001B00PUBLIC00Aceh0web.pdf; Zakout, Wael. (2020, 20 January). "How Joint Land Titles Help Women's Economic Empowerment: The Case of Vietnam." World Bank Blog. https://blogs.worldbank .org/voices/how-joint-land-titles-help-women-s-economic-empowerment-case -vietnam. Accessed 16 November 2020.
26 Girma, Hirut, & Renée Giovarelli. (2013). "Gender Implications of Joint Land Titles in Ethiopia." Focus on Land. http://www.focusonland.com/countries /gender-implications-of-joint-titling-in-ethiopia/. Accessed 5 February 2017; Herrera Arango, Johana, Adriana Beltrán, Pablo Ramos, Mauricio González, Lina Abella, Ana Maria Sierra, et al. (2018). "Context, Figures and Trends in

Governance of Land Tenure in Colombia LANDex – Pilot Experience." On file
with the author; Hildenbrand, Emily, & Rekha Panigrahi. (n.d.). "CARE India
Partners with LANDESA to Increase Women's Land Literacy." http://www
.carepathwaystoempowerment.org/care-india-partners-landesa-increase-womens
-land-literacy/.

27 FAO. (2018). "Realizing Women's Rights to Land in the Law. A Guide for Reporting
on SDG Indicator 5.a.2." http://www.fao.org/3/I8785EN/i8785en.pdf. Accessed
16 August 2018; Massay, Godfrey. (2018). "Addressing Women's Land Rights Using
the SDGs Framework: Experience from Tanzania." Paper prepared for presentation
at the 2018 World Bank Conference on Land and Poverty. The World Bank –
Washington, DC, 19–23 March 2018.

28 Chaves, Patricia, Jolyne Sanjak, & Malcolm Childress. (2017). "Local Movement
Leveraging the Sustainable Development Goals to Strengthen Women's Land
Rights in Brazil." https://www.landesa.org/blog-local-movement-leveraging
-sustainable-development-goals-strengthen-womens-land-rights-brazil/.
Accessed 30 June 2017.

29 Chaves, Patricia. (2018). "Benchmarking Real Change for Women to Secure
Land by Bridging Data and Social Movement." https://gltn.net/2018/07/10
/benchmarking-real-change-for-women-to-secure-land-by-bridging-data-and
-social-movement/. Accessed 16 November 2020.

30 Massay, Godfrey. (2018). "Addressing Women's Land Rights Using the SDGs
Framework: Experience from Tanzania." Paper prepared for presentation at the
2018 World Bank Conference on Land and Poverty. The World Bank – Washington
DC, 19–23 March 2018.

31 USAID. (2018, 2 April). "Land Front and Center in Colombia." USAID Landlinks;
Landesa. (n.d.). "What We Do: Landesa in Liberia." http://www.landesa.org
/what-we-do/sub-saharan-africa/landesa-in-liberia/. Accessed 6 March 2017.

32 Herrera Arango, Johana, Adriana Beltrán, Pablo Ramos, Mauricio González,
Lina Abella, Ana Maria Sierra, et al. (2018). "Context, Figures and Trends in
Governance of Land Tenure in Colombia LANDex – Pilot Experience." On file
with the author.

33 Ibid.

34 Mwangi, Wangu. (2018, 4 October). "Landesa, UNEP and Partners Unveil
Initiatives to Protect Land, Environmental Rights." IISD Knowledge Hub. https://
sdg.iisd.org/news/landesa-unep-and-partners-unveil-initiatives-to-protect-land
-environmental-rights/.

35 Knox, A., A. Kes, & N. Milici. (2007). "Mending the Gap between Law and Practice:
Organizational Approaches for Women's Property Rights." http://www.icrw.org
/publications/mending-gap-between-law-and-practice-organizational-approaches
-womens-property-rights. Accessed 15 January 2020.

36 Sida. (n.d.). "Quick Guide to What and How: Increasing Women's Access to Land,"
6. Women's Economic Empowerment Series. http://www.oecd.org/dac/gender
-development/47566053.pdf. Accessed 9 March 2016.

37 Ibid.

38 UN Economic Commission for Africa. (2015). "Assessing Progress in Africa
toward the Millennium Development Goals MDG Report," 1. https://studylib.
net/doc/12224058/assessing-progress-in-africa-toward-the-millennium-develo...
Accessed 16 November 2020.

39 Government of Rwanda. (2013). "Millennium Development Goals Rwanda: Final Report 2013." http://www.in.undp.org/content/dam/undp/library/MDG /english/MDG%20Country%20Reports/Rwanda/Rwanda_MDGR_2015.pdf. Accessed 6 October 2016.

40 IFAD. (n.d.). "Land Tenure Security and Poverty Reduction." https://www .ifad.org/documents/10180/0f715abf-3f59-41f6-ac08-28403ebd271f. Accessed 14 September 2016; International Women's Rights Action Watch Asia-Pacific. (2010). "Participating in ICESCR and CEDAW Reporting Processes: Guidelines for Writing on Women's Economic, Social and Cultural Rights in Shadow/Alternative Reports." https://www.peacewomen.org/node/90373. Accessed 16 November 2020; IFAD. (2008). "Improving Access to Land and Tenure Security." http:// www.cpahq.org/cpahq/cpadocs/Land%20Access%20Rural%20Communities. pdf. Accessed 30 September 2016; IFAD. (2012). "Land Rights and Agricultural Productivity: Issue Brief." Briefing no. 24, Resources on Rural Transformation in Africa, Brussels Rural Development Briefings; IFAD. (2014). "Irrigation Development in Malawi: A Pillar for Food Security and Improved Nutrition." https://ifad-un.blogspot.com/2014/07/irrigation-development-in-malawi-pillar .html. Accessed 22 January 2020.

41 IFAD. (n.d.). "Land Tenure Security and Poverty Reduction." https://www .ifad.org/documents/10180/0f715abf-3f59-41f6-ac08-28403ebd271f. Accessed 14 September 2016.

42 Land Rights. (2015, 22 October). "Land Rights: An Essential Global Indicator for the Post-2015 SDGs." https://www.landesa.org/wp-content/uploads/Land -Rights-An-Essential-Global-Indicator-Sep-2-2015-Endorsed.pdf.

43 Moser, Caroline. (2007). *Reducing Global Poverty: The Case for Asset Accumulation.* Washington, DC: Brookings Institution Press.

44 Gilbert, Jérémie. (2013). "Land Rights as Human Rights." *SUR 18,* 115. https://sur .conectas.org/en/land-rights-human-rights/. Accessed 1 November 2020; Wickeri, Elisabeth, & Anil Kalhan. (2010). "Land Rights Issues in International Human Rights Law." *Malaysian Journal on Human Rights,* 4(10). Available at SSRN: https:// ssrn.com/abstract=1921447; Rights and Resources Initiative. (2017). "Rights and Resources Initiative 2018–2022. Third Strategic Program from the Rights and Resources Initiative (RRI)." http://rightsandresources.org/wp-content /uploads/2017/12/Strategic-Program-2018-2022_RRI_Dec-2017.pdf.

45 FAO. (2012). "Voluntary Guidelines on the Responsible Governance of Tenure of Land, Fisheries and Forests in the Context of National Food Security." http:// www.fao.org/3/a-i2801e.pdf.

46 Parmentier, Stephane. (2014). "Two Years On: What Became of 'The Guidelines on the Responsible Governance of Tenure of Land, Fisheries and Forests?'" https://blogs.oxfam.org/en/blogs/14-05-13-two-years-guidelines-responsible -governance-tenure-land-fisheries-and-forests; Pearshouse, Richard, & Jurema Werneck. (2020, 19 April). "Land Seizures and COVID-19: The Twin Threats to Brazil's Indigenous Peoples." Amnesty International. https://www .amnesty.org/en/latest/news/2020/04/land-seizures-and-covid-19-the-twin -threats-to-brazils-indigenous-peoples/; Quisumbing, A.R., & J. Maluccio. (2003). "Resources at Marriage and Intrahousehold Allocation: Evidence from Bangladesh, Ethiopia, Indonesia, and South Africa." *Oxford Bulletin of Economic Statistics,* 65(3), 283–327.

47 Gómez, Mayra, & D. Hien Tran. (2012, October). "Women's Land and Property Rights and the Post-2015 Development Agenda," 3. Global Thematic Consultation on Addressing Inequalities.

48 CESCR. (1997, 20 May). "The Right to Adequate Housing." https://www.refworld .org/docid/47a70799d.html; CESCR. (2005, 11 August). "Substantive Issues Arising in the Implementation of the International Covenant on Economic, Social and Cultural Rights." https://www.refworld.org/docid/43f3067ae.html.

49 FAO. (2004, November). "Voluntary Guidelines to Support the Progressive Realization of the Right to Adequate Food in the Context of National Food Security." http://www.fao.org/3/a-y7937e.pdf. Accessed 16 January 2020.

50 Ibid.

51 FIDA-Kenya. (2020). "About FIDA-Kenya." https://www.fidakenya.org/site /history. Accessed 24 November 2020.

52 Kenya Land Alliance. (n.d.). "What We Do at K.L.A." http://www.kenyalandalliance .or.ke/.

53 Uganda Land Alliance. (n.d.). https://landportal.org/organisation/uganda-land -alliance-ula.

54 Jacobs, Krista, Meredith Saggers, & Sophie Namy. (2011). "How Do Community-based Legal Programs Work? Understanding the Process and Benefits of a Pilot Program to Advance Women's Property Rights in Uganda." International Center for Research on Women. http://www.icrw.org/publications/how-do-community -based-legal-programs-work.

55 Ibid.

56 Asia Pacific Forum on Women, Law and Development. (2017). "Campaign Updates." https://apwld.org/campaigns-updates/.

57 Ibid.

58 Human Rights Watch. (2003). "Double Standards: Women's Property Rights Violations in Kenya." https://www.hrw.org/reports/2003/kenya0303/kenya0303. pdf. Accessed 10 February 2017; Human Rights Watch. (2016, 21 October). "Honduras: Investigate Killings of Land Rights Leaders. Regional Body Had Ordered Protection for Peasant Leaders." https://www.hrw.org/news/2016/10/21 /honduras-investigate-killings-land-rights-leaders. Accessed 26 February 2017.

59 Human Rights Watch. (2017). "'You Will Get Nothing': Violations of Property and Inheritance Rights in Zimbabwe." https://www.hrw.org/report/2017/01/24 /you-will-get-nothing/violations-property-and-inheritance-rights-widows -zimbabwe. Accessed 26 February 2017.

60 GI-ESCR. (2014). "Using CEDAW to Secure Women's Land and Property Rights: A Practical Guide (GI-ESCR)." https://www.gi-escr.org/womens-escr-resources /using-cedaw-to-secure-womens-land-and-property-rights-a-practical-guide-gi-escr.

61 GI-ESCR. (2018). "Advocating for Women's Rights to Land and Other Productive Resources." https://www.gi-escr.org/annual-report/womens-rights.

62 FIAN. (2018). "FIAN International Strategic Plan 2018–2023." https://www .fian.org/fileadmin/media/publications_2018/Reports_and_guidelines /FIANInternationalStrategicPlan2018-2023_Preamble.pdf. Accessed 16 December 2019.

63 Ibid.

64 ActionAid. (2012). "Women's Land Rights Project in Guatemala, India, and Sierra Leone." https://actionaid.org/sites/default/files/consolidated_baseline_report _june_2012.pdf. Accessed 16 November 2020.

65 Hildenbrand, Emily, & Rekha Panigrahi. (n.d.). "CARE India Partners with LANDESA to Increase Women's Land Literacy." http://www.carepathway stoempowerment.org/care-india-partners-landesa-increase-womens-land-literacy/.

66 Namati. (2017). *Community Land Protection Facilitators' Guide*. https://namati.org/ wp-content/uploads/2016/02/Namati-Community-Land-Protection-Facilitators -Guide_Ed.2-2017-LR.pdf. Accessed 16 January 2020.

67 Namati. (2019). *Annual Report 2018*. https://namati.org/wp-content/uploads /2019/04/2018-Namati-Annual-Report.pdf. Accessed 16 January 2020.

68 Santos, Florence, Diana Fletschner, & Giuseppe DaConto. (2014). "Enhancing Inclusiveness of Rwanda's Land Tenure Regularization Program: Insights from Early Stages of Its Implementation." *World Development, 62*, 30–41; Prosterman, R., R. Mitchell, & T. Hanstad. (2009). *One Billion Rising: Law, Land and the Alleviation of Global Poverty*. Chicago: University of Chicago Press.

69 Landesa. (n.d.). "Private: Strengthening Women's Tenure Security in Northern Uganda." https://www.landesa.org/northern-uganda-project/partners/.

70 USAID. (2012). "Land Policy and Institutional Support (LPIS) Project. Customary Land Tenure in Liberia: Findings and Implications Drawn from 11 Case Studies." http://www.usaidlandtenure.net/sites/default/files/USAID_Land_Tenure _Liberia_LPIS_Synthesis_Report.pdf.

71 International Land Coalition. (n.d.). "Explore." https://www.landcoalition.org /en/explore/.

72 International Land Coalition. (2020). "National Engagement Strategies." https:// www.triennial.landcoalition.org/nes-1. Accessed 16 November 2020.

73 International Land Coalition. (2017). "Land and the SDGs: Key Takeaways from the 2017 HLPF and What We Need to Do Next." https://landportal.org/blog -post/2017/08/land-and-sdgs-key-takeaways-2017-hlpf-and-what-we-need-do -next. Accessed 16 November 2020.

74 Anseeuw, Ward, & Eva Hershaw. (2000). "How People-Centered Land Monitoring Can Contribute to the Realization of the SDG and VGGTs – The Case of ILC's Dashboard." https://www.oicrf.org/documents/40950/0/107 _Handout_02-04-Anseeuw-535_ppt.pptx.pdf/a1abc551-cdd5-bbff-df50 -bd813f4926aa?t=1560243343603. Accessed 16 November 2020.

75 Human Rights Watch. (2016, 21 October). "Honduras: Investigate Killings of Land Rights Leaders. Regional Body Had Ordered Protection for Peasant Leaders." https://www.hrw.org/news/2016/10/21/honduras-investigate-killings-land -rights-leaders. Accessed 26 February 2017; Asian NGO Coalition for Agrarian Reform and Rural Development (ANGOC). (2019). *In Defense of Land Rights: A Monitoring Report on Land Conflicts in Six Asian Countries*. Quezon City: ANGOC.

76 Stanley, Victoria, & Paul Prettitore. (2020, 5 May). "How COVID-19 Puts Women's Housing, Land, and Property Rights at Risk." World Bank Blogs. https://blogs. worldbank.org/sustainablecities/how-covid-19-puts-womens-housing-land-and -property-rights-risk; Cotula, Lorenzo. (2020, 1 June). "Stopping Land and Policy Grabs in the Shadow of COVID-19." International Institute for Environment and Development. https://www.iied.org/stopping-land-policy-grabs-shadow -covid-19; Namati. (2020). "COVID-19 Justice Challenge Results." https://s25642 .pcdn.co/wp-content/uploads/2020/07/Results-COVID-19-Justice-Challenge.pdf. Accessed 16 November 2020.

77 Pearshouse, Richard, & Jurema Werneck. (2020, 19 April). "Land Seizures and COVID-19: The Twin Threats to Brazil's Indigenous Peoples." Amnesty International. https://www.amnesty.org/en/latest/news/2020/04/land-seizures-and-covid-19-the-twin-threats-to-brazils-indigenous-peoples/; Human Rights Watch. (2020). "Cambodia: Micro-loan Borrowers Face Covid-19 Crisis: Suspend Debt Collection, Stop Coerced Land Sales." https://www.hrw.org/news/2020/07/14/cambodia-micro-loan-borrowers-face-covid-19-crisis#; Jong, Hans Nicholas. (2020, 15 April). "Land Conflicts Escalate with Spread of COVID-19 in Indonesia." Mongabay. https://news.mongabay.com/2020/04/land-conflicts-escalate-with-spread-of-covid-19-in-indonesia/; DAI Team. (2020, 23 June). "In Ethiopia, Keeping Land Rights on the Agenda through the Pandemic." Developing Alternatives. https://dai-global-developments.com/articles/in-ethiopia-keeping-land-rights-on-the-agenda-through-the-pandemic.
78 Land Rights Now. (2020). "Indigenous Peoples Mobilise to Curb COVID-19." https://www.landrightsnow.org/indigenous-peoples-mobilise-to-curb-covid-19/; Land Rights Now. (2020). "Urgent Action Alert: Call on the Ugandan Government to Protect Local Communities from Land Grabbing." https://www.landrightsnow.org/urgent-action-alert-uganda/.

7. Politics and Accountability: Implementing the SDGs

1 UNDP. (2020)."COVID 19 and the SDGs: How the 'Roadmap for Humanity' Could Be Changed by a Pandemic." https://feature.undp.org/covid-19-and-the-sdgs/?utm_source=social&utm_medium=undp&utm_campaign=covid19-sdgs&fbclid=IwAR3S4hs1a7nljr8pLmCa3aNjHUzEgHHZxe1eK92Tkr6KnDQhAfgt3kgFof0.
2 Geohagen, Tighe, & Steve Bass. (2016, December). "Reconceiving the SDGs as a Political Force for Change," 4. IIED Briefing. http://pubs.iied.org/17391IIED/. Accessed 24 May 2017.
3 Hall, Anthony. (2006). "From Fome Zero to Bolsa Família: Social Policies and Poverty Alleviation under Lula." *Journal of Latin American Studies, 38*(4), 689–709. DOI: 10.1017/S0022216X0600157X; ILO. (n.d.). "Financing Social Protection through Financial Transaction Taxes." https://www.social-protection.org/gimi/RessourcePDF.action?ressource.ressourceId=53855.
4 Edwards, Martin S., & Lis Kabishi. (2017). "Using the Sustainable Development Goals as a Weapon against Populism." https://www.opendemocracy.net/en/openglobalrights-openpage/using-sustainable-development-goals-as-weapon-against-populism/. Accessed 17 December 2019.
5 Glennie, Jonathan. (2019). "Countering Populism." https://www.sustainablegoals.org.uk/countering-populism/. Accessed 17 December 2019.
6 Murphy, Erica, Mihir Mankad, & Francesca Feruglio. (2019). "SDG 4: Making Human Rights Count." Data for Sustainable Development UNESCO Institute for Statistics Blog. https://sdg.uis.unesco.org/2019/07/15/sdg-4-making-human-rights-count/. Accessed 19 November 2019.
7 CESR. (2019, 16 July). "South Africa: Is Resource Mobilization Reducing Inequality?" https://www.cesr.org/south-africa-resource-mobilization-reducing-inequality.
8 Rights and Resources Initiative. (2017). "Securing Community Land Rights: Priorities and Opportunities to Advance Climate and Sustainable Development

Goals." http://rightsandresources.org/wp-content/uploads/2017/09 /Stockholm-Prorities-and-Opportunities-Brief.pdf; International Planned Parenthood Federation. (2015). "Sustainable Development Goals. A SPHR CSO Guide for National Implementation." https://www.ippf.org/resource /sustainable-development-goals-srhr-cso-guide-national-implementation. Accessed 17 December 2019; ActionAid. (2009). *Accounting for Poverty: How International Tax Rules Keep People Poor.* London: ActionAid; Anima Mama wa Afrika. (2019). "Progress on Implementation of Sustainable Development Goal 8 on Decent Work and Economic Growth in Uganda." https://www.akinamamawaafrika.org /progress-on-implementation-of-sustainable-development-goal-8-on-decent-work -and-economic-growth-in-uganda-2019/. Accessed 18 November 2019.

9 Amnesty International, CESR, Center for Reproductive Rights, & Human Rights Watch. (2015). "Post-2015 Outcome Document: Redlines and Proposals on Follow -up and Review." https://www.amnesty.org/en/documents/pol30/2131/2015 /en/.

10 Carvalho, S. (2017). "Accountability Is a Lifeline for Sustainable Development Goals but Governments Need to Be Listening." *Huffington Post.* https://www .huffingtonpost.com/savio-carvalho/accountability-is-a-lifel_b_9326168.html. Accessed 5 November 2017.

11 Fredman, Sandra. (2018). *Working Together: Human Rights, the Sustainable Development Goals and Gender Equality.* London: The British Academy.

12 Save the Children. (2017). "Towards a New Accountability Paradigm: An Accountability Framework for the 2030 Agenda for Sustainable Development." http://www.savethechildren.org.uk/sites/default/files/images/New _Accountability_Paradigm.pdf. Accessed 24 May 2017; Save the Children. (2014). "Leaving No One Behind: Embedding Equity in the Post-2015 Framework through Stepping Stone Targets." London: Save the Children. http://www.savethechildren .org.uk/sites/default/files/images/Leaving_No_One_Behind.pdf. Accessed 20 June 2017; Global Partnership to End Violence against Children. (n.d.). "Progress Map." https://www.end-violence.org/progress-map; Independent Accountability Panel on Women's, Children's, and Adolescents' Health. (n.d.). "About the IAP." https://iapewec.org/about/.

13 Together 2030. (2018). "National Civil Society Coalitions on the Sustainable Development Goals: A Mapping"; United Cities and Local Governments. (2016). "Brazil: Enhancing Local Plans and Monitoring & Accountability Systems for the Localization of the SDGs." http://www.cib-uclg.org/news/brazil-enhancing -local-plans-and-monitoring-accountability-systems-localization-sdgs.

14 Galati, Alanna. (2015). "Onward to 2030: Sexual and Reproductive Health and Rights in the Context of the Sustainable Development Goals." *Guttmacher Policy Review, 18*(4). https://www.guttmacher.org/gpr/2015/10/onward-2030-sexual -and-reproductive-health-and-rights-context-sustainable-development. Accessed 14 June 2017.

15 International Planned Parenthood Federation. (2015). "Sustainable Development Goals. A SPHR CSO Guide for National Implementation." https://www.ippf.org /resource/sustainable-development-goals-srhr-cso-guide-national-implementation. Accessed 17 December 2019; Hall, Anthony. (2006). "From Fome Zero to Bolsa Família: Social Policies and Poverty Alleviation under Lula." *Journal of Latin American Studies, 38*(4), 689–709. DOI: 10.1017/S0022216X0600157X.

16 Feminist Alliance for Rights. (2017). "Sustainable Development Goals: Agenda 2030. India. A Civil Society Report." http://www.indiaenvironmentportal.org.in /files/file/Civil-society-Report-on-SDGs.pdf.

17 Equal Measures 2030. (2018). "EM2030 SDG Gender Index: National Launches." https://www.equalmeasures2030.org/sdg-gender-index-launch-national/. Accessed 4 January 2020.

18 Lebada, Anna Maria. (2016). "Colombia, Mexico, Venezuela Present Early SDGs Implementation Actions." file:///E:/UTP%20HR%20SDGs/chapter%206%20 HR%20leverage%20SDGs/Colombia,%20Mexico,%20Venezuela%20Present%20 Early%20SDGs%20Implementation%20Actions%20_%20SDG%20Knowledge%20 Hub%20_%20IISD.html. Accessed 20 June 2017.

19 Hege, Elisabeth, & Laura Brimont. (2018, 18 July). "Integrating SDGs into National Budgetary Processes." Institute for Sustainable Development and International Relations. IDDRI Study, 5, 9. https://www.iddri.org/sites/default/files/PDF /Publications/Catalogue%20Iddri/Etude/201807-ST0518-SDGs-budget-EN.pdf.

20 Cities Alliance. (2015). "Sustainable Development Goals and Habitat III: Opportunities for a Successful New Urban Agenda." https://www.citiesalliance .org/sites/default/files/Opportunities%20for%20the%20New%20Urban%20 Agenda.pdf. Accessed 17 December 2019

21 United Cities and Local Governments. (2016). "Roadmap for Localizing the SDGs: Implementation and Monitoring at Subnational Level." https://www.uclg.org /sites/default/files/roadmap_for_localizing_the_sdgs_0.pdf.

22 Conrood, John. (2017). "Localizing the SDGs in Bangladesh: An Innovative Community-led Approach." https://communityleddev.org/2017/06/15 /localizing-the-sdgs-in-bangladesh/. Accessed 5 November 2017.

23 OECD. (2018). "Official Development Assistance." https://www.oecd.org/dac /financing-sustainable-development/development-finance-standards/official -development-assistance.htm. Accessed 18 December 2019

24 Hearn, Sarah. (2017, 17 May). "What Does the Populist Wave Mean for Global Aid and Development?" *World Politics Review*. http://www.worldpoliticsreview .com/articles/21278/what-does-the-populist-wave-mean-for-global-aid-and -development. Accessed 24 May 2017.

25 OECD. (2018). "Official Development Assistance." https://www.oecd.org/dac /financing-sustainable-development/development-finance-standards/official -development-assistance.htm. Accessed 18 December 2019.

26 Harder, Amy. (2020, 13 July). "How Europe's Green Pandemic Recovery Will Push the Rest of the World." Axios. https://www.axios.com/europe-green-pandemic -recovery-6fabad13-1c3c-4dfb-9316-1ad09a05f858.html.

27 Kenny, Charles. (2015, 27 May). "MDGs to SDGs: Have We Lost the Plot?" Center for Global Development. https://www.cgdev.org/sites/default/files/CGD-Essay -Kenny-MDGs-SDGs-Have-Lost-Plot.pdf.

28 ActionAid. (2009). *Accounting for Poverty: How International Tax Rules Keep People Poor.* London: ActionAid.

29 Long, Cathal, & Mark Miller. (2017). "Taxation and the Sustainable Development Goals: Do Good Things Come to Those Who Tax More?" Overseas Development Institute. https://www.odi.org/sites/odi.org.uk/files/resource-documents/11536 .pdf. Accessed 15 June 2017; Bharali, Ipchita, & Indermit Gill. (2019). "Measuring the Gap between Ability and Effort in Domestic Revenue Mobilization." Brookings

Institution. https://www.brookings.edu/blog/future-development/2019/04/29/measuring-the-gap-between-ability-and-effort-in-domestic-revenue-mobilization/. Accessed 20 January 2020.

30 Moore, Mick. (2007). "How Does Taxation Affect the Quality of Governance?" *Tax Notes International, 47*(1). http://citeseerx.ist.psu.edu/viewdoc/download?doi=10.1.1.504.8376&rep=rep1&type=pdf; UN DESA. (2018, 14 February). "Countries Urged to Strengthen Tax Systems to Promote Inclusive Economic Growth." New York. https://www.un.org/development/desa/en/news/financing/tax4dev.html.

31 ActionAid. (2009). *Accounting for Poverty: How International Tax Rules Keep People Poor.* London: ActionAid; CESR. (2014). "A Post-2015 Fiscal Revolution Human Rights Policy Brief." http://archive.cesr.org/downloads/fiscal.revolution.pdf. Accessed 21 June 2017.

32 Barrett, Scott. (2011). *Why Cooperate? The Incentive to Supply Global Public Goods.* Oxford: Oxford University Press.

33 Fox, J., & L.D. Brown. (1998). *The Struggle for Accountability: The World Bank, NGOs, and Grassroots Movements.* Cambridge, MA: MIT Press; Nelson, Paul. (2001). "Transparency Mechanisms at the Multilateral Development Banks." *World Development, 29*(11), 1835–47.

34 FAO. (n.d.). "Sustainable Development Goals." http://www.fao.org/sustainable-development-goals/tracking-progress/en/. Accessed 18 December 2019.

35 Donald, Kate, & Sally-Anne Way. (2016, 10 June). "Accountability for the Sustainable Development Goals: A Lost Opportunity?" *Ethics and International Affairs.* https://www.ethicsandinternationalaffairs.org/2016/accountability-sustainable-development-goals-lost-opportunity/. Accessed 21 June 2017.

36 Decade of Accountability. (2020). "Campaign for a Decade of Accountability for the SDGs." https://secureservercdn.net/166.62.112.219/9bz.99d.myftpupload.com/wp-content/uploads/2020/05/Flyer_Decade-of-Accountability-for-the-SDGs_HQ.pdf.

37 Williams, Carmel, & Paul Hunt. (2018). "Neglecting Human Rights: Accountability, Data and Sustainable Development Goal 3." *The International Journal of Human Rights, 21*(8), 1114–43.

38 Donald, Kate, & Mahlatse Ramoroka. (2018). "Five Key Takeaways from the High-level Political Forum." Accessed 31 July 2018.

39 Center for Reproductive Rights, Amnesty International, CESR, & Human Rights Watch. (2015). "Accountability for the Post-2015 Agenda: A Proposal for a Robust Global Review Mechanism." http://www.hrw.org/sites/default/files/related_material/Post2015GlobalReviewProposal.pdf. Accessed 15 June 2015.

40 Asia Pacific Forum & CESR. (2015). "Defending Dignity: A Manual for National Human Rights Institutions on Monitoring Economic, Social and Cultural Rights." https://www.cesr.org/sites/default/files/Defending_Dignity_ESCR_Manual_2019.pdf. Accessed 16 November 2020.

41 Brook, Anne-Marie, K. Chad Clay, & Susan Randolph. (2020). "Human Rights Data for Everyone: Introducing the Human Rights Measurement Initiative (HRMI)." *Journal of Human Rights, 19*(1), 67–82. DOI: 10.1080/14754835.2019.1671176.

42 Danish Institute for Human Rights. (2015, June). "SDGs Data, Indicators and Mechanisms." Human Rights Reference Paper. CDP Background Paper 25.

https://www.yumpu.com/en/document/view/54494912/sdg-data-indicators -mechanisms. Accessed 16 November 2020.

43 Danish Institute for Human Rights. (2019, 3 July). *Integrated Review and Reporting on SDGs and Human Rights a Key to Effective, Efficient and Accountable Implementation.* https://www.humanrights.dk/publications/integrated-review-reporting-sdgs -human-rights. Accessed 16 November 2020.

44 Kindornay, Shanon. (2018). "Progressing National SDGs Implementation: An Independent Assessment of the Voluntary National Review Reports Submitted to the UN High-level Political Forum on Sustainable Development in 2018." https:// ccic.ca/third-edition-of-progressing-national-sdgs-implementation/.

45 Ibid., xx.

46 Ibid.

47 CESR. (2018), "Five Key Takeaways from the 2018 High-level Political Forum." https://www.cesr.org/five-key-takeaways-2018-high-level-political-forum.

48 Jensen, Steven L.B. (2020, 4 August). "UN Special Rapporteur on Extreme Poverty and Human Rights Goes Out Guns Blazing against Failure to Address Poverty." Blog, Universal Rights Group. https://www.universal-rights.org/blog/un-special -rapporteur-on-extreme-poverty-and-human-rights-goes-out-guns-blazing -against-failure-to-address-poverty/.

49 Alston, Philip. (2020). "The Parlous State of Poverty Eradication. Report of the Special Rapporteur on Extreme Poverty and Human Rights," 12. Human Rights Council Forty-fourth session, 15 June–3 July 2020. https://chrgj.org/wp-content /uploads/2020/07/Alston-Poverty-Report-FINAL.pdf.

50 Blampied, C., R. Greenhill, M.A.J. D'Orey, T. Bhatkal, S. Chattopadhyay, M.B. Sarwar, et al. (2016, December). "Leaving No One Behind in the Health Sector: An SDG Stocktake in Kenya and Nepal." London: Overseas Development Institute. https://www.odi.org/ publications/10675-leaving-no-one-behind-health-sector -sdg-stocktake-kenya-and-nepal.

51 Ibid.

52 CESR. (2019). "South Africa: Is Domestic Resource Mobilization Reducing Inequality?" https://www.cesr.org/south-africa-domestic-resource-mobilization -reducing-inequality.

53 Donald, Kate. (2017). "The Politics of 'Progress': UN Report Paints a Highly Partial Picture of SDG Implementation." http://www.cesr.org/politics-%E2%80%98progress%E2%80%99 -un-report-paints-highly-partial-picture-sdg-implementation.

54 Donald, Kate, & Matthew Annunziato. (2017). "Low-level Performance at High-level Political Forum." CESR. http://www.cesr.org/low-level-performance-HLPF. Accessed 14 October 2017.

55 Save the Children. (2017). "Towards a New Accountability Paradigm: An Accountability Framework for the 2030 Agenda for Sustainable Development." http://www.savethechildren.org.uk/sites/default/files/images/New_ Accountability_Paradigm.pdf. Accessed 24 May 2017; Save the Children. (2014). "Leaving No One Behind: Embedding Equity in the Post-2015 Framework through Stepping Stone Targets." London: Save the Children. http://www.savethechildren.org. uk/sites/default/files/images/Leaving_No_One_Behind.pdf. Accessed 20 June 2017.

56 Jensen, Steven L.B. (2019, 4 July). "UN Human Rights Mechanisms Proving Effective SDGs Monitor," 1. Open Global Rights. https://www.openglobalrights .org/un-human-rights-mechanisms-proving-effective-sdgs-monitor/.

57 Chattopadhyay, Soumya, & Stephanie Manea. (2019). "The Leave No One Behind Index." Briefing, Overseas Development Institute. https://www.odi.org/sites/odi.org.uk/files/resource-documents/12920.pdf. Accessed 6 January 2020.
58 Ibid.
59 Equal Measures 2030. (2019). "Harnessing the Power of Data for Gender Equality: Introducing the 2019 EM2030 SDG Gender Index." https://www.equalmeasures2030.org/wp-content/uploads/2019/07/EM2030_2019_Global_Report_English_WEB.pdf. Accessed 7 January 2020.
60 Ibid., 2.
61 ARROW. (2015). "ARROW's Sexual and Reproductive Health and Rights Database of Indicators." https://arrow.org.my/introducing-the-updated-srhr-database-of-indicators/. Accessed 7 January 2020.
62 UNICEF. (2017). "Narrowing the Gaps: The Power of Investing in the Poorest Children." https://www.unicef.org/media/49111/file/UNICEF_The_power_of_investing_in_the_poorest_children-ENG.pdf. Accessed 20 November 2019; United Nations Department of Economic and Social Affairs. (2015). "Transitioning from the MDGs to the SDGs: Accountability for the Post-2015 Era. A Background Report by the CDP Subgroup on Accountability." http://www.un.org/en/development/desa/policy/cdp/cdp_background_papers/bp2015_25.pdf. Accessed 25 May 2017.
63 IRC (International Reference Center on Community Water Supply). (n.d.). "SDGs Hub: Wash." https://www.ircwash.org/tags/sustainable-development-goals.
64 Dunning, Casey, & Jared Kalow. (2016, 17 May). "SDG Indicators: Serious Gaps Abound in Data Availability." https://www.cgdev.org/blog/sdg-indicators-serious-gaps-abound-data-availability.
65 UN Stats. (2019). "Tier Classification for Global SDG Indicators." https://unstats.un.org/sdgs/iaeg-sdgs/tier-classification/. Accessed 14 November 2019.
66 United Nations Development Group. (2016). "Tailoring SDG to National, Sub-national, and Local Contexts." https://undg.org/2030-agenda/mainstreaming-2030-agenda/tailoring-sdg-to-national-context/.
67 Eurostat. (2020). "Sustainable Development in the European Union – Monitoring Report on Progress towards the SDGS in an EU Context – 2020 Edition." https://ec.europa.eu/eurostat/web/products-statistical-books/-/KS-02-20-202.
68 Lao People's Democratic Republic. (2019). "National Roundtable Process, SDG Indicators." https://rtm.org.la/sdgs/sdg-indicators/. Accessed 14 November 2019.
69 Government of Colombia. (2019). "How Is Colombia Doing on the SDGs?" https://www.ods.gov.co/en. Accessed 14 November 2019.
70 Chaves, Patricia, Jolyne Sanjak, & Malcolm Childress. (2017). "Local Movement Leveraging the Sustainable Development Goals to Strengthen Women's Land Rights in Brazil." https://www.landesa.org/blog-local-movement-leveraging-sustainable-development-goals-strengthen-womens-land-rights-brazil/. Accessed 30 June 2017.
71 Chaves, Patricia Maria Queiros. (2019, 17 August). "For the First Time Women from Informal Settlements in Bonita, State of Pernambuco, Brazil, Will Be Granted with Land Titles." Land Portal. https://landportal.org/blog-post/2019/08/first-time-women-informal-settlements-municipality-bonito-state-pernambuco-brazil.

72 Sáenz, Luis Hernán. (2019). "Localizing the SDGs in Colombian Cities through the Cómo Vamos City Network." https://static1.squarespace.com /static/5b4f63e14eddec374f416232/t/5cb648867817f738d11ca998/1555449998211 /LDASI-Colombia_April19.pdf. Accessed 20 November 2019.

73 Ibid., 5.

74 Rosga, AnnJanette, & Margaret L. Satterthwaite. (2009, July). "The Trust in Indicators: Measuring Human Rights." *Berkeley Journal of International Law, 27*(2), 315. https://heinonline-org.pitt.idm.oclc.org/HOL/Page?handle=hein.journals /berkjintlw27&id=257&collection=journals&index=journals/berkjintlw. Accessed 16 November 2020.

Conclusions

1 Marks, Stephen P. (2014). "Prospects for Human Rights in the Post-2015 Development Agenda." In Julia Kozma, Anna Müller-Funk, & Manfred Nowak (Eds.), *Vienna +20: Advancing the Protection of Human Rights Achievements, Challenges and Perspectives 20 Years after the World Conference*, 291–306. Ludwig Boltzmann Institute of Human Rights, Studies Series, vol. 31. Vienna: Neuer Wissenschaftlicher Verlag; Brolan, C.E., P.S. Hill, & G. Ooms. (2015, 21 August). "'Everywhere but Not Specifically Somewhere': A Qualitative Study on Why the Right to Health Is Not Explicit in the Post-2015 Negotiations." *BMC International Health and Human Rights, 15*(22). doi:10.1186/s12914-015-0061-z; MacNaughton, Gillian. (2019). "The Mysterious Disappearance of Human Rights in the 2030 Development Agenda." In Rajini Srikanth & Elora Halim Chowdhury (Eds.), *Interdisciplinary Approaches to Human Rights: History, Politics, Practice*, 131–47. New York: Routledge.

Index

accountability: as function of domestic politics, 12, 135, 160–3; human rights, 175–6; Outcomes, Policy Efforts, Resources, and Assessment (OPERA), 176; Social and Economic Rights Fulfillment (SERF) Index, 176; Human Rights Measurement Initiative (HRMI), 177; "taboo" in United Nations, 184–5; and taxation, 171–3; Voluntary National Review Reports for SDGs, 177–8

ActionAid: advocacy on tax policy, 84–5; projects on women's land rights, 155, 167; rights-based approach, 53; monitoring inequalities, 81–2

AIDS, 3, 7, 18, 26, 50, 57, 59, 89, 97, 98, 99, 102, 103, 154, 199, 202

Alston, Philip, report on COVID-19 and SDGs, 11

Asian floor wage, 127

Asia Pacific Forum on Women, Law and Development (APWLD), 153–4

authoritarian populism: and egalitarian strategies, 88; an obstacle to SDGs, 10, 16; in the Philippines, 10; SDGs as a counterweight, 163–4

Ban Ki-moon, 14

Birdsall, Nancy, 68

Cambodia: health equity fund, 94; minimum wage, 127; out-of-pocket health costs, 94

Care, joint work with Landesa on land rights, 155

Center for Economic and Social Rights (CESR), influencing human rights views of SDGs, 34, 81

Center for Global Development, 68, 122, 172, 181

circular economy: Ghana's Suame/Kumasi industrial cluster, 134; Tearfund advocacy, 134

civil and political rights: included in SDGs, 27; omitted from MDGs, 27

civil society: limited access to High-level Political Forum, 169; participation in defining SDGs, 30–1

UTP insights

Books in the Series